CIRCLES *of* SISTERHOOD

"As a timely survey on a century of women's evolving work within and outside one Mennonite church denomination, *Circles of Sisterhood* is expansive in its definition of what constitutes that work—from 'service to others' to 'self-care.' Anita Hooley Yoder's book is commendable especially for its critical eye, for its effort to analyze the racialized nature of church institutions, and for presenting women as neither heroes nor victims but rather as central actors in the history of the Mennonite church."
—***Marlene Epp****, author of* Mennonite Women in Canada: A History

"Mennonite women need each other! Anita Hooley Yoder has traced our history from the early 1900s to the present, from sewing circles at which a male pastor had to open in prayer to Mennonite Women USA, Sister Care, and other current groups where women meet for service and spiritual support. Well written and hard to lay down, *Circles of Sisterhood* updates previous books and essays about Mennonite women's history. If you are a Mennonite girl or woman of any color or cultural background, this is your story!"
—***Reta Halteman Finger****, author of* Creating a Scene in Corinth *and former editor of* Daughters of Sarah

"This landmark history, carefully researched and clearly written, tells the story of the courageous and gifted visionaries who brought about a transformation in the role of women in the Mennonite church. For anyone trying to make sense of the complex fault lines among Mennonites today—be it gender, ethnicity, sexuality, cultural engagement, or church polity—this book offers an illuminating window into the slow and sometimes painful process of transformative change. I highly recommend it."
—***John D. Roth****, professor of history, Goshen College*

"Anita Hooley Yoder puts to rest any lingering question as to whether there has been a Mennonite women's movement. The answer is yes. *Circles of Sisterhood* offers readers a complicated and fascinating story

of empowerment, best summed up in the words of an elderly woman to a younger woman who was headed into a denominational meeting: 'You go, girl!' "
—***Lee Snyder**, president emeritus, Bluffton University*

"With the current rise of global women's movements, Anita Hooley Yoder has given us a timely denominational and cultural history of Mennonite circles of sisterhood from 1917 to 2017. As she artfully narrates the neglected histories of diverse women's groups and organizations within the church, these engaging collective stories will certainly invite and inspire more individual stories of Mennonite women in the genres of biography, autobiography, history, and theology."
—***Scott Holland**, professor of theology, Earlham School of Religion*

"*Circles of Sisterhood* shares the stories of women who struggled, persevered, failed, and tried again. The story of women in the church is the story of the church. We are family on this journey, and it would serve us well to listen and learn from the voices of the past so that we might better support each other as siblings on the road ahead."
—***Jamie Ross**, coeditor of* Anabaptist Witness

CIRCLES *of* SISTERHOOD

A History of Mission, Service, and Fellowship in Mennonite Women's Organizations

Anita Hooley Yoder

HERALD PRESS
Harrisonburg, Virginia

Herald Press
PO Box 866, Harrisonburg, Virginia 22803
www.HeraldPress.com

Library of Congress Cataloging-in-Publication Data
Names: Yoder, Anita Hooley, author.
Title: Circles of sisterhood : a history of mission, service, and fellowship in Mennonite women's organizations / Anita Hooley Yoder.
Description: Harrisonburg, Virginia : Herald Press, 2017. | Series: Studies in Anabaptist and Mennonite History Series ; 51 | Includes bibliographical references and index.
Identifiers: LCCN 2016056937| ISBN 9781513801421 (pbk. : alk. paper) | ISBN 9781513801438 (hardcover : alk. paper)
Subjects: LCSH: Mennonite women--Societies and clubs. | Women in church work—Mennonites.
Classification: LCC BX8128.W64 Y63 2017 | DDC 267/.4497--dc23 LC record available at https://lccn.loc.gov/2016056937

Library of Congress Control Number: 2016056937
International Standard Book Number: 978-1-5138-0142-1 (paper); 978-1-5138-0143-8 (hardcover); 978-1-5138-0306-7 (ebook)
Printed in United States of America
Design by Merrill Miller
Cover photo at left: A mending crew working at the Eureka, Illinois, Home for the Aged in 1951 (*left to right*): Kathryn Hansford, Edna Stutzman, Margaret Shank, Elsie Sutter (MCUSAA–Elkhart). Middle cover photo: Manor Sewing Circle members working on a quilt together (Jonathan Charles). Cover photo at right: Sheron Walcott (*left*) anointing Donna Berry-Holland during the closing blessing ritual at the Sister Care seminar in Trinidad (Carolyn Holderread Heggen).

21 20 19 18 17   10 9 8 7 6 5 4 3 2

To the Mennonite women whose stories I carry in my body—
especially Nettie, Katie, and Julie—
and the many more whose stories I carry in my heart.

Contents

Foreword

Women in the church have often encountered new opportunities for leadership and service amid the instabilities of conflict and expansion. As the early church divided from its Jewish roots, women took up roles as missionaries and deacons. As part of the Anabaptist movement during the European Reformation, women engaged in theological debate with opponents, hosted house churches in their homes, and in some circles, prophesied and preached. The modern missionary movement provided another such opportunity for women to take up new leadership responsibilities beyond traditional roles as wives, mothers, and keepers at home.

In Mennonite churches, the new emphasis on urban and overseas mission toward the end of the nineteenth century created institutional and social needs that Mennonite women were uniquely positioned to fill. By turning "domestic" skills such as sewing and food preparation into publicly valued capacities for meeting global needs, Mennonite women in the twentieth century also learned to engage in the committee work and administrative responsibilities previously associated with male-dominated denominational agencies and structures. By developing the practices of theological and spiritual formation through which women came to understand their emerging role in the church's mission, modern Mennonite women were able to see themselves also as worship leaders and Bible teachers—roles that had been primarily associated with men. These changes in identity led to conflict with some church leaders who came to see women's organizations as either unworthy of recognition or as threats to male authority.

While Mennonite women who sought to serve the world and one another through sewing circles and missionary support societies did not typically view themselves as feminists, the women's movements of the twentieth century did shape the way church leaders and women themselves regarded the work and potential of women's organizations. And in the end, the various organized forms of Mennonite sisterhood did lead to more explicit feminist challenges to both denominational and congregational patriarchy—relationships organized by the exclusive public authority of men.

Anita Hooley Yoder tells this intriguing and inspiring story of social change in the Mennonite church with a well-documented attentiveness to both its personal and collective dimensions. Her account interweaves the lives and leadership of particular Mennonite women with developments and tensions unfolding in denominational and national contexts. In so doing, Yoder illuminates how Mennonite women changed and were changed by the Mennonite church's response to twentieth-century challenges, from the world wars and the Depression to the civil rights movement and globalization.

In telling this story so skillfully, Yoder also sheds new light on the broader story of Mennonite mission and activism in the twentieth century, particularly in the U.S. context. This story is usually told from the perspective of the men who were in charge of the church's institutions and projects. By focusing on women's responses to the church's mission program, Yoder unveils an alternative yet complementary reality that has been unfolding in this story of mission. This alternate story is about Mennonite women's experiences of empowerment and struggle —including the struggle to be acknowledged and recognized for the considerable gifts they had to offer—as they led their church from a position of institutional weakness. Through both service and solidarity, Mennonite women initiated projects and forged relationships marked by a desire for more justice and greater flourishing.

The old story of twentieth-century Mennonite life is that there was a golden age of church institutions and structures, led by men, which are now declining and dying. This new story suggests that—thanks to the resourcefulness and determination of Mennonite women—the faithful church's gospel mission of restoration and reconciliation has only just begun.

Gerald J. Mast, Series Editor
Studies in Anabaptist and Mennonite History

Acknowledgments

My first thanks to the many women (about one hundred of them), plus a few men, whom I interviewed for this project. Whether they took time to host me in their homes, take me out to lunch, or simply answer questions over email, our conversations were memorable. I feel honored to have had the task of creating a vessel to hold their stories, images, and reflections. Many interviewees' names do not appear in these pages. If you are one of them, please know that your conversations were also important in aiding my understanding of this sometimes complicated story.[1]

Many thanks are owed to the Mennonite Women USA staff and board members for choosing me to take on this project and supporting me along the way. Thanks to Ruth Lapp Guengerich and Beth Martin Birky for initial support and to Rhoda Keener and Marlene Bogard for reading many (many!) drafts of certain sections and offering invaluable clarifications, critiques, and affirmations. You have been both careful and generous with how the organization you are so invested in is represented. (And, without both Rhoda's and Marlene's help, this book would have very few photos!) Gerald Mast, Studies in Anabaptist and Mennonite History series editor, made a serious effort to keep the publication process moving and helped me shape this story within a wider context. Many of the clearest and most thought-provoking insights in these pages are drawn from his feedback. Thanks also to Valerie Weaver-Zercher, Amy Gingerich, Malinda Berry, Carolyn Holderread Heggen, and Kathy Bilderback—not only for helpful comments and resource ideas but also for general encouragement of me and my work on this project.

Colleen McFarland Rademaker and Jason Kauffman at the Mennonite Church USA Archives in Goshen, Indiana, provided helpful assistance and interest in the project, as did Joe Springer at the Mennonite

Historical Library. Special thanks to John D. Thiesen at the Mennonite Library and Archives in Newton, Kansas, for helping find (and refind) sources in person and at a distance. Thanks to Gordon Houser at *The Mennonite* and Jamie Ross at *Anabaptist Witness* for providing spaces for parts of this work to be made public in advance of the book. And although it probably doesn't know it, the Cleveland Heights library system played an essential role in this project, providing me with resources, work space, and a free daily printing allotment!

Oak Grove Mennonite Church (Smithville, Ohio) and First Mennonite Church of Christian (Moundridge, Kans.) provided financial backing for the project, and the Schowalter Foundation made it possible for me to travel to meet with Mennonite women in areas that I surely would have otherwise overlooked. Numerous friends and family provided a place to stay and delicious food to eat during trips related to this project or let me use their space for some (relatively) uninterrupted work time, including Brenda and Steve Bachman, Amanda Entz, Julie and Dan Hooley, Emma and Tim Almquist, Mary Ina and Don Hooley, Sylvia and Nick Meyer, and Jane and Dave Yoder. Special thanks to Jane Hooley, a longtime women's organization participant herself, for letting me know about Mennonite Women USA's call for a history writer.

Last but not least, thanks to my husband, Ben Yoder, whose hard work makes it possible for me to do what I love, and who asked me almost every morning (usually while I was still in bed), "What chapter are you working on today?" Thanks for keeping me grounded and keeping me going, even when the answer was the same for many days in a row.

Introduction: Service and Sisterhood

Mary Mellinger was a capable woman. As Mennonite historian John Landis Ruth tells it, a teacher once asked a local Sunday school boy a leading theological question: "Who can do anything?"

"Mary Mellinger," the boy replied.[1]

Mellinger organized some of the earliest recorded meetings of Mennonite women for sewing and missions support. In September 1897, she gathered a sewing circle at her home near Paradise, Pennsylvania. According to notes from the group, the women collected clothing for a Christmas barrel, as well as nineteen dressed chickens and other items for the Methodist Deaconess Home in Philadelphia. In June 1898, the group officially organized and elected Mellinger as their president, a role in which she served for the next thirty years.

By 1911 there were several functioning sewing circles in the area, and Mary Mellinger's brother-in-law John Mellinger suggested a larger organization. Mary became the president of the resulting Associated Sewing Circles of Lancaster Mennonite Conference. By 1914, member groups were meeting in at least fourteen locations. Representatives from the local groups gathered twice a year and heard workers from area Mennonite mission stations share about their needs. Mary Mellinger reported that the associated circles, in addition to helping people in their immediate communities, sewed for "the Welsh Mountain Mission, Columbia Mission, Philadelphia Mission, Lancaster Mission, Old People's Home, Millersville Orphan's Home, the Lancaster General Hospital and the Alms House." Extra goods were sent to Mennonite missions in Altoona, Pennsylvania, and Youngstown, Ohio.

The Lancaster sewing circles did not contribute exclusively to local or Mennonite causes. From their start in 1911 to March 1919, the Associated Sewing Circles supplied the American Friends Service Committee with nearly eight thousand garments, representing about one-fourth of the committee's total intake across the country. After the Friends stopped sending cut garments for Lancaster women to sew together, Mary Mellinger bought a cloth-cutting machine and set up a "cutting room" under the direction of Lancaster Conference's mission board. Over the next twenty years, this cutting room provided the material for a quarter-million garments sent to missionaries and people in need in at least twenty countries.

* * * * *

Joyce Shutt was in her thirties when she served on the literature committee for Women in Mission, the women's organization of the General Conference Mennonite Church (GCMC). As part of her role, Shutt sat in on meetings of the denomination's Commission on Home Ministries and took notes so she could communicate the commission's projects and goals to hundreds of women's groups across the United States and Canada. At such a meeting during the late 1960s, the commission members, all of whom were ordained men, were discussing whom to send to a special evangelism conference.[2]

Suddenly, Shutt heard a voice saying, "You men make me sick. You act is if there's only one kind of person in the world: ordained men. Well, I've got news for you. Over half of the world's population is made of up of women, and the rest are men who are not ordained!" Then Shutt burst into tears. She realized it was *her* voice that had said those words, and she ran sobbing from the room. Before her tears abated, the door of the meeting room opened, and one of the commission members came out. "What you just did was beautiful and prophetic," he said. "You were absolutely right in what you said."[3]

Within a few years, the GCMC's three commissions had all agreed to have female members appointed by the women's organization. The Commission on Home Ministries said they wanted three women, and Shutt herself became a full-fledged member of that group. Her work in this role exposed her to important people and issues in the wider denomination and gave her a chance to exercise her budding leadership skills. Eventually, Shutt decided to enroll in seminary. Her studies spanned a challenging time in her marriage and family life. But after about eight years of intermittent coursework, in 1980 Joyce Shutt was among the earliest women to be ordained in the GCMC. She served her home congregation, Fairfield (Pa.) Mennonite Church, for twenty years, and is now considered a pastor emeritus.[4]

Joyce Shutt, pastor emeritus of Fairfield Mennonite Church.

Shutt credits the women's group in her congregation and her experience with Women in Mission as instrumental in her awakening as a church leader. Her congregational women's group cheered her on when she wanted to quit. The denominational group, led by Gladys Goering, challenged her to channel her angry energy in a constructive way. In a 2014 interview, Shutt recalled her surprise at the sense of sisterhood and empowerment she experienced through Women in Mission, an organization that she expected to be "a bunch of staid old fuddy-duddies." Which, said Shutt, "they *were*, in appearance. But they were very empowering." Shutt remembers walking down a hallway en route to a meeting at the denominational headquarters and passing an old woman bent over and using two canes. "You go, girl!" the woman told her.[5]

* * * * *

When Mennonite Women USA leaders shared an abbreviated Sister Care seminar at the 2014 Native Mennonite Ministries assembly, Suzette Shreffler was intrigued. The presenters were not able to lead a full seminar at the assembly, and Shreffler knew she wanted to experience the entire program. When she returned home, she spoke to Nadine Busenitz, a leader at her church, White River Cheyenne Mennonite in Busby, Montana. Busenitz had heard about Sister Care and was also interested, so the two women made plans to attend a full Sister Care event in Iowa.[6]

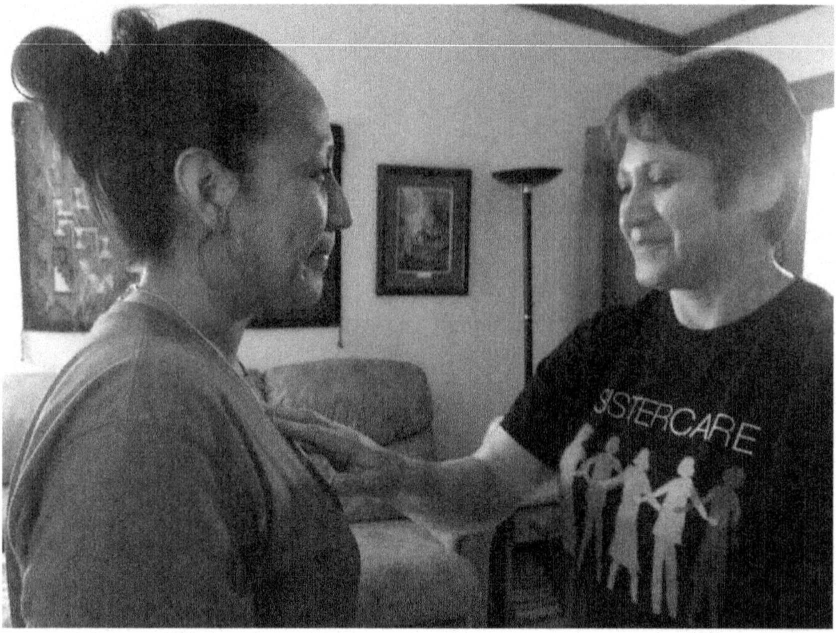

Suzette Shreffler (right) anointing Roslyn Bigback in the Sister Care closing blessing ritual in a seminar led by Shreffler and Nadine Busenitz in Busby, Montana.

"The seminar cost thirty-five dollars or something and we drove over one thousand miles to get there!" Shreffler said, laughing, in a 2015 interview. But the trip was worth it. Sister Care, which provides women with tools for ongoing personal healing and for responding more effectively to the needs of others, helped Shreffler think about how to relate to her son and daughter-in-law, who had just lost a child. Shreffler also saw the program's potential to touch her own life and the lives of women in her community. Shreffler is one of many Native women who have experienced domestic violence, and her openness about her story has prompted others to tell her about their struggles. "Almost on a weekly basis someone comes wanting to share," she said. "Sister Care has helped me be a compassionate listener and helped me deal with my own feelings."[7]

In early 2016, Shreffler began using the Sister Care materials in her weekly visits to a girls' detention center. Though the frequent turnover of attendees makes it difficult to progress through the program, simply reading a blessing from the material has been meaningful. "I read this and the tears start to roll down their cheeks," Shreffler said. "I know it touches them deep in their hearts and gives them hope."[8] Shreffler and Busenitz also started a Sister Care Bible study group with women from their church. "There's such a need for God's healing in the emotional areas of life here," Busenitz said. "We're hoping for a better way of supporting each other."[9]

* * * * *

These three stories—the work of Lancaster's Associated Sewing Circles, Joyce Shutt's challenging of denominational structures, and the various uses of Sister Care in Montana—provide a glimpse of the different purposes Mennonite women's groups have served over the past one hundred years. For some women, these groups have been a way to serve others by sewing clothing, laboring over quilts, rolling bandages, and packing school kits, thus extending God's love in material ways in their own communities and around the world. For others, women's groups have provided an opportunity to test their skills as leaders and give voice to callings they felt. And for just about everyone who has participated in them, women's groups have been a source of support—a place for connection and for sharing the struggles and joys of being women across ages, spaces, and cultures.

From their inception, Mennonite women's organizations have created space for women to serve others *and* to develop a "circle of sisterhood" among themselves. As we will see throughout these pages, the service and sisterhood functions of women's organizations have sometimes been at odds with each other or have created a sense of confusion about the identity of the organizations. More recently, through programs such as Mennonite Women USA's Sister Care, the two functions have merged in a way that seems promising for the future. But even if not explicitly stated, Mennonite women's groups have always had both an outward and an inward focus. Through congregation-based women's groups, Mennonite women have connected with each other, with women around the world, with God, and with the stirrings of their own souls.

This book tells the story of Mennonite Women USA (MW USA), the organization that nurtures and supports congregational women's groups and provides ministries that engage many individual women. MW USA is a constituency group of Mennonite Church USA, a denomination formed in 2002 through a merger of the "old" Mennonite

Church (MC) and the General Conference Mennonite Church (GCMC), both of which had their own women's organizations. In 2017, MW USA celebrated one hundred years of the existence of denominational Mennonite women's organizations.

The story of Mennonite women's organizations is a story of struggles and triumphs, of productivity and misgivings, of questions and celebrations. Uncovering this story has been both a formidable and inspiring journey for me as I read stacks of books and articles, spent hours in archives and historical libraries, and interviewed scores of women. Along the way, I learned not just about an organization but about important historical events, changing church structures, the enduring hopes of women, and the way that God keeps working in all kinds of circumstances.

When I took on this project soon after turning twenty-nine, I knew I had a lot to learn. I did not live through the historical eras or participate in the denominational discussions that shaped so much of this story. Though I have attended Mennonite congregations all my life, I have never been part of one that had a women's group connected to the denominational women's organization. I did not recall ever hearing my mother or grandmothers talk about participating in church women's gatherings.

It was a delightful surprise when my dad, while cleaning out my late grandmother's files several months after I started my research, found a yellowed folder labeled "Hands for Jesus Circle." Inside were event programs, notes for talks, and a reflective article written by my grandmother about the Girls' Missionary Sewing Association group she led at Pleasant View Mennonite Church in North Lawrence, Ohio (see chapter 2). It was interesting to speculate about the significance this role might have had for her, as well as for her church and community.

Another delightful surprise came when I was perusing past issues of *Timbrel*, the magazine of Mennonite Women USA. In the March/April 2010 issue, Anna Groff responded to a question about what helped when feeling lonely in one's community. "I joined a book club about three years ago when I moved to Pittsburgh," Groff wrote. "Meeting regularly with this intergenerational group of women provides a constant reminder that I am not alone in addressing the following: charting my career and family life, my relationship with my church, the influence of my family of origin, the push and pull of significant relationships and more."[10] As an intern at Pittsburgh Mennonite Church, I had worked with an older woman from the congregation to start that book club, and I believe it is still going strong ten years later. We started the book club with the intention of engaging young adults in the area, but it soon morphed into a space for women of different ages and levels of church commitment to connect with each other. That experience, and its continuing significance for those involved, made me consider the value of women getting together to support each other—something I had not given much attention to before. The value of women meeting together as women while grounded in the call of God is something that permeates these pages and sustains this journey through different eras, locations, and cultural contexts.

The book is divided into three parts that cover periods of different lengths. The chapters proceed somewhat chronologically, which should give the reader the sense of an unfolding story and help place the different organization names, projects, and people in their appropriate eras. However, several "interludes" throughout the book allow me to separately discuss important themes or questions that have been present for Mennonite women's groups over the duration of their existence.

Part 1, spanning the early 1900s through the 1960s, narrates the beginning and development of denominational women's organizations in both the Mennonite Church and General Conference Mennonite Church. Chapter 1 includes a brief introduction to women's roles in Anabaptist-Mennonite history and tells of the earliest efforts toward organization of Mennonite women on a denominational level. Chapter 2 gives an overview of what many consider to have been the prime of church women's groups, the 1940s through the 1960s, and concludes before the women's liberation movement noticeably affected the church in the 1970s. This formational period receives just two chapters because it has already been discussed in several books and articles, most notably *Women in Search of Mission* by Gladys Goering (a study of GCMC groups) and *Mennonite Women: A Story of God's Faithfulness* by Elaine Sommers Rich, as well as *Mennonite Quarterly Review* articles by Melvin Gingerich and Sharon Klingelsmith (all MC-related projects). I draw on these works in the first section of this book but add new information and provide a frame of wider events in church and society.

These first two chapters build a basis for understanding the trajectory and significance of the women's organizations in more recent years.

Part 2 begins with the 1970s and ends with 1997, the year the women's organizations from the two denominations merged. The 1970s were a time of great change for Mennonite women's groups, as was the decade for women in general. Both the MC and GCMC women's organizations changed their names in the early 1970s, reflecting a broader focus and more diverse membership as well as shifting relationships with their related denominations. The first chapter in this part (chapter 3) provides context for understanding the events and issues of the 1970s. Chapter 4 discusses the MC women's group, which took the name Women's Missionary and Service Commission (WMSC) in 1971. Chapter 6 discusses the GCMC women's group, which adopted the name Women in Mission in 1974. In between, chapter 5 explores the activities of black and Hispanic Mennonite women, two distinct and vibrant cultural groups most closely related to the MC. To close the section, chapter 7 explores the context of the 1980s and 1990s and the beginnings of collaboration between the two denominational organizations.

Part 3 opens with chapter 8, which discusses the relatively brief existence of Mennonite Women, the merged GCMC and MC organization that included women from Canada and the United States. In 2002, the MC, GCMC, and Conference of Mennonites in Canada formed two national bodies, which led to the formation of Mennonite Women USA (MW USA) and a separate Canadian group (first called Canadian Women in Mission and then Mennonite Women Canada). Chapter 9 covers the major activities of MW USA from its inception to the present. Chapter 10 focuses on Sister Care, the most prominent ministry of MW USA, a program that has had a global reach and has especially gained traction among Latin American women.

Although this is a story of a denominational organization, the real heart of MW USA is the smaller groups of women who meet in congregations and gather for events organized by area conference women leaders. Chapter 11 highlights a sample of activities of local and regional groups of Mennonite women. Finally, chapter 12 puts this continuing story in the context of denominational and societal realities and offers thoughts about the future of Mennonite women's organizations and God's work through women in the years to come.

PART I: 1917–1960s

Let us not become weary in doing good, for at the proper time we will reap a harvest if we do not give up. Therefore, as we have opportunity, let us do good to all people, especially to those who belong to the family of believers.

—Galatians 6:9-10 (NIV)

1
Beginnings of Mennonite Women's Groups

> While the Bruderschaft [Brotherhood] was making the important decisions in the main body of the church, the Frauenverein [women's society] was in the basement, getting the food ready. . . . Mennonite identity, as defined upstairs by the men, may be built on the bodies of the women who offer their labors in the basement.
> —Magdalene Redekop[1]

In 1551, Lijsken Dircks and Jerome Segers, an Anabaptist couple, were arrested as heretics and imprisoned in Antwerp, Belgium. As Anabaptists, Lijsken and Jerome rejected infant baptism in favor of baptism of adults upon a confession of faith and questioned the sacramental system of the dominant church tradition of their time. The couple was jailed separately and eventually martyred separately. Jerome was burned at the stake on September 2, 1551; Lijsken was drowned in the early morning hours of February 9, 1552, after she had given birth to their child.[2]

Martyrs Mirror records several letters the couple wrote to each other from prison. The letters of both writers are filled with Scripture passages, which they used to encourage each other to remain true to their understanding of biblical faith. In one of her letters, Lijsken recorded these words from her interrogator: "Why do you trouble yourself with the Scriptures; attend to your sewing."[3] Jerome wrote in his reply: "And though they may tell you to attend to your sewing, this does not prevent us; for Christ has called us all . . . and Christ also said that Magdalene had chosen the better part, because she searched the Scriptures."[4]

The letters of Lijsken Dircks and Jerome Segers provide a glimpse into the position of women among the early Anabaptists. Jerome addressed Lijsken as both a beloved wife and his spiritual equal, comparing her to the biblical figure of Mary Magdalene and using Scripture to affirm her preference for spiritual study over sewing. Women such as Lijsken likely played a significant role in the Anabaptist movement of sixteenth-century Europe—significant enough to be persecuted for their faith. About one-third of the people listed in the *Martyrs Mirror* are women, some of them described as deaconesses, teachers, or prophetesses.[5]

The Anabaptists, sometimes known as the Radical Reformers, shared in common some ideas with prominent church reformers Martin Luther and Ulrich Zwingli, such as the authority of Scripture alone, salvation by faith through grace, and the concept of a priesthood of all believers. The "radical" stream of the Reformation, however, emphasized the activity of the Holy Spirit, both in individuals and in the gathered community of believers, as part of the interpretation of Scripture. In *Profiles of Anabaptist Women*, C. Arnold Snyder and Linda Huebert Hecht write that this radical spiritual emphasis is crucial in telling of the story of Anabaptist women. Because the Holy Spirit could work in anyone regardless of status or education level, and because of the decentralized nature of Anabaptism, women had significant opportunities for participation in the movement.[6]

As Anabaptism morphed into more settled religious bodies (including Mennonites, Hutterites, Amish, and some Brethren groups), women mostly played behind-the-scenes roles. Mennonite historian Lois Barrett writes that after the creative initial phase of Anabaptism, the status of Mennonite women was comparable to that of other women in European culture.[7] Mennonites, who had taken the name of the Dutch leader Menno Simons and adopted his pacifist convictions, moved to the United States and Canada in various waves starting in the late seventeenth century. In North America, they often settled in close-knit communities that stressed nonconformity to the society around them. While Mennonite women took on leadership roles in some isolated cases, as churches and denominational structures developed, women were generally excluded from decision-making or leadership bodies.[8]

Sewing Circles

By the early twentieth century, Mennonite women may have felt that, like Lijsken Dircks several centuries earlier, they were expected to attend to domestic tasks and leave the more public church or community matters to the men. But as did women from many Christian denominations, Mennonite women across Canada and the United States were beginning to meet in local groups and, in the parlance of the day, "attend to their sewing" together. In doing so, they engaged in work that significantly supported the mission of their congregations and denominations and connected them to each other in new and deeper ways.

One early sewing circle was organized by women from Sycamore Grove Mennonite Church in Missouri. The Mennonite Church's

Five women from the original 1887 Newton (Kans.) Sewing Circle, 1945.

denominational magazine mentions a missions contribution from the "Sycamore and Bethel Congregations Sewing Circle, Garden City, Missouri," as early as 1901.[9] Even before their formal organization as a group, women met in homes to sew together, often making garments and carpet rags and doing mending for their hostess. Each person took a sack lunch; the hostess provided hot drinks. A brief history of the Sycamore Grove church says that the women were paid one dollar for their services and that the money was put into the treasury "to be used for a benevolent cause."[10] The first existing notes of the Sycamore Grove Sewing Circle are from a meeting dated July 8, 1915. The notes record that "the House was called to order by a Song," after which "Sister Sarah Miller led in prayer" and officers were elected.[11] Money was also collected, probably to pay for sewing materials and to donate to missions. The fifty women present that day made forty garments and one quilt. Some of the items were given to "a family of our Home members," and the rest were sent to "Argentine Mission."[12]

Early sewing circle notes also exist from Prairie Street Mennonite Church in Elkhart, Indiana. Even though the group usually included only a handful of women, their commitment was remarkable. Notes from a meeting on October 14, 1908, state that the attendees decided to prepare a box of clothing for the Fort Wayne Mission before Thanksgiving, so they called an extra meeting to supplement their regular monthly schedule. An entry on November 11, 1908, records a three-page list of what they sent, including new and old (presumably mended) garments. The extensive list includes "comfort[er]s," vests, dresses, aprons, suits, petticoats, underwear, "[shirt]waists," socks, stockings, shoes, coats, pants, capes, and "one flour sack dried apple, corn, and beans." Extra meetings were also sometimes called to sew for individuals in the community, perhaps someone who had experienced a fire or other disaster. Notes from a meeting on February 6, 1918, record that "a rush order from Ft. Wayne came between this and the last sewing which was done by several of the sisters." During the 1910s, the group contributed financial aid to "missionary support" and material aid to the "Old People's Home," "Orphan Home," a "poor family," and "unfortunate Belgians."[13]

The Prairie Street and Sycamore Grove groups show the productivity and passion of Mennonite women around the turn of the twentieth century. By the 1910s, sewing groups were being called upon to meet specific needs of people in their communities or at mission stations, as the "rush order" from Fort Wayne to Prairie Street shows. In many Mennonite sewing circles, meetings were opened with prayer by a man,

Many congregations had multiple women's groups, often divided by age. These photos, taken in 1902, show the older and younger women's groups from Bethel Mennonite Church in Mountain Lake, Minnesota.

or the male pastor came to lead a devotional time. But in other groups, like Sycamore Grove, "sisters" led singing and prayers. (Contrary to the typical practice of the day, the Sycamore Grove notes record women's full names preceded by "Sister" instead of a woman's husband's name preceded by "Mrs.") In almost all early sewing groups, women elected their own governing officers, organized projects, and collected and administered monetary funds. Throughout North America, women's sewing circles and missionary aid societies gave women a place to both engage in service and form a circle of sisterhood.

Early Organization

By the mid-nineteenth century, most Protestant denominations in North America were engaged in building institutions and programs. They formed mission boards, Sunday schools, and institutions of higher education. Women saw the benefits of increased effectiveness and enthusiasm that came with organization and collaboration. By 1912, nearly all the major Protestant bodies had organized denominational women's missionary societies.[14] While Mennonites lagged somewhat behind mainstream Protestant denominations in institution building, by 1912, both the Mennonite Church (MC) and the General Conference Mennonite Church (GCMC) had started magazines, established schools for higher education, and embarked on mission work at home and abroad. Marlene Epp points out that this expansion of church programs also happened in a context of great public activity of women in society overall.[15] In Mennonite circles, new administrative and educational institutions provided roles for women as Sunday school teachers, missionaries, deaconesses, writers for religious publications, and leaders in women's groups formed to support mission activity.[16]

Strong interest in mission and biblical education were among the reasons some Mennonite individuals and congregations expressed a desire to organize and meet together in "general conferences" in the mid-1800s. By 1860, this group had become a new Mennonite denomination called the General Conference Mennonite Church (GCMC), as distinct from the "old" Mennonite Church (MC). (Later, many congregations, primarily made up of Mennonites coming from Russian-controlled lands, would join the GCMC without having any previous connection to other Mennonite bodies in the United States.) Women's sewing groups were present in GCMC-affiliated congregations soon after the formation of the denomination—if not before—in places like Donnellson, Iowa, and Bally, Pennsylvania.[17] James Juhnke writes that the first GCMC women's missionary society in the United States was organized in the Salem congregation in Ashland, Ohio, before the denominational mission board existed.[18] Clearly, it was not just the male leaders of the GCMC who were interested in mission. In fact, mission work was one of relatively few acceptable public areas of interest for women in the denomination. Beginning in the early 1890s, GCMC women oversaw an evening mission program at the triennial assembly of the denomination.[19] Women's groups also gave material and financial support to the GCMC's Wadsworth Institute, which trained missionaries and church leaders.

Women's mission societies existed in the Mennonite Church (MC) before the twentieth century as well. The earliest mention of a women's group in a denominational periodical is a note about contributions to mission from a group of "sisters" in 1894.[20] Donations from "sisters" or "Ladies Aid Societies" in Missouri, Pennsylvania, Ontario, Indiana, Illinois, Ohio, and Kansas are mentioned before 1900.[21] Some people, such as Clara Eby Steiner, saw a potential benefit to organizing the work of these widespread women's groups. Clara Eby Steiner was the wife

Missionaries often started sewing circles in the areas where they served. Taken about 1900, this photograph shows, according to notes, a "Sewing class of Mrs. Marie Petter in Cantonment, Oklahoma, composed of Northern Cheyenne women."

Clara Eby Steiner (seated) in 1920 with her infant grandson Hugh Hostetler, father Tobias Eby, and daughter Charity Steiner Hostetler.

of prominent MC mission leader Menno Simon Steiner, and she often assisted her husband with church activities. Menno died in March 1911, leaving Clara with a family to raise and bereft of the active role she had held in the denomination as Menno's spouse and partner.[22] By August 1911, Clara had begun writing letters and making visits to local MC sewing circles to encourage wider organization among the women.[23] Her goal was to better connect the women's groups to each other and to the church's missionaries—especially to female missionaries, who made up more than half the MC mission force at the time.[24]

Steiner's organizing activities yielded results, and a first general meeting of MC sewing circle women was held at the denomination's biennial assembly near Wauseon, Ohio, in 1915. "Several hundred interested sisters from a number of States and Canada" attended the gathering.[25] At a second general meeting, held in 1916 just before the Ohio Sunday School Conference, three officers were elected to give leadership to a denominational women's group: Steiner, Mary Burkhard, and Ruth A. Yoder.[26] The organization met again in connection with the June 1917 Ohio Sunday School Conference and a fourth time during the August 1917 MC assembly at Yellow Creek Mennonite Church (near Goshen, Ind.). At the August 1917 meeting, women elected fourteen district representatives for the organization, which later took the name Mennonite Woman's Missionary Society (MWMS).[27]

Already by 1918, the MWMS had begun supporting a female missionary in India.[28] In the following years, the organization continued contributing funds and sewing clothes for missionaries and projects in India, and it began raising money to build an orphan's home in West Liberty, Ohio.[29] A 1921 report that collected information from

124 women's groups reported more than 21,000 garments made and more than $15,000 contributed.[30] To facilitate communication from the executive committee to local groups, Steiner started the *Monthly Letter* in 1919. The publication contained letters from missionaries and relief workers, short descriptions of what various women's groups were doing, financial reports, and the organization's book recommendations. In 1924, the MWMS began issuing a *Booklet of Prayer for Missions of the Mennonite Church*, a devotional guide to focus the prayers of its users; this project has continued in various forms to today.[31]

The year 1917 was a significant point in the formation of the MC women's organization, as the election of district officers solidified and expanded the reach of the network. The same year saw the beginning of a denominational women's organization in the GCMC. At the 1917 triennial GCMC assembly at First Mennonite Church in Reedley, California, women conducted a business meeting and elected a three-member executive committee "for the purpose of bringing the mission and sewing societies of our conference into closer touch with our foreign missionaries."[32] The new executive committee—Susannah Haury, Martha Goerz, and Anna Isaac—had its first official meeting in a parked car on the church grounds.[33] The organization soon took the name Women's Missionary Association (WMA). The denominational organization united approximately seventy congregational women's societies that were actively involved in mission programs.[34]

The WMA eventually took over the intermediary task of handling requests, sometimes for specific clothing items, from missionaries to local sewing groups. The denominational organization contacted missionary families about their needs and developed "wants lists." Each women's group was assigned a mission station and missionary family, and personal relationships often formed between group members and the missionaries they supported. Gladys Goering writes that during this time, church mission circles "became veritable factories in the production of goods."[35] Women made and sent clothing to domestic mission outposts ministering to Native Americans in Montana and Arizona and to city mission stations. The most donations were sent to India, though; from 1917 to 1934, groups sent 54,560 pounds of materials to India alone.[36] WMA leadership also had a goal of informing congregation members about mission activity. They appointed a literature committee to issue pamphlets, and a magazine called *Missionary News and Notes* began publication in English and German in 1926.

It appears that the new denominational women's organizations were quickly accepted and affirmed by female missionaries. Agnes Wiens, a GCMC missionary, had spoken in favor of such an organization during her time back in North America. She later wrote, "We want to let you know that we are very glad a committee of ladies has been formed to act as mediator between the sewing societies and the missionaries."[37] A 1924 letter from Emma H. Shank, an MC missionary in Brazil, spoke of her visits to sewing circles affiliated with the MWMS while home on furlough. She wrote, "This is encouraging and we hope that you may continue to try to know our field and work better, for the more you know the more definitely can you pray for us, and the more intelligently give and do for the support of the work."[38] Also writing in 1924, missionary Lydia Lehman reflected on her careful reading of the previous year's report from the MC women's organization. She wrote, "Think of what can be accomplished in the future if the Women's Missionary work grows in the next ten years as it has in the last ten."[39] Some missionaries even discovered that they could get a quicker and more favorable response by writing directly to the women's organization or congregational women's groups rather than by going through the denomination's mission board.[40]

Tensions and "Takeover"

Despite the support from missionaries—or perhaps partially because of it—the fledgling denominational women's organizations experienced tension with the all-male mission boards of their denominations. WMA leaders were frustrated by the lack of public recognition of their work by the GCMC and its Foreign Mission Board, even though they were working closely with that agency. As Gladys Goering relates in *Women in Search of Mission*, although "voluminous reports" of the mission board's work appeared in church papers in the early 1920s, the work of the Women's Missionary Association was never mentioned. After repeated requests for such recognition, which WMA leaders thought would help validate their young organization, a report from the mission board finally appeared in the church papers. It contained the sentence "The sisters have done good work, and the board will allow them further mediation." In a letter to the WMA executive committee, Frieda Regier expressed her surprise at the reference, which she said struck her as "rather peculiar." She added, "I think it sounds rather weak, at least the last part. But I may misunderstand the good man entirely." WMA leaders continued to lament the lack of publicity for their organization. While their submissions were regularly printed in *Der Bote* (the German-language denominational periodical), the editor of *The Mennonite* (the English-language periodical) often chose not to print what they submitted or otherwise scattered it throughout the magazine. Advocating for a regular column for the group, Martha Goerz wrote, "This may sound like Women's Rights, but I think it should be done for the good of the cause." Goering writes that the reason for the denomination's opposition to publicizing the work of WMA is unclear, though she quotes a 1925 letter from Goerz saying that "it is hard for some of our men to realize that women can do other things besides keeping house and raising families."[41]

Although many Mennonites in the early 1900s lived in rather insular communities, Goerz's comment about "Women's Rights" reveals that the events and debates of wider North American society were also present for Mennonites. While the United States' entrance into World War I in April 1917 was surely the most pressing contemporary event for pacifist Mennonites, the politics of the Progressive Era and the women's suffrage movement were also on the minds of church members. Scholars have dubbed the feminist activity of women during the nineteenth and early twentieth centuries as "first-wave" feminism. Much of women's activism during this era focused around gaining legal rights, culminating in North America with national suffrage for white women in Canada in 1918 and in the United States in 1920. Many Mennonites during this time did not vote and discouraged any engagement with the political system, but the changing status of women in society certainly affected the formation and development of church women's groups and the discomfort some male leaders had with them. Women leaders sometimes had to defend themselves against involvement in "worldly" causes; in a 1918 letter to Daniel Kauffman (a prominent MC leader), Clara Eby Steiner assured him that the women she was organizing were not suffragettes.[42]

Most writing by and about early Mennonite women's organizations stresses the spiritual and ecclesial motivations for the groups. The early women leaders saw their work as closely tied to the existing programs of their respective denominations. However, Mennonite denominational women's organizations were formed at a time of exponential growth for women's associations in broader society.[43] Although early women's group leaders rarely refer to other organizations, it seems likely that Mennonite women were influenced in some way by the activities of groups such as the Women's Christian Temperance Union (organized in 1873) and the Women's International League for Peace and Freedom (formed in 1915), as well as women's missions groups in other denominations. In general, women's mission groups did not see themselves as part of the women's movement of the late nineteenth and early twentieth centuries; Wendy Mitchinson concludes as much in her analysis of women's societies in several Protestant denominations in Canada.[44] Yet, as Mitchinson points out, congregational women's groups provided a meaningful outlet for their participants' energies and ended up contributing to an increased role for women in society at large.[45] In *Women and Twentieth-Century Protestantism*, Margaret Bendroth and Virginia Brereton make a similar point, claiming that women in missionary societies "were not, on the whole, cultural radicals."[46] Bendroth and Brereton write that women in early mission organizations did not challenge male hegemony but rather built power in separate institutions.[47]

Early Mennonite women's group leaders would hardly have been labeled as radicals by most people outside their denominations. But some in the Mennonite Church (MC) especially saw the women's organization leaders as, if not radicals, then at least liberals. To understand this characterization, one must grasp the context of the time. By the 1920s, within Christian circles a debate was raging, a debate now called the fundamentalist-modernist controversy. While this doctrinal battle between more conservative (fundamentalist) and liberal (modernist) Christians had its roots in the Presbyterian Church, its effects were felt in most Christian denominations, including among Mennonites. During a period of rapid societal change, some Mennonites, particularly in the MC, were drawn to fundamentalism, though it was often expressed in a form different from that of other Protestant groups. For example,

Jennifer Graber writes that rather than take issue with the fashions of the day because they posed a danger to men or violated the Victorian cult of domesticity, Mennonites advocated for plain, modest dress as an expression of community nonconformity.[48] Paul Toews writes that some Mennonites saw fundamentalism as a way to "codify doctrine, reassert churchly authority, and redefine cultural boundaries."[49] While Mennonite men, especially church leaders, were encouraged to wear the plain coat (a suit with no tie), many of the dress restrictions were directed toward women. Using 1 Corinthians 11:1-16 as justification, church leaders stressed that women should wear a devotional head covering in all situations, not only in prayer or worship, as was the traditional practice in many places.[50] Wearing a covering was seen mainly as fulfilling a biblical commandment but also as a sign of women's subordinate status in the order of creation.[51]

This greater attention to the distinct place of women was no doubt one reason that men sometimes viewed women's organizations with suspicion. In addition, organizing to promote missions—and simply organizing about anything—was still somewhat controversial in the MC. Paul Toews notes that in the early 1900s, MC leaders "clearly were troubled at any kind of freelance organization."[52] Desires to organize as a denomination, to engage in mission, and to start Sunday schools had contributed to the original break of GCMC congregations from the "old" Mennonite body, and these things were still regarded with caution by some in the MC. In some places, women were permitted to give talks to mixed-gender groups at Sunday school conferences and mission meetings, but this was not allowed in general church settings. Thus, the organization of women's mission societies (as well as the Sunday school movement) had a liberal or progressive connotation for many people at the time.

The additional involvements of the leaders of the Mennonite Woman's Missionary Society also surely contributed to the perception of their endeavor. In a *Mennonite Quarterly Review* article on women in the MC, Sharon Klingelsmith discusses the conservative-liberal debate of the early twentieth century and writes that MWMS leaders "for the most part, would have to be placed on the liberal side in that struggle." Clara Eby Steiner's daughters and sons-in-law had participated in the Young People's Movement in the MC, a group that expressed dissatisfaction with the slow movement of denominational leadership, and Steiner herself had given a talk at one of their conferences. Ruth A. Yoder (the first MWMS treasurer) and Crissie Shank (MWMS secretary of literature) were both on the editorial team for the *Christian Exponent*, a short-lived Mennonite journal that attempted to provide an alternative voice to the more conservative main body of the MC denomination.[53]

It was in this atmosphere of conservative-liberal tension that the MC women's organization was effectively subsumed by the denomination. Sometime before November 4, 1925, Clara Eby Steiner wrote a letter to Emma Stutzman Yoder asking her to take charge of the sewing orders from overseas mission stations, since Steiner's health was failing.[54] Emma Yoder never wrote back, but her husband did. S. C. Yoder, who was the executive secretary of the Mennonite Board of Missions and Charities at the time, replied that his wife could not take on this task and said that people had been asking for a central committee to receive all sewing orders.[55] A March 1925 issue of *Gospel Herald*, the MC periodical, carried a letter from S. C. Yoder announcing that the mission board had appointed a "Committee of three sisters" who were to "have charge of the distribution of the Sewing Circle work."[56]

The leaders of the women's organization wondered what was happening, but they received no reply when they wrote to denominational leadership asking for an explanation.[57] Since the organization saw overall promotion of mission—not just sewing—as its goal, it continued operating for several years in addition to the committee appointed by the mission board. This arrangement was not tenable, however, and in late 1927 the executive committee of the women's organization announced that they "in joint session with the committee appointed by the General Board and at the suggestion of their committee give the further planning and work of this society over to the General Mission Board or such other persons as they see fit to sponsor it."[58] This completed what was essentially a takeover of the relatively young women's group by the denominational structures. The June 1929 *Gospel Herald* carried this statement from the mission board:

> The church has not looked with favor on such a movement, not that it was not interested in women's work but because it was

> feared that the organization of such a society would have a divisive influence. We can see a reason why there should be a women's sewing organization, for this is distinctly woman's work.
>
> With a separate mission society this is different.[59]

A "Final Report of the Mennonite Woman's Missionary Society" in July 1929 reported that the MWMS handed over its funds and any further work of the women and girls to a committee appointed by the mission board.[60]

The MC women's organization was not alone in experiencing a takeover by its denominational mission board in the early twentieth century. It was a time of business mergers and consolidation in the secular world, and Christian denominations were not exempt from the impulse toward amalgamation and efficiency.[61] During this time, male-led mission boards in many Protestant denominations made moves to more closely tie, or even subsume, female-led mission groups to denominational structures. For example, in the Christian Church (predecessor of the Disciples of Christ denomination), a male leader arranged the election of several men to the female-led National Benevolent Association in 1917. Loretta Long notes that the women soon "lost control over their activities and never again exercised so much power over reform efforts among Disciples."[62] In the Presbyterian Church, a major reorganization in 1923 subsumed various women's boards under the denominational mission structure. While church leaders assured women that they would have representation on the broader mission boards, women's organization participants resented church leaders for taking such an action without consulting them.[63] In 1927, three out of four Congregationalist women's boards of mission were absorbed into the male-led foreign mission board. The women voted for this arrangement, but with it they lost control over their money and their direct connection to female missionaries.[64] Susan Yohn suggests that women's mission groups in various denominations were "takeover" targets during this time because the women were so successful at fundraising and at developing their work.[65] In the process of consolidation, though, male leaders "raised a host of questions about the efficacy of women's endeavors, not the least of which called into question women's motivations in building an enterprise and their ability to administer the funds they raised."[66]

Regardless of whether MC leaders had such qualms about the women's motivations, their actions certainly made the women feel that their efforts were being questioned. One can imagine that it was indeed confusing to have two denominational groups communicating with missionaries and organizing projects. But to the women involved—and to many Mennonite women hearing this story in later years—the actions of the mission board seemed inconsiderate at best and oppressive at worst. In her 1983 narration of these events, Elaine Sommers Rich connects the men's desire to relegate the women to a sewing role with the story of martyr Lijsken Dircks.[67] She notes that women's group leaders Clara Eby Steiner, Martha Steiner, and Crissie Shank all died in the late 1920s, amid the confusion with the mission board. "Did they die at least partially of broken hearts?" Rich asks.[68] After consolidating the denomination's mission support, the mission board may have been able to operate more efficiently, but the connection between congregational women's groups and denominational efforts waned. In 1927, the Mennonite Women's Missionary Society counted 8,629 members; the new women's sewing committee appointed by the mission board reported around 3,000 members in 1931.[69]

The so-called takeover of the MC women's organization raises the question of why the GCMC Women's Missionary Association fared differently. Partially this had to do with the different (and less significant) way that fundamentalism affected the GCMC. As James Juhnke writes, many GCMC members were more recent immigrants and were at a different point in the acculturation process.[70] Their struggles during and beyond the 1920s were about cultural and linguistic assimilation, and the fundamentalist-modernist debate in wider North American religious contexts did not influence them in any uniform way.[71] The GCMC body was also organized in a less hierarchical manner and, unlike the MC, lacked bishops to promote adherence to church authority. The MC women's organization may also have fared differently because of the status of its leaders. Besides their involvement in so-called liberal causes, at the time the Mennonite Church's MWMS was formed, its three leaders were all unmarried: Clara Eby Steiner and Mary Burkhard were widows and Ruth A. Yoder was single. By contrast, the three original leaders of the GCMC Women's Missionary Association were all married, and their husbands were significant leaders in the mission field or in the denomination.[72] Toews writes that GCMC mission leaders "actively sought the women's cooperation"; starting in the 1930s, the mission board invited two members of the women's association to its meetings and integrated projects the women initiated into its work.[73]

The Dual Purpose of Mennonite Women's Groups

Of course, the maneuvering of denominational structures did not necessarily affect the thousands of women who continued to gather in church basements and living rooms to sew, talk, and worship together. Some local and regional groups had never joined the denominational women's organization in the first place because of pressure from area church leaders or their own uncertainty about the value of wider cooperation.[74] Yet the women continued working in their local groups, leading meetings, organizing sewing projects, giving devotional reflections, making presentations, and recruiting more women to join their efforts. At many gatherings, mothers brought their children, who played beneath quilt canopies and heard stories of missionaries in faraway lands.

Aside from questions about their organizational independence, the material work of Mennonite women was undoubtedly needed. As World War I ended, Mennonite women responded to urgent calls for aid, both for people dealing with the war's effects abroad and for new immigrants to North America. A 1922 *Monthly Letter* reported that the Mennonite Relief Commission (an organization of the MC mission board) had decided to work though the sewing circles rather than make appeals directly to congregations.[75] The women apparently rose to the occasion, sending many items to Russia in particular. By the end of 1923 the need had abated, and Crissie Shank wrote, "Thank God the Russian Relief work is closing! It has been a time not soon to be forgotten for the methods of work it developed and for the accomplishments it achieves."[76]

GCMC members were particularly involved with relief to Mennonite immigrants who came from Russia to Canada, since some shared family ties with the new arrivals. The Women's Missionary Association provided material aid and helped raise funds for homes for immigrant girls who came to Canadian cities to work.[77] GCMC women's groups in Canada did not organize nationally until 1952, at which point they established a closer relationship with the WMA. But sewing circles had been present in Canadian Mennonite congregations before the twentieth century—the first one perhaps at Gretna, Manitoba, in 1895 or 1896.[78] Mennonites coming from famine-stricken Russia to Canada often quickly formed their own circles once they had settled there. Esther Patkau writes of a group formed in 1929 in Yarrow, British Columbia: "They themselves had experienced what it meant to suffer. A group of thirteen women formed a 'Maria Martha Verein' (sewing circle), their name indicating their character: to meet for spiritual encouragement and to serve."[79]

Patkau's description highlights a central theme of this book: the dual purpose of Mennonite women's groups. In their organizations, women came together to *work*—to meet the needs of others, often with amazing dedication. But they also *came together* to work—to meet their own needs for fellowship and community. Meeting regularly with other women to collaborate on projects and gather funds was an outlet for serving others, but it also provided opportunity for social connection and spiritual growth. In *The Work of Their Hands*, Gloria Neufeld Redekop identifies "three foci"—service, fellowship, and worship—as primary for Mennonite women's societies.[80] Throughout this book, I will most often speak of two foci, or a dual purpose, discussing how the groups functioned, and continue to function, as spaces for service and sisterhood. Through their material and monetary support of mission stations and, later, of relief agencies like Mennonite Central Committee, women's organizations gave Mennonite women a tangible way to participate in Jesus' call to serve others. The groups also allowed Mennonite women to experience a circle of sisterhood. Though early twentieth-century Mennonites may not have used the term *sisterhood*, the language of "sisters" was common. Especially in MC congregations, church women called each other sisters and were also referred to that way by the "brothers." Meeting regularly with other women and worshiping with them, often without the presence of men, allowed women to bond with each other and develop a sense of personal empowerment. For some, this sense of sisterhood extended to the female missionaries they backed and, later, to women theologians they supported around the world.

The interplay of service (or mission) and sisterhood (or fellowship) is apparent both in the reflections of early women's group participants and in the work of scholars who have written about them. In her study of several sewing circles in Wayne County, Ohio, Valerie Rake notes that the groups' explicit focus involved support for missions and service to "the needy."[81] But, she writes, "an implicit focus—and one that shows up clearly in the oral histories—is Christian fellowship among the women of the congregation."[82] While service was the initial impetus for most early Mennonite women's groups, it seems likely that women continued to meet because of the sense of sisterhood they experienced. Notes from a 1921 gathering of Ohio women's group leaders list benefits derived from the district meetings. "Souls are warmed by the influence of others," the list states. "It keeps us in touch with the work the Master has given us."[83] Writing from a Canadian context, Marlene Epp notes that while women's groups formed out of a desire to do material mutual aid, the groups also provided a much-needed social outlet, especially for women in isolated rural communities.[84] Epp quotes one woman who said that her church women's group provided recreation and relief that were of "great personal value"; another woman said the meetings were "even therapeutic."[85]

This dual function of women's groups was not limited to Mennonite contexts. Discussing Protestant women's organizations in general, Rosemary Skinner Keller writes that beneath the duty to others "lay a duty to self, the need for women's society members to find deeper purpose for their individual lives."[86] While they worked to meet the needs of churches and social service agencies, women explored personal vocations, helped each other grow as leaders, and "developed bonds of sisterhood that previously had been inconceivable."[87] Early Mennonite women's group participants probably did not think of themselves as performing a "duty to self" when they attended their regular sewing meetings. But they certainly received support and encouragement as they worked together. And the leadership development aspect of the groups would come to the forefront later in the twentieth century, when women's group participants began to take prominent roles in congregations and the wider denominations.

While the close of the 1920s brought some uncertainty about the role of an MC women's organization and its relation to the denominational structure, the GCMC group seemed to be finding clarity about its identity and role. The first constitution and bylaws of the Women's

Missionary Association were written in August 1929 and set six-year terms for officers, stipulated that meetings were to be held every three years at the triennial GCMC assembly, and noted that all women's societies were expected to pay ten cents per member.[88] The organization's stated purpose was "to glorify God and serve the Conference and its missionary representatives (1) in the support of home and foreign missions; (2) in the spread of mission interests; (3) in the promotion of cooperation between mission societies and missions; and (4) in the production and dissemination of missionary literature."[89] This statement shows an entirely external focus, with missions referred to in each point. It was not until years later that the organization's purpose statement would articulate the fuller function (mission *and* sisterhood) that it actually served.

The Great Depression that began in late 1929 affected all society, including Mennonite denominations, congregations, and families. Mennonite women would sense more than ever the importance of contributing material and financial aid not only to faraway mission stations but also to individuals and groups closer to home. They would also continue to seek to care for the souls and spirits of those reached by international missionaries and of their "sisters" who sat beside them in the sewing circle. In chapter 2, we turn to the development of Mennonite women's organizations in the 1930s and beyond.

2
Years of Quiet Faithfulness

> We strive toward the vision of concerting the efforts of every Mennonite woman and girl to the total program of the Mennonite Church so that wherever the church is found, in city or country, at home or abroad, in charitable or educational institutions, in community efforts, in relief to the ends of the world, there we may be found enhancing the attractiveness of the Gospel and giving expression to the love of Jesus.
> —Minnie Graber[1]

Elaine Sommers Rich describes the 1930s and beyond as "years of quiet faithfulness" for Mennonite women's groups.[2] Many new groups formed in congregations, sometimes despite resistance from male church leaders. Area conferences (or "districts") and provinces formed regional organizations, each with their own president, treasurer, secretary of girls' groups, literature committee chairperson, and sometimes other positions. In denominations that were still overwhelming rural, interest grew in "home missions," especially for projects in urban centers.[3] Along with reports from India and China, women's groups began to hear about children in Kansas City and young women in Vancouver, and they often rallied their efforts around new home missions in their areas. A list of activities of Oregon Mennonite women during this time serves to describe the work of Mennonite women across North America: they sewed clothing, quilts, and comforters; they mended used clothing; they dried fruit and sent it to missionaries; they gave money and materials for local community and congregational needs;

they scrubbed, painted, and decorated in mission churches, homes for the aged, and parochial schools.[4] Congregations and mission agencies began to depend on the aid women's groups provided.

The Depression Era

Women's groups were significant forces in their denominations during the difficult Depression years. In *Mennonites in American Society*, Paul Toews writes that the stock market crash of 1929 did not immediately affect many Mennonites.[5] But subsequent falling crop prices did, and the new economic realities, coupled with the ongoing conservative-liberal tensions, were especially hard on Mennonite institutions.[6] In 1931, the Mennonite Church considered shutting down Hesston (Kans.) College. Toews writes that "as much as anybody, women of the surrounding congregations saved it from that fate."[7] Throughout the Depression, women made bed and window coverings for dorm rooms at Hesston and contributed canned foods for the cafeteria.[8] Women's groups in areas near other Mennonite schools likely supported them in similar ways. It is difficult to track the activity of the MC denominational women's organization during this time, since it was now simply a sewing circle committee under the mission board. Elaine Sommers Rich notes that the committee began supporting nurses at the La Junta (Colo.) Mennonite School of Nursing in 1934 and set up a "sheet and blanket fund" in 1937.[9]

The Women's Missionary Association (the GCMC group) and its local societies kept up their work during the challenging Depression era. In 1931, GCMC women's groups collaborated to raise money for a car for a missionary in China, a school in India, a hospital in Winnipeg, and Russian Mennonite refugee students.[10] Women also raised significant amounts of money for their congregations and denominational institutions. A history of British Columbia Mennonite women's groups records that when a group of Mennonite settlers arrived in Coghlan, British Columbia, in 1934, "the women were called upon to raise money by sewing articles and selling them, thus establishing a church construction fund."[11] Six women gathered, each donating twenty-five cents to purchase materials. Using the items they created as well as others donated by the surrounding community, their first sale in 1936 raised eighty-three dollars.[12] During this time and beyond, many church kitchens, nurseries, and libraries were furnished and financed by women's groups. Goering reports on women's groups purchasing pianos, carpeting, curtains, pulpits, hymnals, pews, and land for a church site. One group bought a "very formal" suit for their minister, which he "modeled for the ladies."[13]

While many denominational institutions, including the GCMC mission board, struggled financially during the 1930s, the annual income for WMA projects remained relatively steady. In 1933, WMA leadership passed a resolution: "That we thank our Heavenly Father that even through this depression our books show a credit rather than a debit and we recommend that we speak of the many blessings rather than the depression."[14] In 1935, the WMA took on the Incapacitated Missionaries' Fund of the GCMC mission board as one of its projects. The women's organization asked all members to contribute "two cents a week and a prayer" for this fund, which was used to pay pensions to returning missionaries. By 1945, women's groups were contributing at least two-thirds of the receipts for this fund.[15] The groups were becoming essential to the basic functioning of congregational and denominational programs.[16]

Since most Mennonite women of this era did not earn salaries, they found creative ways to raise money for their group dues or donations. GCMC women were encouraged to save their "Sunday egg money" (income from selling eggs their hens produced on Sundays) for their contributions.[17] Fanny Stoll recalled that at the beginning of the sewing circle at Lakeview Mennonite Church (an MC congregation near Wolford, N.Dak.), the group had no money to work with. "The church took pity and gave us ten dollars, with the understanding that we were on our own after that," she wrote in a *Voice* article.[18] For her monthly contribution to the group, Stoll used money from the weekly sale of a five-gallon can of cream, which was hers to use for household expenses. Each week she put some of the change in her "sewing circle bowl" in the cupboard. "After four weeks I had my offering for circle," she wrote.[19] Many groups raised money by holding auctions or raffles, selling items they sewed and baked, and by serving dinners at community events.

In an essay about Protestant women's groups, Barbara Brown Zikmund points out that the fundraising and service projects these groups engaged in took a great deal of time—and any activity involving a significant time commitment is bound to promote feelings of belonging and identity among participants.[20] Even as demand for homemade clothing dwindled, Mennonite women still met together to produce goods or plan events that could garner financial contributions. Since most women could not quickly and individually give money to aid others, they participated in activities that bonded them with each other and nourished their own souls, establishing a secondary and growing sisterhood function of the organizations.

World War II

With the onset of World War II, women found that their material work was again in demand, both internationally and at home. In 1941, leaders in the historic peace churches (Church of the Brethren, Religious Society of Friends, and Mennonites) set up the Civilian Public Service (CPS) program as an alternate to military service. CPS camps were funded by church agencies; Mennonite Central Committee (supported by the MC, GCMC, and other related groups) administered about sixty camps. Women's groups helped prepare "camp packs" for CPS participants, which included bedsheets, towels, toiletries, and other personal items.[21] Camp directors also requested that women's organizations provide curtains, caps for food workers, towels, rugs, and bedding.[22] Paul Toews writes that "virtually every unit kitchen relied on the generosity of home congregations," noting that camp newsletters contained many expressions of appreciation for the contributions.[23] Goering reports that women's organization leaders estimated that the Mountain Lake, Minnesota, community singlehandedly sent four thousand jars of canned food.[24]

Mennonite Central Committee (MCC) was originally created in 1920 as a collaboration of several Mennonite-related relief committees. The organization gained prominence during World War II and beyond and became an important vehicle for engaging sometimes separatist-minded Mennonites with the needs of the world. Scholars such as Calvin Redekop have described MCC as "probably the most important institution or sub-structure of the Mennonite society, pervading all aspects of Mennonite life and thought."[25] Toews writes that as Mennonites engaged with society during the war years, often through MCC programs,

Esther Weber, Cora Cressman (back turned), and M. C. Cressman in the basement of First Mennonite Church, Kitchener, Ontario, surrounded by yards of material to be packed into bales for MCC, circa 1945–50.

they transformed "from a parochial and withdrawn people to a people of global involvement and service."[26]

Women's groups were essential to MCC's impact during World War II. In 1944, Maria Siemens claimed that without the women's sewing circles, it would not be possible for Mennonite Central Committee to "have the results that it enjoys today."[27] Lorraine Roth wrote that women "were almost entirely responsible" for the collection, sewing, and processing of bedding and clothing sent to Europe during the war.[28] Women's groups developed close ties with international MCC workers, some of whom sent lengthy letters and diagrams to groups detailing exactly what kinds of clothing were needed.[29] The work women did for MCC was also significant for the women themselves. Marlene Epp writes that women's material aid work during World War II both contributed to their country and expressed the pacifist religious beliefs their husbands, brothers, and sons were embodying in CPS camps.[30] In 1945, the GCMC women's group leadership reflected that participating in the CPS effort had brought women and girls "into fellowship" with the men who were serving and gave them "a feeling of responsibility to thus witness to the way of Christian love in action."[31]

Some Mennonite women did work at CPS locations, either alongside their husbands or more independently as "CO Girls," or COGs. In *Women against the Good War*, Rachel Waltner Goossen discusses the impact of CPS on female participants.[32] Through CPS, Mennonite women explored new ways of caring for their families, participating in the labor force, and volunteering.[33] "In so doing they stretched the boundaries of conventional gender role expectations," Goossen writes.[34] Rachel S. Fisher shared her experiences in Albert Keim's book *The CPS Story*.[35] When Rachel's husband, Bob, was drafted and started CPS work in 1942, she decided to find work near him, first taking a job as a maid in Illinois and then as a secretary in Idaho when Bob's camp moved there. When her husband transferred to the state hospital in Ypsilanti, Michigan, Rachel went along and started working at the hospital as one of about twenty-five other "CPS wives." Rachel recalled many new and interesting experiences from her three years in Ypsilanti, including learning to know and love GCMC Mennonites, playing tennis, owning a motorcycle, hitchhiking to visit relatives, and visiting small Mennonite congregations nearby. After Bob was discharged from CPS, the couple volunteered with MCC for two years in Belgium and Poland before returning to farm in their home community.

During World War II, MCC and some other Mennonite bodies started voluntary service programs. MCC's Voluntary Service units arose out of summer service programs that were offered for young women who were not part of CPS.[36] (The Mennonite Voluntary Service program exists to this day; administered by Mennonite Mission Network, it recruits primarily young women and men to spend a year or two living together and serving in locations around the United States.) During World War II, female Voluntary Service and CPS participants were mostly college students or young wives. Few of these women were closely connected to congregational women's groups, which served mostly in behind-the-scenes roles during the war. Still, the broadening engagement and ecumenical (or at least inter-Mennonite) work of women in and beyond women's groups would affect the direction of those groups in the coming years.

World War II also affected women's groups in other denominations, though in somewhat different ways. Like most Americans, Protestant women in general were supportive of the war. African American Christian women in particular endorsed the military participation of their brothers and husbands as a matter of social equality.[37] However, many women's groups (including those from African American denominations) were also becoming interested in collaboration and in peace efforts. In December 1941, leaders from three interdenominational women's organizations met to form the United Council of Church Women, which later became Church Women United and exists to the present day.[38] The new organization's first action was to urge the United States to join the United Nations and "take its full responsibility in a world organization."[39] In 1943, as the war continued, Church Women United started celebrating an annual World Community Day for study and worship around the theme of peace.[40] In some Protestant denominations, having many ministers and seminarians in the armed forces during the war opened up greater church leadership roles for women. In a few denominations, such as the United Church of Canada and the African Methodist Episcopal Church, women began to be ordained as pastors in the 1940s and 1950s.[41] Many women's groups, though, continued to focus on women's roles as wives and mothers, especially in the postwar baby boom era.

At Home

While some Mennonite women explored new roles and involvements in society during the war years, most women's organization participants remained within the boundaries of conventional gender expectations. In doing so, they often provided significant service to congregations and church-related institutions. For example, when the Virginia Conference (MC) annual assembly was held at Warwick River Mennonite Church in 1946, the congregation's sewing circle was asked to supply the meals. The women served anywhere from one hundred to five hundred people a day for four days—in a building with no stove, refrigerator, or sink.[42] In 1942, the moderator of the Conference of Mennonites in Canada requested that Manitoba sewing circles participate in a scholarship fund for girls in need who attended the Mennonite Collegiate Institute in Gretna.[43] A group of women immediately gathered to support this project, which was a forerunner to the scholarship funds that continue to the present day.

Local women's groups received from as well as gave to their congregations; some groups in Iowa-Nebraska Conference (MC) received a portion of the Sunday school or regular church offering and eventually were included in the church budget.[44] In a region where some

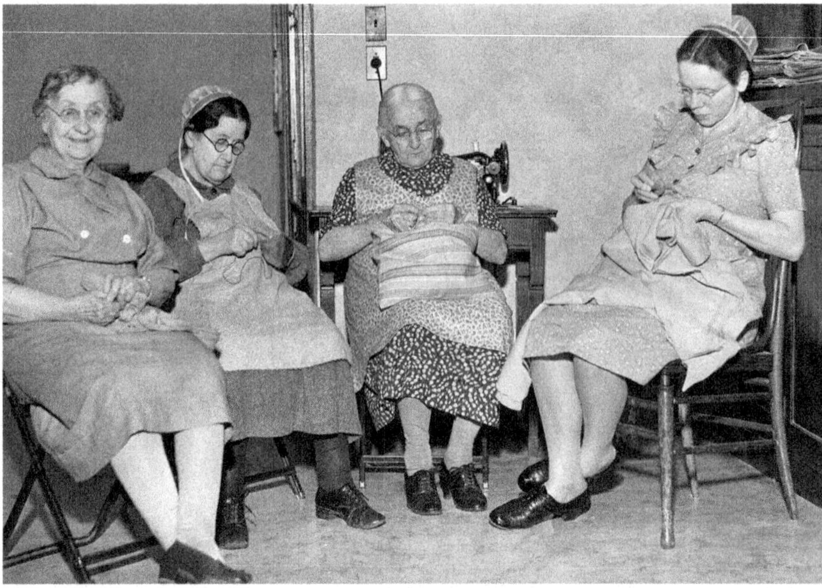

A mending crew working at the Home for the Aged in Eureka, Illinois, in 1951. (Left to right) Kathryn Hansford, Edna Stutzman, Margaret Shank, and Elsie Sutter.

church leaders had been reluctant to give their approval to women's groups when they first formed, this financial support shows how important the groups had become to congregational life. Marlene Epp notes that Mennonite church building or remodeling plans in the 1940s and 1950s often included a sewing circle room, indicating the valuable place of these groups in the congregation's program.[45]

In 1947, the MC women's organization name changed from the General Sewing Circle Committee of the Mennonite Board of Mission and Charities to the Women's Missionary and Sewing Organization (WMSO). The organization was described as an "auxiliary" to the denomination's mission board. In the mid-1950s, the group appointed its first paid executive secretary (later called "coordinator" or "director").[46] The organization's name changed again in 1955 to the Women's Missionary and Service Auxiliary, substituting the term *sewing* with the broader *service* and highlighting the organization's relationship to the mission board. Minnie Graber, WMSA president, explained: "This new strain of interest involved the total life of women. They met in fellowship groups, missionary meetings, sunshine circles, in prayer groups, homemakers groups, home builders—and many other types of groups."[47] During this time, women's groups in some regions started meeting together for annual "jubilee" Saturdays, a precursor to the Day of Inspiration events many area conferences host today. An article in the WMSA magazine describes these gatherings as times for gaining inspiration, reuniting with old friends, making new friends, and sharing program ideas.[48] Though the organization still had a primary focus on service to others, the inclusion of "fellowship groups" and "prayer groups" in Graber's list—as well as the idea of "jubilee" meetings primarily for inspiration—reveals the growing sisterhood and self-renewal aspects of their gatherings.

The GCMC women's organization retained its name, the Women's Missionary Association (WMA), throughout this period. By 1947 the organization had its first office, a paid employee, and an official budget.[49] When the GCMC revised its constitution in 1950, it mentioned the WMA for the first time and classified it as an auxiliary to the denomination.[50] In general, WMA members seemed to be satisfied in their "auxiliary" role and in funneling their contributions through the denomination's mission board, though there was one notable point of tension. It involved the Missionary Pension Fund (formerly known as the Incapacitated Missionaries' Fund), toward which many women's group members were still contributing "two cents a week." In 1952, the trustees of the fund (members of the mission board) asked WMA leadership for full control of the account so they could draw on the principal as needed.[51] At the 1953 national WMA meeting, the gathered women refused the mission board's request, which had been affirmed by the WMA executive committee, and voted instead to keep building the fund as a permanent endowment.[52] Goering calls this action of local and regional women's group leaders "a rare display of independence."[53] Perhaps while organizing their own mission and service efforts, women in congregations had developed skills that assured them they could make monetary decisions with as much acumen as male church leaders.

During the 1950s, some opportunities for wider church service were emerging for Mennonite women. In 1950, an MC study (conducted by three men) concluded that women could serve as members of church boards, although they should not be given chief executive or administrative responsibilities.[54] In 1956, the GCMC updated its deaconess program to become Women in Church Vocations, an organization

Lois Warkentin, Willa Kuyf, and Tina Block (left to right) working in the GCMC mission board office in 1956. Tina Block (Ediger) was a champion of women's leadership in the church and the mission field.

for women who were giving full-time service to the church, usually through care for the sick or elderly. This program recommended one year of seminary study, for which the WMA provided some financial assistance.[55]

The 1950s also saw an increased emphasis in wider society on women's roles as wives and mothers. Combined with the subordinating biblical interpretation upheld by most church leaders, women's organizations were still the most accepted place for Mennonite women to engage in significant activity and spiritual leadership outside the home. Even within women's groups, many presentations and conversations focused on the importance of cultivating a Christian home atmosphere. In 1950, Ruth Brunk Stoltzfus, a member of a prominent MC family, started a radio broadcast for mothers called *Heart to Heart*. Many Mennonite women's groups supported and listened to the popular broadcast, which (to use today's terminology) advocated for traditional Christian family values.[56]

Girls' Groups

The postwar baby boom years also brought a special focus on girls in the congregations. While sewing and mission groups for girls had existed in some places for almost as long as women's groups, they received the greatest attention during the 1940s and into the 1960s. Frieda Amstutz, a significant leader in her local church (Kidron Mennonite in Ohio), served as the MC organization's secretary of girls' activities in the late 1950s.[57] She issued a handbook for girls' group leaders that stressed connection both to the congregational women's group and to the larger denominational organization. The purposes of girls' groups as listed in the guide were to develop a Christian girlhood, to be friendly to all other girls, to learn about missions, to find a place to work in the church, to do Christian service in daily life, to work with the WMSA, and to learn to be a good leader.[58] Girls' groups were designed to include girls from age nine through high school and beyond, with the young participants filling the officer roles and making decisions to shape their own groups under the supervision of sponsors. In a time when children had few extracurricular options and congregations often discouraged participation in "secular" organizations like the Girl Scouts, many Mennonite girls looked forward to activities especially geared to them.

In some places, like the large First Mennonite Church in Berne, Indiana, girls of different ages participated in separate "mission bands," of which a main purpose was familiarizing participants with the work of missionaries the congregation supported. Some congregations planned themed nights where girls experienced food, music, and crafts associated with a place they were raising money for. Many girls' groups did material work as well. Eleanor Yoder reports that in the 1950s, girls' groups in Iowa-Nebraska Conference made baby quilts, layettes, scrapbooks, and stuffed animals; they canned vegetables and raised dried beans; they bought linens and other needed items; and they rolled bandages.[59] Both the MC and GCMC denominational organizations designated special projects for the girls' contributions. One well-remembered MC girls' group project was "Mules for Mildred"—which

Stitches of Cheer, the junior sewing circle of the North Lima Mennonite Church congregation in Ohio, in 1952.

raised funds for a female church planter who traveled the Brazilian countryside by mule.[60]

Girls' groups, such as the group at Pleasant View Mennonite Church (North Lawrence, Ohio), also provided an opportunity for outreach. After mission work started at nearby East Greenville, the girls' group sponsors—who included my grandmother, Nettie Hooley—began to reach out to the "newly born again" girls there. In a 1956 article in *WMSA Monthly*, Hooley reported that the group had "girl-to-girl discussions on the meaning of baptism, communion, the devotional covering, and subjects related to the beginning Christian life."[61] Since many of the girls did not know how to sew, the group did simple projects such as packing relief kits and textile painting.[62] The Pleasant View girls' circle apparently also had a goal of education—biblical and otherwise. In my grandmother's files, I found, stapled together, an invitation to a mother-daughter banquet, a dramatic reading based on Matthew 25, notes for a presentation on the positive and negative examples of various biblical women, and a pencil drawing of the female reproductive system.

Girls' groups tended to embody the dual purpose of women's organizations—outward-focused service and self-empowering sisterhood—more explicitly than most women's groups did. A significant part of their purpose was to develop leadership and spiritual growth in the young participants. Less explicitly stated was the leadership opportunity these groups gave their adult sponsors. Phyllis Baumgartner had always felt she was called to special service to God, though not to overseas mission.[63] When she moved to Berne, Indiana, a close-knit community, she was asked to work with the church's Intermediate Mission Band. This role helped her quickly feel included in the congregation and was something meaningful she could do even while raising a large family. Baumgartner later took on other leadership positions, such as president of the women's organization of Central District Conference and member of the Mennonite Biblical Seminary board.

A Golden Era

The 1940s through 1960s were in many ways "a golden era for the women's association," as Gladys Goering writes.[64] Goering reports that during the 1940s and early 1950s, about 55 percent of all women and girls aged twelve to sixty-five in GCMC congregations belonged to mission societies; in some smaller congregations there was 100 percent involvement.[65] In the MC, about half the women were involved in missions groups as well, according to numbers from the late 1950s.[66] In 1966, J. C. Wenger wrote that there were about as many women's group units organized as there were MC congregations, plus several hundred children's groups.[67] During this time, some congregations started additional groups that met in the evening and were often geared toward younger women. Many groups invited women from the community to attend, sometimes bringing new members into the congregation. For example, Marilyn Miller wrote that the women's group at Evangelical Mennonite Church in Fort Dodge, Iowa, was "a service group as well as a vital congregational outreach during the beginning years of the church."[68]

While Goering is referring specifically to the GCMC women's organization when calling the 1940s and beyond a "golden era," women's organizations flourished in many denominations in the mid-twentieth century. In an article about the the groups that became the United Church of Christ, Barbara Brown Zikmund writes that after

Women unpacking gifts of food and supplies at the Home for the Aged in Eureka, Illinois, in 1950.

World War II, homemakers and mothers "flocked to local churches."[69] Through congregational groups, these women found encouragement in the midst of their changing lives, and they continued to learn about mission and support the church's work in the world.[70] Participation in women's groups in the United Church of Canada reached an all-time high in the mid-1960s after the merging of the denomination's Woman's Missionary Society and its Woman's Association, which had described its members as "the home-makers of the Church."[71] Peak membership in women's organizations in the Presbyterian Church in the United States occurred in the 1960s as well, though Joan LaFollette points out that the rise (and subsequent decline) in group membership roughly parallels the trend in the denomination as a whole.[72]

Gloria Neufeld Redekop's study of women's groups in Mennonite and Mennonite Brethren churches in Canada found that the formation of new societies peaked between 1953 and 1959 and that during this time, most women who were members of Mennonite congregations were also members of a Mennonite women's society.[73] Redekop also notes that several women's groups changed their names during this period, largely from names referencing sewing to names denoting fellowship.[74] The 1950s saw an increased emphasis on women's roles as wives and mothers in church and society. This focus on the domestic sphere may have led to feelings of isolation for some women, perhaps

The Mennonite Mission Society in Beatrice, Nebraska, 1952.

stimulating an increased emphasis on the sisterhood/connective element of women's gatherings.

Mission work, both international and domestic, remained a central concern for Mennonite women's groups, however. From their beginning, the denominational women's organizations had promoted involvement in missions and provided education about the contexts of church mission work through their publications. From very early on in their formation, both the MC and GCMC organizations published magazines or newsletters with letters from missionaries and information about local group activities. In the 1960s, both denominational organizations changed the name and format of their magazines as they tried to keep pace with the shifting interests and needs of their members.

In 1961, the MC group renamed their magazine *WMSA Voice*, which became known simply as *Voice*. The refashioned magazine's first editor was Lois Gunden Clemens (who will be discussed more in chapter 3). In her first *Voice* editorial, Clemens wrote that the publication was intended to "speak to every woman in all churches. . . . We want it to make her aware of her special calling in the missionary and service outreach of the church."[75] As the 1960s began, the denominational women's group was clear that its role was not just to pass on information about missionaries. Rather, it sought to empower women in their own contributions to God's work in the world through the denomination. The women's organization leaders were also stating that the magazine—and the organization—was for all Mennonite women, regardless of whether they belonged to a sewing group, or to any group at all.

The GCMC organization retained the centrality of *mission* in the new title of its magazine, which changed from *Missionary News and Notes* to *Missions Today* in 1965. The *today* in the new title suggested, perhaps, that mission today was not quite the same was it was yesterday. The new magazine exhibited not so much a change of direction as an attempt to build a larger circulation by reaching entire families rather than just women's groups participants.[76] The subscription base did not broaden substantially, but even if only women read the magazine, its reach was significant. Most Sunday school teachers and children's group leaders were women, and many children heard the magazine's missionary stories repeated in their classrooms or homes.[77]

Magazines were not the only publications of the women's organizations. Early on, both denominational groups appointed literature secretaries and literature committees. These committees gave guidance to the magazines but also produced pamphlets, prayer guides focused on church mission projects, handbooks for group leaders, reading lists for women and girls, and by the 1960s, devotional guides for women to use in group or personal study. Supporting women's needs for fellowship and personal spiritual growth had always been at least a by-product of women's organizations, but this area of focus was beginning to be more explicitly stated and affirmed. The desire for women to be encouraged in their whole beings, not just for the service they could provide to others, would significantly shape the future direction and mission of Mennonite women's groups. Part 2 of this book explores this new direction and the forces that shaped it.

"More Than Sewing"

"We're about more than just sewing!" This refrain has echoed from the lips of Mennonite women's organization leaders for one hundred years. Even as the organizations have tried to redefine themselves over the decades—or have simply tried to stress that not *all* groups are sewing groups—the typical picture most people have of a "Mennonite women's group" is a circle of elderly women around a quilt. To be sure, many women (and not just elderly ones) still do find fulfillment and express generosity through stitching quilts, knotting comforters, and created crocheted gifts. But denominational women's groups have consistently resisted the tendency to be thought of only in terms of the handiwork of their members.

The strongest evidence that the original MC denominational women's group was not just concerned with sewing is the fact that when the mission board appointed a Sewing Circle Committee in 1926, the Mennonite Woman's Missionary Society kept operating. Clara Eby Steiner had written in 1917 that the newly formed MC women's organization was not to be only an organization of sewing circles "but a general organization of Home and Foreign Missionary Endeavor, including Sewing Circles, Mothers Meetings, Ladies Aids, Missionary Societies, Young Peoples and Childrens [*sic*] Circles or Societies, Individual Sunday School Classes."[1] According to Sharon Klingelsmith, the organization's early leaders saw the sewing groups as an important foundation, but they "tended to see sewing as a stepping stone to more important work."[2] This more important work was not necessarily the spiritual nurture and leadership development that later versions of the organization would stress. Rather, the denominational women's organization wanted to help ordinary Mennonite women join and promote the burgeoning missions movement of the wider church.

In the GCMC context, there was also a sense that the denominational women's society was about more than coordinating sewing projects. When the Women's Missionary Association treasurer ordered the organization's first stationery, it had "Sewing Societies" in the heading. But when it was time to reorder, Susannah Haury made sure the word *sewing* was changed to *missionary*. Haury wrote, "I think the latter [Sewing Societies] is a misnomer, because of the societies which *do not sew*, but they are all 'Missionary Societies,' even if they don't."[3] Like the MC organization, the wider thinking of the GCMC leaders meant including all groups interested in mission activity, which did not need to involve sewing.

As chapter 2 discusses, reformulations of organizational names and resources show that women were expanding beyond sewing throughout the 1950s and 1960s. But it was the greater women's movement of the 1970s that prompted a much stronger push for women's groups to do "more than sewing" and for women's groups to articulate that they were relevant for women who were not interested in sewing for mission. The context and activities of the 1970s and beyond will be explored in the coming chapters; what follows is simply a glimpse of how women's organization leaders continued to grapple with the sewing theme.

Reflecting on her time with the GCMC women's association in the late 1960s and early 1970s, Lora Oyer recalled that congregational groups were "just doing what needed to be done," things like sewing for missionaries and making blankets for babies.[4] Oyer vividly remembers the leadership she saw displayed by young women at an inter-Mennonite Women's Caucus she attended in 1972. "With renewed emphasis I carried this message back to our [GCMC women's group leadership] that we needed to do more at our meetings than sew, to prepare our women for greater involvement as leaders," she said.[5] As Oyer's comments indicate, in the 1970s, the "more than sewing" sentiment became less a call for wider involvement in mission and more a refocusing at a time when new roles were becoming available to women in church and society.

The leaders of the MC organization, then known as the WMSC, also saw that a wider purpose was needed since sewing circle members were growing older and younger women were not joining. Vel Shearer, editor for the WMSC in the late 1970s, recalled, "WMSC had been historically perceived as women who sat around and quilted, and rightly so—I love to quilt." But, she added, "younger women couldn't relate. There was real talk about how to reach some of those younger women."[6] WSMC executive committee minutes attest that the organization did talk at length about reaching younger women and trying new activities, but its sewing circle identity did not disappear. A 1989 *Gospel Herald* article promoting a new direction for the women's organization said, "Ask people, including women, what they think of when WMSC is mentioned and the answer overwhelmingly is 'sewing' or 'quilting.' "[7]

Even well into the twenty-first century, the "sewing circle" identity seems to haunt Mennonite Women USA leadership. In a 2015 interview, Kathy Bilderback, chair of the MW USA board, commented that part of the struggle the organization faces is "getting beyond the sewing circle idea" to the notion that all women in Mennonite churches are "Mennonite Women."[8] Soon after she was hired as Mennonite Women USA executive director in 2015, Marlene Bogard observed that plenty of sewing circles are still thriving. But she went on to say, "I want so deeply to help Mennonite women everywhere realize that we can be more and we can do more together beyond the traditional structures of sewing circles."[9]

The sewing circle identity can feel like a barrier to inclusion for various cultural groups. In a 2012 interview in *The Mennonite*, Carol Roth spoke about her desire for more Native Mennonite women to connect with the women's organization. Roth said, "They need to know that today's women's groups are no longer all about quilting all day."[10] Hyacinth Stevens, MW USA board representative for the African American Mennonite Association, said that past representatives in her position "spent so much time just trying to get past the sewing circle concept."[11] For some people, the sewing circle image seems culturally specific, unwelcoming, or simply uninteresting. For some Mennonite women, there likely also lingers the history of people like Lijsken Dircks, the Anabaptist martyr who was told to cease searching Scriptures and "attend to her sewing" (see chapter 1). At times throughout their history, Mennonite women have been limited to certain acceptable roles and activities—the sewing circle being one such activity—and many women now resist such classification.

* * * * *

And yet sewing circles, and the act of sewing on one's own, have been and continue to be meaningful for many Mennonite women. In a 2014 interview, Joan Wiebe (a past director of the GCMC women's organization) recalled how important quilting was for her mother. Wiebe's mother met as frequently as two afternoons a week with a group in Newton, Kansas. "I mean, my mom was in her nineties, quilting," Wiebe said. Someone read an informative or inspirational book out loud while the group worked, and coffee breaks gave the women time to connect with each other.[12]

Esther Yoder, my husband's grandmother, also continued sewing into her nineties. As a younger woman she had worked at a quilt shop, which gave her skills and resources she contributed to her Ohio congregation's sewing group. The group met for a full day, with a break for lunch. "We worked hard, but it also—I wouldn't say it was social—but I missed being with the ladies when I didn't go," she said. Even after she no longer attended a sewing group, Yoder continued making bags for school kits distributed by

Esther Yoder showing her special "double-cinched" style of closure for the school kits she sews.

Mennonite Central Committee. She made thirty-five kit bags in the fall of 2014 at the age of ninety-two. "I've never been able to give a big offering," she said. "This is something I can do."[13]

Gatherings of women to sew also made an impression on the children around them. Elaine Widrick, a leader among Mennonite women in New York State, remembers not wanting to go to school when the sewing circle met at her home. She enjoyed listening to the women's stories and was deeply influenced by the depth of their spiritual walk. "A lot of them had very little material wealth, but they were so willing to share," she said. "That made a big difference in my life."[14] Carolyn Holderread Heggen remembers going to the sewing circle with her grandmother in Idaho when she was four or five. She would sit under the quilt with her cousin and pretend the needles poking through the fabric above them were scary dragons. "Mostly we loved hearing the women talking and laughing," she said.[15] Even in more recent times, attending a sewing group has been meaningful for children. Carmen Miller regularly took her children, Ginny and Clint, to the sewing circle at Harrisonburg (Va.) Mennonite Church while she was homeschooling them in the years from 2008 to 2015. In a large congregation where activities are often segregated by age, the women's group provided a space to cultivate relationships with an older generation. "My children really own those friendships," Miller said.[16]

While sewing is often seen as a traditional and perhaps exclusionary Mennonite activity, in some contexts it has helped connect people across ages and cultures. In 2008, College Mennonite Church in Goshen, Indiana, started a Passing on Traditions program to connect women quilters in the congregation with college students hungry for connections (and the homemade soup the women provided). A variety of male and female Goshen College students attended the group, which created comforters and quilts as well as offered individual instruction in knitting, crocheting, and embroidery. One student, Kelly Frey, commented, "I learned that quilting and knitting with women equals quality conversation and bonding."[17]

The Manor Sewing Circle, a collaboration of several congregations in Lancaster County (Pa.), has found renewed energy since

Manor Sewing Circle members packing school kits together.

Karen refugees joined the group in the late 2000s. Many of the Karen attendees, who fled persecution in Burma, received a handmade blanket themselves while living in a refugee camp in Thailand. Hearing the stories of these women "helps us have a face to put to projects that we have worked at for many years," said Rhoda Charles, a leader of the group.[18] The sewing circle, which used to draw only a handful women, now has thirty to forty people attending each month. Elderly white Mennonite women mingle with Karen women, teenagers, and children in their monthly meetings as they knot comforters, pack school kits, and share a devotional time together.

Another significant cross-cultural sewing experience happens annually in Gulf States Mennonite Conference, where women from Native, Latina, African American, Anglo, and other backgrounds come together to work on a conference quilt.[19] Edith Michalovic, who grew up in a GCMC Mennonite family in Chicago, learned to quilt from Choctaw women when she joined a Gulf States church in Philadelphia, Mississippi. Michalovic enjoys quilting with the bigger stitches and creative designs the Choctaw women use, and she has purchased several of the conference quilts herself.[20] Serena Tubby, a member of the Mississippi Band of Choctaw Indians and a friend of Michalovic, said that the time flies by at the annual quilting event as the women work, talk, and eat together. She described the gathering as "like a family" and "a loving, blessed day."[21] For the diverse participants in Gulf States Conference, the Manor Sewing Circle, and the Passing on Traditions group, engaging in communal service through sewing has provided an opportunity for a kind of "sisterhood" relationship.

* * * * *

Through the years, Mennonite women's groups have always been about "more than sewing" *and* have always been associated with sewing. Sewing and material projects have been significant both for those who engage in them and for those who receive items or the proceeds from the sale of those items. However, the automatic association with sewing—and only sewing—is something that the women's organization leadership has not always found helpful. The notion that Mennonite women's groups were concerned mainly with cultivating a separate space for women to get together to sew contributed to some of the criticism the organizations received as feminist thinking arose in Mennonite circles in the 1970s. We turn to the context of the eventful 1970s in chapter 3.

Part II: 1970s–1997

Each of you should use whatever gift you have received to serve others, as faithful stewards of God's grace in its various forms. If anyone speaks, they should do so as one who speaks the very words of God. If anyone serves, they should do so with the strength God provides, so that in all things God may be praised through Jesus Christ.

—1 Peter 4:10-11a (NIV)

3
Woman Liberated

> The current women's liberation revolution happening in secular society is also happening in Mennonite circles throughout North America. It may be subtle, it may be quiet, but it is happening. Every area of life, every institution, every place where women have a role (or lack one) is being exposed and questioned.
> —Dorothy Nickel Friesen[1]

In 1970, Lois Gunden Clemens was invited to give the Conrad Grebel Lectures, the first woman to do so in the lectureship's twenty-year history.[2] At the time of her lectures, Clemens was serving as the editor for the MC women's organization as well as in several other denominational and academic roles. Her lectures, published in 1971 as *Woman Liberated*, upheld a complementarian view—that men and women have distinct roles and skills that complement each other. Clemens did not challenge typical (perhaps stereotypical) notions of gender and femininity, but she also advocated for a new look at Scripture passages traditionally used to subordinate women. And she called for women to have a greater voice in the church and world. "The church has not yet made use of even a tithe of the vast reserve of talent and devotion to be found in its female members," she wrote.[3]

Lois Gunden Clemens is a fitting—if extraordinary—example of a Mennonite woman navigating the changing times of the mid-twentieth century. In the early 1940s, she went to France to direct a children's home administered by Mennonite Central Committee. During the tumultuous war years, she saved several Jewish children from

Fern Yoder (left) and Lois Gunden Clemens.

likely imprisonment in concentration camps and was held as a German prisoner herself for thirteen months.[4] (In January 2016, she was honored posthumously as Righteous among the Nations, a prestigious award from Yad Vashem that only three other Americans have received.) After she returned to the United States, she taught at Goshen College, worked with Mennonite Voluntary Service, earned a PhD, married Ernest Clemens, and served on several MC denominational boards. She was also a personal inspiration to women in many settings, including those involved with the MC women's organization. Jocele Meyer, who was board president for the organization in the 1970s, remembers being inspired by the "caliber" of women she interacted with in that role, including Clemens. They were so knowledgeable and well-read, she said, that "it was kind of like a second college education."[5]

For many years, Mennonite women of Clemens's ilk had found a place for their skills and leadership ability within church women's organizations. But by the 1970s, women were beginning to envision new avenues of involvement. Marlene Epp writes that Mennonite women had been serving as church leaders in isolated situations before the 1970s: when there were no men available, on the mission field, and among children or other women.[6] But, Epp writes, it was the feminist movement of the 1970s and onward that truly opened the door for women to hold official church ministry positions.[7] The feminist movement elicited varying responses from Mennonite women. But it greatly affected the future of church women's organizations and the individuals involved in them.

Women's Liberation and the Church

Historians often describe feminism as one ongoing movement with several "waves" or surges in activity. The first wave included actions advocating for women in the late nineteenth and early twentieth centuries, actions that had connections to the abolitionist movement and culminated with women gaining the right to vote. As Flora Davis describes in *Moving the Mountain*, after the 1920s, women continued to participate in activist organizations, but feminism was often ridiculed by the media, and women rarely referred to themselves as feminists.[8] Second-wave feminism arose from and was inspired by the civil rights movement, as the work of Davis and others like Sara Evans shows.[9] This new surge of feminist activity grew steadily though the 1960s and exploded in the early 1970s.[10] Both Davis and Evans distinguish between a "liberal feminism" arising among older, professional women and a somewhat independent "women's liberation movement" embraced by younger radicals who were part of the New Left in American politics.[11] For people on the fringes of this activity, including most Mennonites, feminism and "women's lib" were somewhat synonymous and somewhat mystifying—suspicious to some and intriguing to others.

One significant early event in second-wave feminism was the 1963 release of a report commissioned by U.S. president John F. Kennedy. Davis and Evans point out that the report was moderate in tone and perhaps meant to defer interest in an Equal Rights Amendment (an effort to add women's rights explicitly to the U.S. Constitution).[12] But the report catalogued substantial inequities in the lives of women and renewed general interest in "women's place in society."[13] Another factor in this renewed interest was the publication of *The Feminine Mystique* by Betty Friedan, also in 1963. In the book, Friedan discussed the widespread unhappiness among suburban women who had bought into the "mystique" that fulfillment came only through being a good wife and mother. Friedan advocated for women to pursue education and meaningful work, not just a serene family life. The book and the wider discussion around its topics were on the minds of some Mennonite women, though few embraced the emerging feminist movement without reservation.

In 1966, Katie Funk Wiebe, a prominent Mennonite Brethren woman, wrote a lengthy two-part review of *The Feminine Mystique* for the *Canadian Mennonite*, a newspaper reaching various branches of Mennonites across Canada. Wiebe noted some problems with the book, namely that it lumped all women together and was written from a "selfish viewpoint," as if self-fulfillment for women were the only thing that mattered.[14] Steeped in a tradition that stressed humility and "yieldedness" for both women and men, the concepts of self-care and self-empowerment were not yet embraced by many Mennonites, who often viewed the ties of family (and the church community) in positive ways. But women were beginning to question the disparity in the roles of women and men, especially in the church context. Wiebe affirmed Friedan's book overall and even stated, with her religious context in mind, that the author did not go far enough in exploring the limited role to which women had been relegated. "Too many women in our churches have yielded to a silence which is less than biblical," Wiebe wrote, asking, "Is there a Mennonite feminine mystique?"[15]

Some Mennonite women, perhaps especially rural, older women, seemed untouched by the feminist conversation or saw it as an unwelcome intrusion. In a 1967 article in *Gospel Herald* (the MC periodical), Susan Martin Weber wrote that American women, including Mennonites, were "fighting against their natures. . . . They are discarding their innate feminine qualities and trying to create in themselves the qualities of men."[16] Elsie Flaming, an Ontario woman who was involved in the GCMC women's organization during the 1970s and 1980s, grew to appreciate the contribution of women who were pushing for more inclusion in the wider church. At the time, though, she remembers feeling like "this women's liberation kind of thing" was a frustration, "because we had just never heard of that; it was a challenge."[17]

Some Mennonite women, though, were having their own experiences of awakening. Joyce Shutt read Friedan and other early feminists as a young mother. "Their writings touched something deep within me, even though I'd convinced myself I was completely happy being a housewife and mother," she recalls in her essay in *She Has Done a Good Thing: Mennonite Women Leaders Tell Their Stories*. When difficulties arose in her relationship with her husband, Shutt "cracked up," realizing that she felt truly unfulfilled. "Then," she writes, "wonder of wonders, in 1968 I was appointed to the literature committee [for the GCMC women's organization]." The writing assignments, trips for meetings, and relationships with other women that came with this role introduced new options for Shutt, who, as mentioned earlier, went on to other denominational and congregational leadership positions.[18]

Lora Oyer began serving as vice president of the GCMC women's organization in 1968. Oyer said that she had been "turned off" by Friedan's book and things she heard about the secular women's movement. But she also wondered what churches were doing. She asked herself, "Why did we Mennonites always lag so far behind society in voicing the concerns of women?" She wrote to seminaries asking about women's leadership conferences but received no information. She researched women's issues and leadership traits at the library. Oyer's reading and her interaction with younger women in the church convinced her that preparing young women as leaders should become part of the agenda of the women's organization. Her commitment shaped the organization's activity and focus into the 1980s.[19]

Reta Halteman Finger grew up in an MC congregation in Pennsylvania. Though she was never closely connected to the denominational women's organization, she played an important role in the 1970s and beyond in developing the feminist sensibility of Christian women from a variety of backgrounds. In 1973, Finger was living with her husband and son in Germany. While looking through a stack of Mennonite publications at a friend's house, she came across a one-page article in *Gospel Herald* titled "Woman's Place" by Phyllis Pellman Good.[20] The article made an unequivocal statement against limiting women to stereotypical roles. Finger marveled that the Mennonite Church back home was so bold and forward thinking on the issue. Then she read the angry letters in subsequent issues about the article and the topic of women's equality. She was struck by how these letters quoted Scripture seemingly out of context, and she decided to research what the Bible actually said about women, searching for any English resources she could find in a German library. Finger's study led her to write, in separate 1975 issues of the *Gospel Herald*, two articles in which she advocated for gender equality based on passages in the New Testament. In "Who Does the Dirty Work of the Kingdom?" she wrote:

> My thoughts wander to the women who prepare the fellowship suppers while the men put on the program. To the women who make quilts in the sewing circle and teach the Sunday school

> while the men plan the future in the building committee, teach the adult class, or serve on the board of trustees. . . . The only unsettling thing about this neat system of traditional roles for men and women is that Jesus did not go along with it.[21]

"And then the angry letters were directed at me," Finger said—though later *Gospel Herald* issues also carried several letters affirming her work or calling for greater roles for women.[22]

If Finger had come across the GCMC periodical, *The Mennonite*, in 1973, she would have encountered even more discussion on the changing role of women. The March 20, 1973, issue was devoted almost entirely to that topic. The cover article by David Augsburger asserted that when the gifts of anyone, male or female, are denied, the whole community suffers. Lois Barrett, assistant editor of the magazine, profiled three outstanding women in Anabaptist-Mennonite history and, in an article titled "Games People Play about Women and the Bible," presented a strong refutation of typical interpretations of Scriptures used to subordinate women. Perhaps the most cautionary article in the issue came from Lora Oyer, who mentioned both benefits and challenges of women entering the workforce. Letters in subsequent weeks reveal about an equal amount of appreciation and disgust for the March 20 issue. Several letter writers expressed a desire that women be afforded more respect by men, though they also thought that women's roles should be separate from men's and not include congregational leadership.[23]

Finger's ecumenical connections and interest in a scriptural exploration of women's place led her to the emerging journal *Daughters of Sarah*. The journal arose out of the Evangelical Women's Caucus, which formed in 1973 within Evangelicals for Social Action.[24] Finger edited *Daughters of Sarah* from 1979 to 1994. Some Mennonite women (including members of Mennonite women's organizations) subscribed to the journal, finding it a welcome voice that engaged societal developments but also valued Scripture and church tradition. Oyer said that in the 1970s she replaced her reading of *Ms.* magazine with *Daughters of Sarah* and other Christian-focused publications.[25] Rhoda Keener, future director of the Mennonite women's organization, was also a *Daughters of Sarah* reader. She contributed a poem to the Spring 1993 issue, likening herself to an Amish doll: "No eyes or ears, no nose or mouth / . . . a thousand threads to quell my voice."[26] In a 2015 interview, Finger said that she still meets Mennonites who express how much they appreciated *Daughters of Sarah*. "That magazine, probably in ways we don't really know, raised the consciousness of Mennonite women in the seventies and eighties," she said.[27]

Women's Liberation and Race Relations

During the 1970s, consciousness raising among Mennonites was about more than just women's issues. The civil rights movement of the 1950s and 1960s had attracted some white Mennonites who were drawn to Martin Luther King Jr.'s ethic of nonviolence.[28] The civil rights movement came at a time when Mennonites were also grappling with their role in American society. Some, following Harold S. Bender's influential 1942 address, "The Anabaptist Vision," continued to stress an ideology of "separation from the world," even while many moved into cities and engaged in global and domestic mission projects.[29] In *Latino Mennonites: Civil Rights, Faith, and Evangelical Culture*, Felipe Hinojosa writes that Mennonites, who were "steeped in rural traditions, a 'quiet in the land' reputation, and overwhelmingly white," struggled with how to engage the civil rights movement.[30] Traditional Mennonite understandings of nonconformity to society and "nonresistant" pacifism made many hesitant to address racial issues, to the frustration of leaders such as Vincent Harding, a prophetic African American Mennonite pastor and Mennonite Central Committee leader in the late 1950s and early 1960s.[31] In *Mennonites in American Society*, Paul Toews writes that Mennonites during this time "were not wholly strangers to the concerns and struggles of others," including racial minorities, but he also notes that Mennonites were "often preoccupied with their own status and problems."[32]

The MC had passed a resolution in 1955 linking its nonresistant stance with a call to rise above practices of racial discrimination; the GCMC passed a similar resolution at its 1956 gathering. Hinojosa puts these statements and Mennonite concern about race in the context of the waves of revivalism and mission programs that were shaping evangelical Christianity in the mid-twentieth century.[33] Because of their involvement in mission and service activities, Hinojosa writes,

"Mennonites and other evangelical groups were unwillingly thrust into a conversation over segregation, race, and power."[34] In the 1940s and through the 1960s, the MC had organized about twenty-seven African American and seventeen Latino churches in the United States, plus twelve in Puerto Rico.[35] In the GCMC, mission churches among Native populations had been present for decades, and small groups of Asian immigrants had begun organizing their own congregations connected to the denomination. The face of Mennonitism was changing even as questions of race and identity were gaining prominence in wider society.

By the late 1960s and early 1970s, some of these mission congregations were developing strong leaders within their worshiping communities. In 1968, an Urban Racial Council was established for greater integration of people of color into the MC; it took the name Minority Ministries Council in 1969. In July 1972, a Cross-Cultural Youth Convention brought together young MC leaders and increased the visibility of the concerns of black and Latino Mennonites.[36] In 1973, the Minority Ministries Council was disbanded, and two separate groups formed: the Black Caucus and the Concilio Nacional de

Lee Ella Ireland, Elmeda Martin, and Nancy Taylor (left to right) peruse a Women's Missionary and Service Auxiliary reading display.

Iglesias Menonitas Hispanas (National Council of Hispanic Mennonite Churches). The Mennonite establishment was slowly beginning to take the interests of its members of color more seriously; in turn, those members were redefining who a Mennonite was.

African American and Hispanic Mennonite women were involved in cross-cultural leadership and in vibrant gatherings for their respective groups in the 1970s (more on this in chapter 5). But leadership of Mennonite women's groups at the denominational level remained mostly white. Mennonite women who were awakening to the limitations placed on them because of gender did not necessarily make connections to the limitations placed on others because of race. In fact, sometimes they actively jettisoned such connection. In 1969, Eleanor High was the first female delegate to an MC biennial assembly, where voting participants were traditionally ordained men. In a letter to Beulah Kauffman (president of the MC women's organization), High recounted her impressions of the assembly, where much of the first day's discussion focused on a proposed new structure for the denomination and the representation of various groups within it. High spoke during the open sharing time, pointing out that during the discussion "women had been classed repeatedly with minority groups."[37] High wrote to Kauffman, "That brought a laugh." At the assembly, High had spoken against segregating women as a separate group, advocating instead for more inclusion in the total work of the church for women, who should be elected to positions based on their qualifications.[38] The laughter of the delegates in 1969 is difficult to analyze many decades removed from its context. But it perhaps reveals that Mennonite leaders on the cusp of the 1970s were not prepared to seriously consider how the white-dominated, patriarchal culture of their tradition affected both women and people of color.

New Directions for Mennonite Women

To be fair, most members of the dominant culture in the 1960s and 1970s were not making connections between intersecting forms of oppression either. In fact, second-wave feminism is often criticized for its myopic focus on the concerns of middle- and upper-class white women. Flora Davis writes that second-wave feminism was "sometimes derided as a white woman's movement."[39] White feminists advocated for things like equal opportunities in the workplace, legal protections, and reproductive rights, taking the white, middle-class, heterosexual woman as the female norm.[40] Many black women, for example, were already in the workforce out of necessity and had equal if not more pressing concerns about social equality based on their race or class rather than their gender.[41] Some white feminists felt it was better to first focus on achieving results for white women and then deal with the concerns of other groups. In other words, the "daughters of Sarah" were not ready to listen to the "Hagars" in their midst (see Genesis 16 and 21).

The women's movement did stimulate significant changes in society. Legal victories in the United States included passage of the Equal Pay Act of 1963, banning sexual discrimination in the workplace as part of the Title VII amendment to the Civil Rights Act of 1964, and the Educational Equity Act of the early 1970s. In the matter of reproductive rights, many feminists lauded the rising availability of the birth control pill and the so-called relegalization of abortion that came with the Supreme Court's 1973 *Roe v. Wade* decision.[42] In Canada, a report released by the Royal Commission on the Status of Women in 1970 outlined 167 recommendations to promote equality for women.[43] Not all the leading feminist concerns were realized. In the United States, President Nixon vetoed a bill that would have established federally funded daycares, and the aforementioned Equal Rights Amendment failed to be ratified by the requisite number of states. But there is no question that social attitudes about women and their place in the world were changing. Flora Davis concludes that "the movement's single greatest achievement was that it transformed most people's assumptions about what women were capable of and had a right to expect from life."[44]

Not everyone thought the changing attitudes about women were a good thing, of course, including people in the church. Many Mennonites and other Christians ascribed to the "headship" of men over women, as Christ has "headship" over man (see 1 Corinthians 11:3 and Ephesians 5:23). Some Mennonites, though, saw a biblical case for equality of women. They celebrated Jesus' interactions with women as well as passages like Galatians 3:28: "There is neither Jew or Greek, there is no longer slave or free, there is no longer male and female; for all of you are one in Christ Jesus." Probably most Mennonites (and other

Christians) took a kind of middle ground during the eventful 1970s, welcoming some advances for women, like equal employment opportunities, but not supporting other feminist causes, such as access to abortion procedures. Of course, some Mennonite women chose to simply continue their regular activities of sewing and service. While they surely had conversations about the debates of the day around the quilt frame, many older women voiced no concerns about the way their lives were unfolding and seemed happy to keep faithfully working in their separate sphere.

Other Mennonite women, including many outside the women's group structure, advocated for more attention to women's issues and more utilization of women's leadership both in the church and around the world. One Mennonite-related outlet for more intentional conversation about women's issues was a task force established by the Mennonite Central Committee board. In 1971, MCC invited the women's organizations from the MC, GCMC, and Mennonite Brethren denominations to each appoint a woman to the Peace Section of its board. The women initially hesitated, and the Mennonite Brethren women never officially accepted the invitation, perhaps because of pressure from male church leaders.[45] Eventually, Fern Umble was appointed by the MC group and Lora Oyer by the GCMC group. In February 1973, these women—along with Dorothy Yoder Nyce, incoming appointee from the MC, and Luann Habegger Martin, an MCC staff person—made the case to Peace Section members that the injustice faced by women was a peace issue.[46] The Peace Section appointed a subcommittee, composed of the women members plus Ted Koontz, an MCC staff person, to explore the topic.

The subcommittee was named the Task Force on Women in Church and Society, later called the Committee on Women's Concerns. One of the committee's main interests was the underrepresentation of women within MCC leadership. The group also organized a conference on the family in Washington, D.C., in 1974, with speakers including leaders in national women's political groups, a congresswoman, and soon-to-be-renowned feminist theologian Rosemary Radford Ruether. Another major endeavor was a newsletter eventually called *Women's Concerns Report*. Several issues per year were published for the next three decades, giving space for women across MCC's constituency to share stories and express concerns. Reflecting on her time editing the first editions of the report, Habegger Martin recalled her satisfaction in "connecting women who might otherwise have felt marginalized in the Mennonite church."[47] Katie Funk Wiebe was one of those women; she eventually joined the task force as a Mennonite Brethren representative, though she was not appointed by the denomination. In a 2005 reflection on the early years of the task force, Wiebe recalled that during this era she was carefully watching and researching developments in the conversations about women's roles among Mennonites and others. "I clung to these contacts like a rope flung to someone who is drowning," she wrote.[48]

The Committee on Women's Concerns faced challenges and resistance. People within MCC and other Mennonite institutions questioned whether women's issues were indeed peace issues. The initial task force was composed of all white members from the United States in the context of a binational organization that was trying to be more inclusive of people from various racial and ethnic backgrounds. After hearing a speech advocating for more women in advanced MCC staff positions, an African American MCC executive committee member reminded the group that "white women are also part of the privileged class."[49] Like many second-wave feminists, Women's Concerns members seemed most aware of issues facing white, middle-class women and were not as articulate about the privilege they carried in relation to other groups. This awareness would broaden somewhat as the task force's work continued, morphing into the hiring of part-time MCC staff members for women's advocacy in the United States and Canada. This position ended in Canada in 2002 and in the United States in 2011, when women's concerns became part of the restorative justice and anti-oppression programs of MCC U.S.[50]

Many other women-related endeavors took place in Mennonite contexts in the 1970s. A Consultation on the Role of Women in the Church was held at Mennonite Biblical Seminary in 1973, and the first of several inter-Mennonite Women in Ministry conferences took place in 1976. Leaders from the denominational women's organizations (particularly the GCMC group) were involved in both events, though many of the women who planned and attended them were not connected to their denomination's women's organization. In fact, in some ways these conferences and the Women's Concerns Committee came into being because the needs and interests of Mennonite women were not being fully served by existing women's groups. (The interlude entitled "Are Mennonite Women's Groups Feminist?" explores this topic further.)

Mennonite women had been serving as leaders in congregations for many years—in some sense, they had been doing so since the beginning of the Anabaptist movement. However, the ordination of the first women for pastoral ministry within Mennonite congregations did not happen until the 1970s.[51] In July 1973, Emma Sommers Richards was ordained at Lombard (Ill.) Mennonite Church, an MC congregation, where she served as copastor with her husband. Conference leaders made it clear that her ordination was not necessarily intended to set a precedent for ordination of women in general. The MC issued no denominational statement on women's ordination during this time, leaving the topic to be discussed and discerned by its area conferences. In 1974, the GCMC passed a resolution on ordination stating that "neither race, class, or sex should be considered barriers in calling a minister."[52] The first ordained female minister within a GCMC congregation was Marilyn Miller in 1976, who served as a copastor at Arvada (Colo.) Mennonite Church. By the late 1970s, a handful of ordained women in both denominations were serving congregations. Many other women kept doing "the dirty work of the kingdom" without official recognition, and some congregations and area conferences continued to bar women's ordination. But in places where it was received, official ordination for women offered legitimacy and a sense that significant progress was happening regarding women's roles.

In this decade of new directions, the established women's mission organizations also felt the need for new vision, at least on the denominational level. Both the MC group, known as the Women's Missionary and Service Commission (WMSC) beginning in 1971, and the GCMC group, which took the name Women in Mission in 1974, would shift their focus and their place within the denomination in the coming years. And new gatherings of Mennonite women would provide spaces for women from different cultural groups to connect with each other and grow in their personal faith. We take a closer look at the activities of the WMSC, black and Latina Mennonite women, and Women in Mission in chapters 4–6.

4
Women's Missionary and Service Commission

> We are encouraging women to accept positions on boards and committees, to participate in the work of the church on all levels. But we are still keeping a WMSC because not all women care to give their gifts in the same way, and there will always be some things . . . that women love to do in their homes and with each other. We want to continue to provide opportunities to serve one another and reach out into the community.
> —Doris Lehman[1]

In 1971, the Mennonite Church (MC) reorganized its structure, and the women's organization became a commission of the newly formed Board of Congregational Ministries. To reflect the new relationship, the organization changed its name slightly from the Women's Missionary and Service Auxiliary to the Women's Missionary and Service Commission (WMSC). This change reveals two shifts for the women's organization. First, it became, in name at least, a more essential part of the denomination's work, replacing the term *auxiliary* and its evocation of a supplemental body that supports the main work of a restricted group. Doris Lehman was the WMSC board president at the time. Married to a dentist, she explained the name change using an example from her personal life. "I have no objection to being a member of a dental auxiliary, because I'm not a dentist," she said. "But some of us didn't think it was appropriate to be an auxiliary of the church. . . . I am a Christian along with my husband, and we're in the church together."[2]

The other shift was away from the mission board. The denominational reorganization redistributed many of the mission board's responsibilities. Even so, it seems significant that an organization that at one point had been run by the mission board was now associated with a different aspect of the denomination. The women's organization still gave a large portion of its funds to mission board projects (the only group that consistently received more contributions was Mennonite Central Committee). But the 1975 WMSC handbook reveals a strong congregational focus. The organization's listed goals were to:

> unite the women and girls of the church, and to coordinate their activities;
> help women and girls find and articulate faith;
> encourage regular and disciplined Bible study;
> promote strengthening the quality of family life;
> develop an awareness and appreciation of our Anabaptist heritage;
> help women and girls discover, develop, and utilize their individual gifts;
> help develop leadership potential among women and girls;
> encourage cultivation of person-to-person relationships;
> motivate creativity in planning programs and activities;
> respond as Christ's representatives to community and worldwide needs.[3]

Only the final goal in this list has an international mission connection. The women's organization was perhaps following a sense in the wider denomination that "mission" was needed within congregations and communities as well as among people in faraway places (this topic is discussed further in the interlude "A Mission to Themselves"). The organization was also explicitly articulating a move from an outwardly directed mentality to a greater focus on the well-being of women's groups and their members. In other words, the women's organization was shifting from a primarily service orientation toward a desire to foster sisterhood among its participants.

Retreats and Spirituality

One way that the MC women's organization developed its sisterhood, or inward focus, was through the development of retreats. In the 1960s, Christian women in many places had begun participating in retreats, including some Mennonites in congregations and regional groups. Mennonite women from Lancaster Conference in Pennsylvania first gathered for a retreat in 1962 organized by Mary Hottenstein Lauver and Beulah Diffenbach.[4] Over the next twenty years, these women, with help from others, would coordinate 118 retreat events for Lancaster women, offering "a time and place where one could go for deep spiritual enrichment and nurture."[5] In 1965, the denominational women's organization held a retreat for district women's group leaders, with input from an Anglican woman. Dorothy Shank, a leader among Mennonite women in Virginia, was one of the participants. She felt privileged to receive training that enabled her to lead retreats for women in her area. "It was a significant mile marker for me in my own spirituality as well," she said.[6] That first retreat filled Shank with a desire for a richer prayer life and led to an experience of personal healing. Through retreats, Mennonite women connected with God and with their own innermost selves, and they were eager to extend the experience to others.

Women around the fire at a retreat in the 1960s.

District retreats sometimes took on the feel of a family reunion, with women spending most of their time in conversations and activities. Beulah Kauffman, executive secretary of the WMSC from 1967 to 1978, felt that Mennonite women generally gave too much time to activities and conversations and not enough time to simply being, and she began promoting the concept of a silent retreat.[7] The WMSC held a silent retreat for its officers, equipping them to travel in pairs to replicate the event in every district. Angie Williams, who served on the WMSC board in the 1970s, attended the first training, where women were encouraged to spend time listening for God's voice. "Being a Mennonite almost all of my life, it was just not what we were used to doing," she remembered. "I mean, God talked to you *personally*?"[8] But a few women who had experience with the idea made the group feel comfortable, and Williams found herself entering fully into the practice and encountering God in ways she never had before. "To this day I still do some teaching that feeds back into that," she said in a 2015 interview. "I tell people that this has been the single source of the most spiritual growth in my life."[9]

The WMSC's silent retreats were part of a general interest in spirituality among Mennonites and others in the 1970s. In their history of Mennonites in North America, Royden Loewen and Steven Nolt write that many Mennonites were part of the small group movement that "swept the North American evangelical world" in the 1970s.[10] Some small groups focused on Bible study, while others were designed to support individuals with ongoing needs or to foster interpersonal connection.[11] Small groups were not universally accepted. For example, Grace Brunner recalls the caution her mother expressed when Brunner told her about the women's small group she was forming.[12] "She just wasn't sure it was a good idea for women to be sharing so intimately," Brunner writes.[13] But Brunner found great benefit from small groups. She brought her interest in them and in the spiritual growth of women into her role with the WMSC, for which she served as board president from 1979 to 1987.

During this time, Mennonites were also becoming interested in spiritual practices that could aid their personal faith journeys, thanks in part to Marlene Kropf, who worked with worship and spiritual formation in various denominational positions.[14] Kropf was concerned about what she perceived as Mennonites' "lack of a direct encounter with God."[15] The WMSC, for its part, encouraged women to encounter God through its retreats and its biennial devotional guide. The organization had been producing devotional resources for many years, usually including Bible study questions and program ideas for groups. The 1978–79 guide, titled *From Monologue to Dialogue*, departed from this format and instead guided readers through the practice of reflective journaling, encouraging them to imaginatively enter biblical texts and conversations with Jesus and to share their insights with each other. The guide was cowritten by Dorothy McCammon, who had been a missionary in Asia (with her husband, Don), and Mary Herr, who later (with her husband, Gene) founded The Hermitage, a center specializing in personal silent retreats. The next WMSC devotional guide, written by Angie Williams, was called *I Will Hear What God the Lord Will Speak* and again focused on intimately connecting with God. The efforts of the women's organization in the late twentieth century surely helped fuel the interest in spirituality that persists among some Mennonites today. Speaking in 2010, Kropf commented that Mennonites were now more "ready to acknowledge that God works and speaks in material ways, in words, silence, relationships, symbols, mystery—in fact, in any way God chooses."[16]

Quiltmaking and Relief Sales

In the mid-twentieth century and beyond, Mennonite women strikingly combined their commitments to service, sisterhood, and spirituality through their contributions to Mennonite Central Committee relief sales. The first sale to raise funds for MCC's work around the world was held in a Pennsylvania barn in 1957, and annual sales have become fixtures in more than forty places across Canada and the United States. Since the early days of the sales, women's groups have supplied a large portion of the labor and donated items. Since MCC is an inter-Anabaptist organization, women's groups from a variety of traditions contribute to the sales.

Quilt auctions are a highlight of relief sales, and women's groups from many contexts create stunning quilts that fetch considerable prices. In a doctoral dissertation titled "Engendering the *Imago Dei*," Elizabeth McLaughlin discusses the quiltmaking of the women's group at Holdeman Mennonite Church (Wakarusa, Ind.), which has contributed to the Michiana Relief Sale since the it began in 1968.[17] McLaughlin claims that by making quilts for the sale, group members participate in Christ's way of peace and express themselves as women made in the image of God.[18] The group gives serious attention to their craft, noting the prices each item brought and which colors and patterns were popular. These observations inform their choices for the next year's quilts so they can raise as much money as possible for MCC's work.[19] Valerie Rake makes similar observations in her study of Wayne County (Ohio) sewing circles. She notes that quilts (mostly made by Anabaptist-related women's groups or individuals) have become an increasingly important factor in the financial success of the Ohio Mennonite Relief Sale.[20]

As mentioned in the "More Than Sewing" interlude, for some people, sewing and quiltmaking are synonymous with Mennonite women's groups. Of course, quiltmaking is not a uniquely Mennonite practice. But for Mennonite women in the past, especially in more conservative communities, quiltmaking was often one of the few acceptable outlets for their creativity energy. In his history of Lancaster Mennonite Conference, John Landis Ruth writes that "making quilts was a simple

Quilt auction at Michiana Relief Sale, 1969.

joining of usefulness and social enjoyment, and not addressed by the conference rules."[21] Ruth's comment describes quiltmaking as an integration of the dual purpose of Mennonite women's groups. Quilts are often sold to benefit others, in line with the service aspect of women's groups; quilting together also nurtures a sense of sisterhood as women talk, share devotions, and eat together during their work days. McLaughlin points out that the making of a quilt itself, which usually includes a designed top that is pieced or appliquéd, a layer of filling material, and a bottom backing layer, is a process of bringing together individual pieces into "a socially constructed community."[22] Both the quiltmaking process and the conversation that happens at a sewing meeting foster circles of sisterhood as well as selfless service.

Aside from its service and sisterhood functions, quiltmaking can also take on a spiritual aspect. In a 2005 *Mennonite Quarterly Review* article, David Born traces the developing perception of Mennonite quiltmaking from utilitarian to aesthetic to iconic purposes.[23] Recalling a display of quilts he saw on the communion table in a Mennonite sanctuary, Born offers the quilt as an icon that could correct what some consider to be the Mennonite overemphasis on the cross and the martyrs.[24] At least on the face of things, Born writes, the quilt is "a celebration of life" and "has much to offer in terms of a theology of solidarity."[25] In her dissertation, McLaughlin describes quiltmaking as a "potential Anabaptist sacrament" that can fuse an inner commitment to Christ's way of peace with outer realities.[26] Drawing on Jesus' parable of the sower, McLaughlin suggests that "the kingdom of God is like a quilt auction," and analyzes the Michiana Relief Sale as "a parabolic expression of the peace tradition, inviting the world into the kingdom."[27]

Mennonite women's group members may not see themselves as participating in parabolic or sacramental practices when they quilt or labor in other ways to support their local relief sale. But the sales do display their commitment to participating in the work of God in the world. Many women's groups undertake impressive efforts for the sales. For example, the women's group at Zion Mennonite Church in Pryor, Oklahoma (now part of the Conservative Mennonite Conference), has organized congregation members to annually make vast quantities food for the Oklahoma Relief Sale since the sale's inception in 1978. Each year they can hundreds of quarts of apple butter; one year they

Attenders browsing through baskets at Michiana Mennonite Relief Sale, 1981.

made 319 angel food cakes, and another year they made 845 pounds of noodles.[28]

Relief sales have also provided an outlet for the material work of women in an era where sewing clothing is no longer common and it often makes more sense to send money rather than material goods to international locations. In her 1989 history of WMSC groups in Iowa and Nebraska, Eleanor Yoder reflected on the shift from making economical clothing and serviceable bedding for those in need to creating sought-after art forms. "Currently our service has taken a new form than in years past, that of converting our creativity into cash to support the world-wide relief program," she wrote.[29] Women enable the success of relief sales, and relief sales enable women to keep enacting their faith in a tangible manner while connecting with others.

International Mission and Domestic Concerns

While MCC relief sales (and later, thrift shops), rather than international mission stations, became the primary outlets for the material work of women's groups in the mid-twentieth century, missions did remain a focus for some WMSC groups. The Virginia Conference women's organization wanted to specifically support "missionary wives," so they appointed a mission needs secretary. The secretary wrote to missionary wives and received lists of what they needed. Then the women's organization had to figure out how to gather contributions from their members to meet the needs. As E. Jane Burkholder remembers it, Ruth Stauffer (likely the mission needs secretary at the time) woke up in the middle of the night and had a vision of charts on easels with numbers on them. Stauffer brought her idea to the women: a number would represent a need, which would be described in the program booklet (for example, fifty kimonos, two quilts, or thirty dollars for a household improvement).[30] On the conference's annual missions day, women gathered in a church sanctuary and stood to indicate their interest in choosing a number, bringing money their women's group had collected over the year or making individual contributions. Numbers came off the board as they were chosen by women in different sections of the sanctuary. "They took up thousands of dollars in fifteen minutes," Burkholder remembered.[31] The day usually also included an inspirational speaker, music, and lunch. Alma Yoder recalled that one year the author and missionary Elisabeth Elliot, the widow of missionary Jim Elliot, was the guest speaker. Elliot had barely heard of Mennonites before but was impressed when she saw the numbers come off the board and needs taken care of so quickly. "Where have you Mennonites been?" she asked in astonishment.[32]

The denominational women's organization also remained involved in mission projects. The WMSC highlighted the stories of female missionaries at the women's public session of annual mission board meetings and during its own gatherings at denominational assemblies. The WMSC also supported missionaries through the Books Abroad program. In the early 1980s, administration of the program was transferred from the mission board to the WMSC, and the name was changed to Books Abroad and At Home. WMSC leaders solicited books (and financial contributions) from women to distribute internationally, to give to returning missionaries, and to stock church libraries. The WMSC had been significantly involved with the program even before taking full responsibility for it. A 1974 *Voice* magazine carried two letters from missionaries expressing thanks to the women's organization for reading material they received. Bertha Beachy wrote that reading helped her better face her problems and that she had averaged a book a week since going to Somalia almost twenty years earlier.[33] Audrey Shank wrote from Jamaica: "The gesture [of giving free books] always makes us feel thought about and cared for, and we need that."[34] Sponsoring this program was a natural fit for the WMSC, since reading and promoting good literature had always been part of the organization's identity. As with the organization's previous publications, *Voice* magazine continued to carry book reviews and reading lists and sometimes included profiles of female Mennonite authors as well as articles about the value of reading.

The WMSC supported other mission-related endeavors as well. The organization provided modest scholarships for young women at Mennonite colleges and seminaries who planned to do service or church-related work. Barbara Reber, WSMC executive secretary during the 1980s, started a project called "A Nickel a Day . . . a Prayer a Day." The women's organization distributed small banks for people to deposit coins into as they remembered to pray for mission projects. "It was a very good feeling when I presented $15,000 raised through this project to Mennonite Board of Missions during General Assembly," Reber recalled.[35] The WMSC also contributed smaller amounts to other church women's events, such as Women in Ministry gatherings or the emerging Hispanic Mennonite women's conferences. And rather than simply supporting mission workers in faraway places, the organization began making international connections itself, sending Jocele Meyer and Grace Slatter to a gathering of Mennonite women in India in 1977.

The WMSC also began exploring connections with different cultures within its denomination in the 1970s. Angie Williams was the first African American woman on the WMSC executive committee. She was nominated by a committee and then elected into office by district women's group leaders at their biennial meeting, and began her term as WMSC vice president in 1973. Williams saw her mandate as providing spiritual leadership for all Mennonite women, not any particular subgroup. "There was an awful lot of talk about race in those days," she said. "I was not the one doing the talking. It was not an issue to me."[36] Williams's WMSC term came amid increased activity around race in church and society. In 1969, for example, James Forman's "Black Manifesto" had demanded reparations from white congregations.[37] Conversations about marginalization and discrimination were happening in the MC's own Urban Racial Council, as they would at later black Mennonite women's retreats (see chapter 5). But Williams felt that she did not have any "special needs" as an African American Mennonite. "I wanted to promote togetherness," she said. "Our spiritual needs are the same."[38]

Maria (also known as Mary) Bustos joined the WMSC executive committee in 1975 specifically as a representative of Hispanic Mennonite women. Women in Spanish-speaking Mennonite churches had organized into a conference several years earlier, and Bustos facilitated communication between the two organizations. She advocated for *Voice* to include Spanish articles, which did appear sporadically throughout the 1970s, and for Spanish translation of the devotional guide, which happened for several years as well. Perhaps having closer ties to the Board of Congregational Ministries (rather than the Board of Missions) had helped the WMSC become more aware of the various cultures and concerns it could explore within the denomination's existing congregations.

The WMSC's *Voice* magazine also showed concern for subjects affecting life for a variety of North American Mennonite women. The magazine still carried reports from missionaries, explanations of MCC projects, and stories from people in so-called third-world countries. But magazine themes in the late 1970s through the 1980s included topics such as women in the church, living simply, Mennonites in the city, motherhood, marriage, "the inward journey," ministering to the elderly, women in the marketplace, and divorce.

Vel Shearer, who was editor of the magazine during this time, especially remembers one issue she published on the topic of domestic violence. Shearer heard many stories of abuse through her work at a domestic violence center in her community and recalls little conversation within the church about the topic. She decided to devote the January 1986 magazine to the issue and included informational articles like "Common Myths about Family Violence" as well as stories that provided a glimpse into the personal experiences of women. Shearer's editorial, which mentioned a domestic violence survivor she called

"Meg," was titled "On the Possibility That There Are Megs in the Mennonite Family." The editorial counseled women being abused by their husbands to seek counseling "through a mental health or social agency or your pastor."[39] After the issue appeared, Shearer received a letter from a reader asking, "What if your pastor is also the husband who is abusing you?"[40] Shearer recalls that the woman said she had talked to her bishop, but had received the unfortunately common response that if she just treated her husband nicely, the abuse would stop. Shearer remembers trying to respond with empathy and encouraging the woman to contact a counselor or social agency in her community or a trusted friend in the congregation.[41]

In the mid-1980s there were few resources or procedures for dealing with abuse perpetrated by Mennonite church leaders. In 1984, John Howard Yoder, the most prominent Mennonite theologian at the time, had been forced to resign from Associated Mennonite Biblical Seminary after repeated instances of sexual abuse against women associated with the seminary.[42] But as Rachel Waltner Goossen describes in a detailed 2015 *Mennonite Quarterly Review* article, attempts in the 1980s to hold Yoder accountable were largely kept quiet and were largely unsuccessful.[43] While it would not be until the 1990s (and beyond) that conversations about abuse by church leaders would come to the forefront in Mennonite contexts, in the 1980s there was a slowly growing awareness among some Mennonites regarding gender-based violence.[44] Issues of MCC's *Women's Concerns Report* dealt with rape and family violence in the late 1970s, though the newsletter tended to reach women on the more progressive end of the Anabaptist spectrum. The WMSC's *Voice* magazine, by contrast, was often distributed to every member of an MC women's group or even to every woman in a congregation. The magazine's January 1986 issue, and the response Shearer received, shows that the WMSC was indeed touching on topics relevant to contemporary Mennonite women.

Another way that the WMSC sought to engage contemporary women was by developing a Business and Professional Women (BPW) wing of the organization. Barbara Reber became aware of a BPW unit that had formed in Lancaster Conference under the leadership of Mim Book, and Reber invited Book to help the WMSC work at better including "professional" women. Book remembers that to some people, who associated the WMSC with sewing projects, it felt like a big stretch to think about including businesswomen in the organization.[45] Even though the WMSC's stated philosophy included "young women, middle-aged women, work-at-home-women, and professional women," Book said that the employed women she interacted with felt neglected by local WMSC groups, who often met on weekday mornings.[46] The women's liberation movement of the 1970s was facing a backlash in many circles in the 1980s, and Reber recalled that among Mennonites there was "a wide gulf between professional women and those who stayed at home."[47] Some older professional women found BPW groups especially valuable, as they had few places to share with peers about their experiences as Christian women in the workplace.[48]

Mim Book met with WMSC leadership for several years before becoming a full board member in 1983 with responsibility for developing and connecting BPW programs in various regions. Some area conferences and congregations did already have groups for professional women. For example, a 1967 *Voice* article describing an anniversary celebration of the Ontario women's organization noted that "members of the Business and Professional Women's Association, dressed in centennial costume, served homemade cookies and tea."[49] By Book's time on the WMSC board, BPW groups were probably not often dressing up in costumes and serving cookies! Rather, there was a sense that many women in the workplace were not participating in WMSC activities and perhaps felt distanced from the Mennonite Church in general.

By the early 1980s, women composed nearly half the American workforce, and mainline Protestant denominations were boosting their numbers of women in church leadership roles.[50] But in many Mennonite congregations, women still encountered expectations that they would primarily be wives and mothers. Grace Brunner, WMSC board president during the 1980s, recalled that the organization was concerned that employed women might feel "they had to go to some other denomination or some other church because there was no place for them to express themselves in our denomination."[51] In a 1985 *Gospel Herald* article about BPW, Book described a sense of excitement, especially among older professional women, that the WMSC was trying to do something specifically for them. "They feel that now they can share their stories, their challenges, and frustrations, and not be put down," she said.[52]

Only a handful of area conferences developed BPW organizations, but congregational BPW groups proved meaningful for many participants, even if they only operated for a few years. A typical group might meet for a monthly breakfast on a Saturday morning to hear from an inspirational speaker, discuss work-family balance, and connect with each other. Besides providing meaningful connections for the women involved, the existence of BPW helped create change in the wider denomination. Book recalls that Mennonite Economic Development Associates (MEDA) did not include women at that time, except for those who attended meetings with their husbands. MEDA leaders sought ideas from Book about how to better involve women in their organization.[53]

Business and Professional Women also served as an agent for change within the women's organization. Susan Gingerich, who gave leadership to BPW in the early 1990s, remembers that there were always older women who thought the future of the WMSC was about sewing, because that was how the organization had started. BPW signaled that some women needed something different. "I think it helped balance the two together and to show women that there is something beyond quilting," Gingerich said.[54] Although BPW leaders did not necessarily use language associated with the wider feminist movements of the day, supporting women in the workplace was perhaps one way the WMSC sought to adopt a more feminist identity. For some younger educated women, though, having a separate profile for professional women may have supported the idea that regular WMSC activities were not relevant for them.

Of course, participants in congregational Mennonite women's groups were engaging in a variety of activities besides the traditional sewing and quilting. Many groups regularly volunteered at homeless shelters, hospitals, and homes for the elderly. A group from Lee Heights Community Church (Cleveland, Ohio) gave a monthly program with refreshments at a local state hospital, including hosting a summer cookout on the hospital roof.[55] The Holdeman Mennonite Church women's group connected with the Hope Rescue Mission in South Bend, where they regularly painted and cleaned, served meals, and attended meetings.[56] At East Union Mennonite Church (Kalona, Iowa) women brought baked goods and fruit plates to each meeting to share with community members who had experienced sickness, a death in the family, or a new baby.[57] The WMSC report to delegates at the 1987 MC assembly highlighted a variety of things women's groups were doing: hosting children through The Fresh Air Fund (New York State), writing letters to elected officials about justice and poverty issues (Northwest Conference), sending Christmas bags to a Navajo reservation (Ohio), helping Salvadoran refugees (South Central Conference), providing a safe home for abused women and children (Atlantic Coast Conference), and marching against abortion (Ontario).[58]

Women's groups in culturally diverse congregations often both embraced and expanded typical notions of Mennonite women's activities. For example, the women's group at New Holland (Pa.) Spanish Mennonite Church, with participants from ten or more Spanish-speaking countries, started an International Spanish Food Festival in the late 1980s. The festival has become an anticipated community event that draws over five hundred attendees; the whole congregation participates in preparations.[59] Part of the income from the festival supports congregational projects such as youth group trips and building improvements, and part goes to the women's group (mostly to help people attend Hispanic Mennonite women's conferences). Women in this congregation have also met for Bible study, to support women who have lost their husbands, and to deliver groceries to new families in the area. Wanda Gonzalez Coleman, who was involved in the congregation for many years, said the group even tried to do a bit of quilting, though, she added, "that wasn't our forte!"[60] But the women liked the idea of working on something together and made a quilt that included the names of all the families in the church. They passed the quilt around and committed to pray for the congregation's families when the quilt was in their home.[61] For the New Holland women, a quilt—an item associated with the traditional service commitment of Mennonite women's groups—also fostered a sense of sisterhood as they worked on it together and used it to unite the congregation in prayer.

During the 1980s, groups for mothers and children formed in many congregations. Some of these groups worked on material projects, but usually the main purpose of the gathering was to give mothers time to connect with each other. Kathy Zendt, from Staunton (Va.) Mennonite

Church, remembered having "what we called a sewing circle," which mostly women with young children attended. "The project was not as important as getting together with our children," she said. Zendt still meets people who say, "Remember how we used to get together and not get much done!"[62] The existence of a sewing circle that "didn't get much done" is a striking expression of the dual purpose of service and sisterhood and perhaps reveals a shift in that purpose. In the 1980s and beyond, many groups more fully embraced their sisterhood function, deemphasizing service projects or missions support in favor of Bible study or informal conversation.

In the 1970s and 1980s, the Lancaster Conference WMSC developed an organized Women and Preschool program. At one point, about fifty congregations participated in the program, which still exists today, though it is not closely tied to the conference women's organization. Besides serving as a refreshing time for the mothers and a fun event for the children, the program "developed women's gifts in amazing ways," said Rhoda Charles, one of the group's leaders.[63] Local groups received a booklet with names of potential speakers, and women who were on that list received dozens of invitations to give presentations. In a conference that would not ordain women as pastors until 2008, women's groups provided a place for women who were gifted speakers and leaders to use their skills.

Leadership and Relationships

Developing leadership skills in women—whether they were serving at congregational, regional, or denominational levels—was an important function of the MC women's organization, even if it was not a large part of its stated purpose. In the 1980s, the MC was just beginning to permit women to serve in official pastoral leadership positions, and women's groups were often the first place women tested their leadership abilities and callings. Some churches had "WMSC Day," during which a leader from the organization gave the Sunday sermon (or at least a "talk," perhaps while standing to the side of the pulpit). Grace Brunner recalls that five people who were on the WMSC board during her time later went to seminary and became pastors, including herself. "I am sure that if I had never done WMSC I would never have been ordained," she said in a 2015 interview. "I mean, my whole life changed because of WMSC. And I think it did for some of those women too."[64]

Donella Clemens, who was WMSC's secretary of girls' activities during the 1980s, later served on the General Board of the denomination and became the first female moderator of the MC in 1993. Her involvement with the WMSC helped her learn about the broader church and develop connections across the United States and Canada. "Certainly being part of the women's committee helped me a great deal to feel comfortable in that type of leadership role," she said, reflecting on her time as moderator, though she noted that participating in male-dominated denominational structures was very different from being part of the women's group.[65] Mim Book looked up to WMSC leaders, first in Lancaster Conference and then at the denominational level, and in them found women who affirmed her own call to leadership.[66] After her time on the WMSC board, Book became the associate general secretary for the MC General Board and later served in a variety of pastoral positions. "WMSC paved the way for [female] pastors and other denominational leaders; I just know that," she said in a 2015 interview.[67]

Levina Huber, who was the WMSC's secretary of peace and social concerns in the 1980s, found that this role was a "springboard" to other church work, such as service on the denominational publications board.[68] What stands out most for WMSC leaders from the 1970s and 1980s, however, is not their personal development or organizational accomplishments, but their relationships. Huber, Clemens, Book, and Shearer all lived in Pennsylvania when they served on the WMSC board. They often traveled together to meetings and retreats, having what both Clemens and Shearer describe as "hilarious" interactions along the way. Shearer said that their fun spirit carried over to the board meetings, and their close relationship probably also allowed them to be more comfortable confronting each other or asking hard questions.[69] Angie Williams also spoke about the lifelong friendships that developed out of her work with the WMSC. "WMSC was a tremendous support group, as well as a group that offered opportunities to grow," she said. "I looked forward to our meetings twice a year, I really did."[70] In an article reflecting on her time directing the organization, Barbara Reber recalled, "It was a very good, very satisfying time. I received much more than I gave by way of friendships and affirmation."[71]

Relationships within congregational groups were also significant for participants and were a major reason why women kept meeting even as many of them took on more responsibilities in the workplace and in the wider church. The WMSC made relationships between women the theme of its 1985–86 devotional guide, which explored the story of Ruth and Naomi. The organization asked Ruth Brunk Stoltzfus to write the guide. Although Stoltzfus was recovering from cancer, she agreed to work on the guide with Eve MacMaster, who would soon become WMSC editor. MacMaster and Stoltzfus embodied the Ruth-Naomi relationship as they collaborated on the project.[72] The material made an impression on many women, including Elaine Widrick, who recalled its significance in an interview. Prompted by suggestions in the resources, Widrick asked a woman she respected to be a "Naomi" to her and to meet once a month to share together. Even though the woman had nineteen children, she immediately said yes, and a delightful friendship formed.[73]

In the 1980s, many congregational women's groups dwindled in numbers. But the WMSC found several ways to celebrate both its past and its future. The organization commissioned a book highlighting three hundred years of Anabaptist-Mennonite women's history, which was written by Elaine Sommers Rich and published in 1983. Reber called the book "the greatest contribution of WMSC to the total church."[74] In the book's chapter on the MC women's organization, Rich detailed "the takeover" of the young organization by the denominational mission board, drawing on the work of Sharon Klingelsmith, whose 1980 *Mennonite Quarterly Review* article set those events within the context of women's roles in the MC.[75] Many Mennonite women heard this story for the first time through the work of Klingelsmith and Rich or when it was later publicized in *Voice* articles in 1990 and in presentations by Ruth Lapp Guengerich. "The takeover," and the faithfulness of the women throughout it, became a significant formational story for the MC women's organization, spurring on participants at later times when the organization faced difficulty or critique.

In 1985, the WMSC celebrated eighty-five years of Mennonite women's groups and presented a reading highlighting the history and current activities of the organization to the delegate body at the MC biennial assembly. (It is unclear why the organization chose 1900 as the year to mark the start of Mennonite women's groups.) The reading proclaimed: "Our foremothers' vision was that our coming together as Mennonite women was not just to sew, but that we would use our gifts and that we would support all the programs of the church."[76] Again, the women's organization was striving to reach well beyond its sewing identity. In a 1985 *Gospel Herald* article about the WMSC, Alice W. Lapp reported a balanced budget in 1984 with disbursements totaling over $181,000. "WMSC is now an organization of the women of the Mennonite Church whatever their talents may be," Lapp wrote. "It has a remarkable record of accomplishment." Lapp expressed hope that the WMSC had a future "on the growing edge of the church."[77]

Elaine Sommers Rich, author of Mennonite Women: A Story of God's Faithfulness.

Not everyone during the 1980s and beyond felt that church women's organizations were filled with promise for the future, however. Some women and men viewed separate women's organizations as relics of the past and questioned whether they were relevant for people who were embracing the contemporary expression of the feminist movement. The intersection of Mennonite women's groups and feminism is worthy of our consideration.

"Are Mennonite Women's Groups Feminist?"

There are probably as many different definitions of *feminism* as there are people who consider themselves feminists. In *Feminism Is for Everybody*, theorist bell hooks defines feminism as "a movement to end sexism, sexist exploitation, and oppression."[1] Leonard Swidler, author of *Jesus Was a Feminist*, describes a feminist as "a person who is in favor of, and who promotes, the equality of women with men, a person who advocates and practices treating women primarily as human persons (as men are so treated) and willingly contravenes social customs in so acting."[2] Perhaps most applicable here is *Merriam-Webster's* simple second definition of feminism: "organized activity on behalf of women's rights and interests."[3]

After I gave a presentation on the history of Mennonite women's organizations at the 2015 Mennonite/s Writing Conference, an audience member asked, "Are Mennonite women's groups feminist?"[4] I did not have a ready reply. Mennonite women's organizations have not always been on the forefront of social movements to promote women's equality. (Recall Clara Eby Steiner's comment that the early women's group leaders were not suffragettes.) And there are certainly members of Mennonite women's groups today who would not claim the feminist label or want to belong to a group that did. However, Mennonite women's group leaders and members, often working behind the scenes and within established structures, have promoted an empowering, egalitarian—and perhaps feminist—view of women for more than one hundred years.

* * * * *

By the 1960s and 1970s, some Mennonites were questioning the value of sewing circles and denominational women's organizations. Unlike in the early twentieth century, when women's group leaders were sometimes viewed as too progressive or potentially dangerous, this time the critique came from those who thought the organizations were too slow to embrace the changing roles of women. For some, the very existence of separate women's groups was a hindrance to the fuller incorporation of women into general church leadership. In 1963, the *Canadian Mennonite* carried an article by Katie Funk Wiebe that voiced doubts about church women's groups. She asked, "Is the women's church organization of today really the vital arm of Christ it purports to be or merely a crutch under the arm of the men?"[5] But a 1969 article in the same periodical defended women's groups as the best way for women to be involved in the church, a sentiment shared by many who participated in them.[6]

Questioning and criticism of women's mission organizations happened across denominations during the 1960s and 1970s. Barbara Brown Zikmund writes that at first, most Protestant women were "ambivalent and even hostile" to the women's liberation movement.[7] While older women often said that church organizations were actually where they felt the most liberated, younger women were less sure.[8] In her analysis of Presbyterian women's organizations, Joan LaFollette writes that in the early years the groups were often "a welcome refuge for progressive women who wanted to be active in church life."[9] However, by the time the women's movement had gained momentum, Presbyterian women's groups often shied away from and sometimes even resisted involvement in work for women's rights. As other groups emerged in the denomination to espouse the feminist cause, "traditional women's groups were often unfairly viewed as outdated," LaFollette writes.[10]

The perception that established women's groups were outdated was present in Mennonite circles as well. New endeavors, such as Women in Ministry conferences, consciousness-raising groups at Associated Mennonite Biblical Seminary in Elkhart, and the initiatives of Mennonite Central Committee's Task Force on Women (later Committee on Women's Concerns) drew women from Mennonite denominations who were more outspoken feminists. In an article on the history of the MCC Task Force, Dorothy Yoder Nyce recalls that the task force, more than established denominational women's groups, connected with women who were younger, more professional, and more on the "fringe" of church life.[11] Nyce relates an anecdote that illustrates the variety of views among Christian women in the 1960s and 1970s. Ruth Brunk Stoltzfus's *Heart to Heart* radio broadcast for Christian homemakers was supported by many Mennonite women's groups, especially in the Mennonite Church. She left the program in 1958 and Ella May Miller took over as host, strongly promoting traditional roles for women in society. A 1968 letter from Miller to the president of the MC women's organization praised women's groups from New Mexico to Missouri to Ontario for distributing *Heart to Heart* leaflets in creative locations.[12] In 1975, two MCC Task Force members attended a women and religion conference in Saskatoon, where they were given *Heart to Heart* leaflets as examples of "church literature that perpetuates sexism."[13] To some people, the projects that traditional Mennonite women's groups supported seemed at odds with efforts for broader opportunities for women.

Mennonite women's group leaders were sensitive to the issues of their day, but they also did not want to belittle women who fully embraced their roles as wives and mothers. In a 1974 *Gospel Herald* article, Beulah Kauffman, then WMSC director, stated that she did not identify with the "Women's Lib" movement "per se," because she saw a "kind of bondage" in its harsh ideology.[14] But, she continued, "I do not agree with the person who feels no questions should be raised, no changes should be expected or introduced, no new dimensions to personhood should be explored."[15] A *Voice* article about Kauffman's time with the WMSC bore the title "Cautious Progress in a Time of Change." The article noted that while some people wanted rapid change, Kauffman "thought it was more important to be sensitive to the feelings of all women in the church and not cause division by moving too fast."[16]

Beulah Kauffman, director of the WMSC from 1967 to 1978.

In 1980, Joyce Shutt, chair of the literature committee for Women in Mission (the GCMC women's organization), wrote an expansive readers theater for performance at the triennial GCMC assembly. The piece highlighted the important function of women's groups over the years and addressed negative perceptions from the younger generation, as this excerpt demonstrates.

> **R 4:** Our young girls, not understanding what went before, curl their noses,
>
> **R 3 & 5:** "Mission groups!"
>
> **R 2:** She's quiet, her needle flashing in and out.
>
> **R 3:** They'll learn they can't walk in other's shoes.
>
> **R 1:** We women have to find our own, a whole new way in Christ.
>
> **R 4:** They'll birth a child, hold a lover in their arms, and learn that love's never out of date.
>
> **R 5:** Love wears many faces.
>
> **R 3:** We also serve who sit and sew.
>
> **All:** We also serve.[17]

Shutt's litany weaves together songs, biblical passages, historical anecdotes, literary references, and information about the women's organization.[18] Reading the entire piece conveys the sense that women's organization members (or Shutt at least) were well read, talented, and practically bursting with creative energy—and the women's organization was one place they could use this energy to build up the church and participate in God's work around the world.

Because of the role of Women in Mission in securing women representatives on its denomination's commissions (see chapter 6), the GCMC group may have been perceived as more "feminist" than the MC organization. Women in Mission did not explicitly claim a feminist label, though. In a 1992 article on the history of the organization, Gladys Goering wrote that Women in Mission "does not exist to promote women's rights."[19] But, she added, "that happened as leadership skills, otherwise overlooked, were encouraged in women's groups."[20]

One point of critique about women's organizations had to do with their separate nature. As the wider church and society became more open to women in leadership, many wondered about the continued necessity of a women-only endeavor. Marian Hostetler, who started as WMSC director in 1987, recalled that some of the early women pastors thought the activities of the women's organization undermined the progress that female church leaders had made. The sense was that "we were making a place for women in this safe little secluded place instead of encouraging women to make their way into the church proper," she said.[21] At a 1982 inter-Mennonite conversation about the changing role of women in the church, Harold Peters-Fransen (a GCMC participant) commented that "women are not going to be equal until the women's organizations disappear."[22] Peters-Fransen said he appreciated the function of women's organizations, but he advocated using the organizational skills of women in all areas of the church.[23]

The separate nature of church women's groups may have nurtured a different kind of leadership and connection than was possible in mixed-gender organizations. That is Rosemary Skinner Keller's argument in a 2006 article about Protestant women's organizations. Keller claims that separatist women's societies developed a leadership style that was alternative to the "traditional male hierarchal model."[24] With a vision of "building bonds of sisterhood" and creating "communities within communities," women's organizations promoted shared authority, teamwork, support, and cooperation—in contrast with individual competitiveness and highly centralized authority, which is sometimes associated with traditionally male patterns of leadership.[25] Mennonite women's organizations may not totally fit Keller's description, and Mennonite organizations run by men may not either (especially with the Anabaptist emphasis on a "priesthood of all believers"). However, reflections from members of Mennonite women's organizations clearly indicate the value of the relationships formed through the groups. Furthermore, the women speak of their experiences with an intensity that is likely different from how most men would talk about their organizational involvements. Building sisterhood and creating community were indeed goals of Mennonite women's organizations, even if they did not use exactly those words.

Susan Jantzen directed the GCMC women's organization from 1990 to 1997 and codirected the merged (GCMC and MC) women's organization for several years. In a 2014 interview, she described how women's organization meetings, held across Canada and the United States, felt very different from the church as a whole. "There was a lot of attention paid to almost rituals of hospitality," she said, remembering beautiful environments, lovely food, and songs and poetry. There was awareness of the fact that "we're souls coming together, and we're women souls who care so deeply for our families and for the church," she said. Even when things were uncertain during the merging process, meetings were always "relationally rich." Jantzen also expressed frustration that women's organizations were sometimes seen as a stepping stone to work in the wider denomination or in congregational leadership. "No, the good Lord would smile on what happened at a women's group as much as what happened at a [regular Sunday morning] worship service," she said. "Both have fully arrived, in my opinion."[26]

A somewhat similar perspective comes from Ivorie Lowe, a longtime member of Community Mennonite Church (Markham, Ill.). Lowe served in many churchwide positions, sometimes as both the first woman and the first African American. She also participated in many women's group activities and attended Central District Conference women's retreats for over thirty years. In a 2015 interview, Lowe noted that traditional activities of women, such as knotting comforters and cooking food, are important, but they need to be *seen* as important. "The fried chicken, the collard greens, the zwieback: all those kinds of things are the things that move a nation, move a people forward," she said.[27] Lowe's ability to both value traditional women's activities and hold prominent roles in the wider denomination is something that Mennonite women of color seemed particularly skilled at, perhaps in part because of their constant experience with negotiating multiple identities (more on this in chapter 5).

Irene Bechler is another example of a woman who held together more "traditional" and "progressive" concerns. Bechler, a white Mennonite, was involved in several multicultural Mennonite churches pastored by her husband, Le Roy Bechler. She served as vice president of the WMSC board from 1985 to 1991. She notes that during this time the organization was working to change its direction and to bring in a broader range of women, which she observes the current women's organization (MW USA) still trying to do. In a 2014 interview, Bechler observed that in doing this, we "have to constantly reach back into our congregations to make sure we're also bringing them along in whatever way we can." She articulated a strong concern for including women with a variety of viewpoints and for empowering women in the nation and around the world. "Women can so quickly revert to or be placed in a lower position," she said. There needs to be a place where women can become aware "that God has called us to be who we are, to lead, to nurture, to teach, to preach, to do whatever he gives us gifts and callings to do."[28]

For Bechler, the place that nurtured awareness around women's callings was the denominational women's organization. It has not always served that function for everyone, though. Sylvia Shirk remembers an experience she had with the WMSC in 1984, after she had been overseas with the mission board and returned to North America for a short-term assignment. She heard that someone from the women's organization was coming to meet with her. "I thought, wonderful, someone is going to talk to me about my needs, what it's like to be a woman in ministry," said Shirk, who also had a young child.[29] Instead, the person gave her a quilt and told her to let the organization know if she needed a crib or any furniture. "I was really shocked and disappointed," Shirk said (though she mentioned that her family did use the quilt for many years).[30] Shirk, who is now a pastor in New York City, has since been involved with the Mennonite women's organization in other ways, but her experience highlights how an organization that excelled at meeting physical needs could fail to minister to the full concerns of all Mennonite women.

The sense that the needs of all Mennonite women were not being met by the denominational women's organizations contributed to the formation of other organizations, such as MCC's Task

Force. Another initiative was Womensage, a resource center established in 1982 by a group of GCMC, MC, and Mennonite Brethren women mostly in northern Indiana. The group's goal was to "tailor our expression of God to women's experience," noting that "many of our spirits are not nurtured."[31] While Womensage never gained widespread recognition, its emergence shows that some Mennonite women were longing for something different from what they sensed they could find in existing organizations.

A current Mennonite women-related initiative is the Women in Leadership Project, which has an explicit goal of naming and transforming sexism in Mennonite Church USA.[32] While the project emerged from a conversation initiated by Mennonite Women USA (MW USA), the Women in Leadership Project, coordinated by Jennifer Castro since 2015, has a more overt concern with challenging institutional forms of oppression and also has a goal of including men in its transformation work. The leaders of MW USA and the Women in Leadership Project see each other as collaborators. "Empowerment, which is central in our mission statement, is a very close cousin to advocacy," said Marlene Bogard, executive direction of MW USA. "It is important that [the Women in Leadership Project's] effort toward dismantling sexism is rightly placed and funded by the denomination."[33] Castro noted that she has had helpful conversations with MW USA leadership, though she is not sure how many members of congregational women's groups would align with the vision of the Women in Leadership Project. "I hope for the opportunity to continue to collaborate with Mennonite Women," she said in a 2015 interview.[34]

* * * * *

If I could go back and respond to the audience member's question, I would say that Mennonite women's groups were and are feminist, though of course it depends on what definition of feminism you are using. The vision statement of MW USA "invites women across generations, cultures, and places to share and honor our stories, care for each other, and express our prophetic voice boldly as we seek to follow Christ."[35] This statement describes a wide, inviting kind of feminism that focuses on individual women rather than primarily on movements or structures. In pursuing this vision, MW USA has empowered a variety of women, from faithful sewing circle members to pioneering female pastors in Latin America, as they embark on personal healing journeys and connect with God's liberating ways in the world. As Claire DeBerg, MW USA communications manager in the mid-2010s, pointed out in an interview, women's organization members had to be bold throughout the years as they faced the expectations of their eras and the limitations of their church structures. "I feel proud to be part of an organization that has to be bold," she said.[36]

5
Hispanic Mennonite Women's Conferences and Black Mennonite Women's Retreats

> We [black Mennonite women] are not the ladies auxiliary. We are not a decoration; we are not a bonus. We are a fully equal part of the flesh, blood, and bones of the Mennonite Church. The church needs us active, questioning, demanding. It needs our labor. It needs our wisdom, not as an added blessing, but for its very survival as a Christian church.
> —Wilma Ann Bailey[1]

At the 1973 Mennonite Church (MC) assembly, about 450 women gathered for a prayer breakfast. They were mostly white women connected with the denomination's women's organization, WMSC. A *Voice* article by Ella May Miller described the event and quoted a Hispanic Mennonite woman identified only as Maria. "I experienced something this morning I've been waiting to see for twenty years!" Maria said. "You shared yourselves—your needs, your problems, your joys, your heartaches. You wept and laughed together. Praise the Lord!" Miller commented that this quote had come from "a sister who has come into the Mennonite Church from another culture." Miller continued, "She knows that only as we bring our emotions and feelings into our Christianity can we become 'whole persons.' "[2]

This *Voice* excerpt highlights several things about the interactions between white Mennonite women and Mennonite women of color, a relationship that in the 1970s was just starting to develop on an institutional level. First, it shows the commitment of women like Maria who were willing to keep engaging with a group that rarely worshiped or conversed in ways that felt comfortable to them, at least at denominational gatherings. Second, it shows the emerging awareness of white Mennonites who were beginning to articulate the ways their faith could be enriched by the perspective of others. Ella May Miller's article also characterizes the Mennonite Church as a culture—and one that Maria did not share. While today many adherents stress Mennonitism as a faith commitment rather than a subset of white European culture, participating in denominational gatherings in the 1970s surely felt like entering another culture for many Mennonites of color (as it still does for some today). But Mennonite churches and related gatherings populated by people of "other cultures" were growing. In the 1970s, Hispanic and African American Mennonites organized to strengthen their own identities through the Concilio Nacional de Iglesias Menonitas Hispanas (National Council of Hispanic Mennonite Churches, or "the Concilio") and the Black Caucus. These groups would later become known as Iglesia Menonita Hispana (IMH) and the African American Mennonite Association (AAMA).[3]

Hispanic and black Mennonite women also started meeting in their own conferences and retreats in the 1970s. These gatherings began independent of the denominational women's organization and were more related to their respective cultural organizations (named above). However, the organized gatherings of black and Hispanic women led to more formal interaction between them and the WMSC. (While some GCMC women participated in the retreats, there were far fewer black and Hispanic GCMC churches, and the Concilio and Black Caucus were MC-based.) Since this book focuses on the history of the denominational women's organizations, my aim for this chapter is to simply give an overview of the conferences and retreats, with particular attention given to their connections to WMSC leaders and structures. I hope that others will soon write histories of the Hispanic and African American Mennonite women's gatherings from more of an insider's perspective.[4]

Hispanic Mennonite Women's Conferences

The first Spanish-speaking Mennonite women's conference was held in April 1973 in Moline, Illinois. Maria Bustos, wife of pastor Mac Bustos, coordinated the gathering, along with Lupe Bustos and Maria Rivera Snyder. Several reasons were given for the one-day event, which was called a *servicio de inspiración*. Seferina De León described it as an opportunity "to have a group of our own to listen to each other and figure out how we can help each other."[5] The organizers specifically wanted to gather women whose husbands were involved in church work and spent much time traveling so that the women could have a meaningful time together while their husbands stayed home.[6] In a *Voice* article about the conference, Lupe Bustos wrote that the gathering arose from a concern for women who could not speak English and had never had the benefit of participating in the WMSC.[7] As a woman of "American-Spanish descent," she had been encouraged by attending WMSC meetings and wanted to provide similar encouragement for Spanish-speaking women.[8]

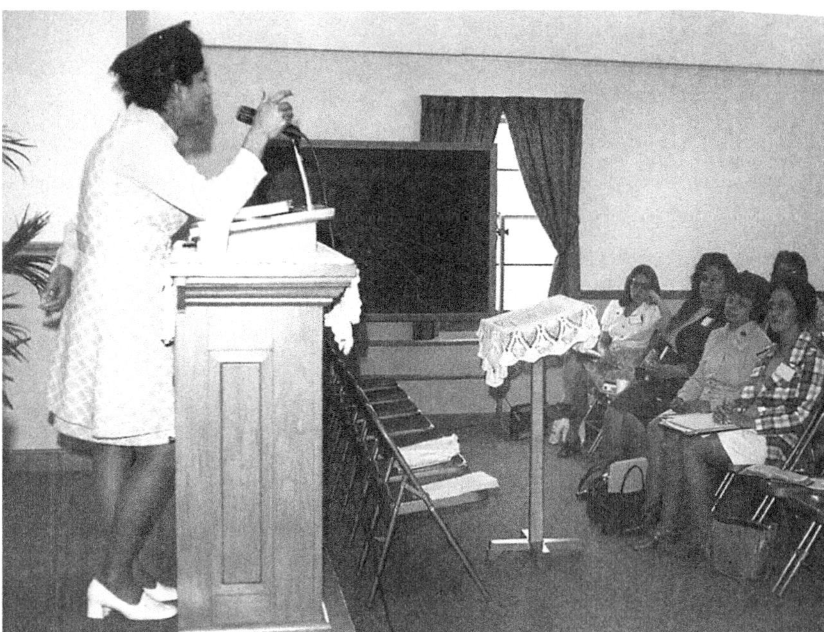

Seferina De León speaking at a Hispanic Mennonite women's conference in the 1970s.

At the first conference, about sixty women gathered from churches in several Midwestern states as well as New York and Texas. Lupe Bustos's article described the event as having women's marks of creativity and care: hospitable overnight hosts, corsages for each participant, a craft project fashioning crosses out of a variety of materials. But the most memorable aspect of the event was the spiritual presence that pervaded it. The Spirit-led singing, prayer, and testimonies came to a climax when the women gathered to take communion. Mac Bustos wished to join the group for the communion service, which was led by pastor Mario Bustos. Suffering from leg pain and other health complications so severe that he was planning to give up his pastoral work, Pastor Mac was assisted into the sanctuary. Women nearby laid hands on him as they prayed and praised God. Suddenly, Mac got up and said, "Praise the Lord, all pain is gone!" He went up and down the steps to show his increased mobility.[9] "Tears just streamed from all of us," Lupe Bustos wrote. "We realized that God still performs miracles; and a miracle happened to all of us there, because we were renewed again in Him."[10]

The conference's leaders viewed the miraculous healing of Mac Bustos as confirmation of God's presence with them and as encouragement to continue their gatherings. At the October 1973 Minority Ministries Council meeting, they made plans for another conference and also adopted the name Conferencia Femenil Hispana Menonita (Hispanic Mennonite Women's Conference). This is the name the group uses today, after a several-year period of using the name Sociedad de Damas Cristianas en Acción (Society of Christian Women in Action).

A 1974 gathering was planned for Lancaster, Pennsylvania. The first gathering was presumably paid for by the women themselves; Maria Bustos listed "faith" in the finances column on a chart showing figures for the early conferences.[11] To help with the second conference, the Concilio leaders wrote to the WMSC requesting a grant of $3,000 for "las hermanas." The WMSC executive committee decided to make the money available, even though it required some temporary reallocation of funds. Beulah Kauffman, WMSC director, wrote a letter to the WMSC district presidents explaining the move and reminding them of the WMSC meeting at the 1973 MC assembly (perhaps the same gathering referred to at the beginning of this chapter). At that meeting,

An ensemble singing at an Hispanic Mennonite women's conference in the 1970s.

women had expressed that they would "stand ready to help in whatever ways possible" when "clearly defined" needs of Spanish-speaking members were presented.[12] Kauffman described this request as just such a need and expressed hope that women across the denomination would consider making the Hispanic women's conference their annual giving project.

The WMSC money was apparently the only outside funding received for the 1974 conference. Women from many Hispanic churches contributed through offerings, craft sales, and other fundraisers, either to support the conference in general or to fund the travel of their own members. Lois Gunden Clemens attended the gathering as a WMSC representative. She reflected in a July 1974 *Voice* article: "It has been good for me at various times to be a minority within a Christian group representing a cultural heritage different from mine. My heart has been strangely warmed in sensing the oneness I could feel with them. This was true again when I joined our Spanish-speaking sisters gathered together in their Lancaster meeting."[13] Enriqueta Díaz summed up her sentiments about the conference in an August 1974 *Voice* article: "It is marvelous that in a reunion like this we can share with each other ideas, emotions, and thoughts, all in our own language and in a cordial environment. Praise God for His love!"[14]

After the 1974 gathering, Maria Bustos wrote to Kauffman presenting the Hispanic women's organizational plan (five regions with a president and secretary for each) and their decision to hold a conference every two years. "All this was done in prayer and not with intentions of being a separate group, but with a desire in our hearts to fulfill the needs of our people, and at the same time be part of the General WMSC groups and work together with you as much as possible," Bustos wrote.[15] Kauffman sent a letter to WMSC executive committee members, enclosing the information from Bustos and noting that she thought the Hispanic women should have the freedom to organize however they saw fit. "However," Kauffman added, "I believe it would mean a great deal to them to be affirmed in their action by our committee."[16] The committee presumably had a positive response, and Maria Bustos was invited to join the WMSC executive committee beginning with its April 1975 meeting. Through Bustos's presence, executive committee members learned about and were inspired by the active Latina organization. Encouragement also happened the other way. "We looked up to the WMSC group," Seferina De León said in a 2015 interview, remembering that Bustos would bring back ideas about things like governing documents and officers' roles, which the Hispanic women incorporated into their young organization.[17]

Hispanic Mennonite women gathered again in 1976 in Corpus Christi, Texas. Lois Gunden Clemens gave greetings from the WMSC, and each region shared about the activities of their groups. A *Voice* article about the conference mentioned a beautiful sunrise service and a vespers service by the bay that included special music and inspiring testimonies.[18] The article also noted that "some sisters made a decision to accept Christ as their personal Savior."[19] Maria Bustos reported about 150 women in attendance and over $9,000 in "finances," which included contributions from the WMSC and the Mennonite Board of Missions in addition to many donations from Latino churches.[20]

A fourth conference was held in 1978 at Goshen College. One reason for this location was to introduce women to the many Mennonite-related institutions in the area. An announcement specifically invited women to attend from Anglo WMSC groups in area conferences that had Latino churches. The announcement also promised a musical and poetry contest, a parade of banners representing the conference theme

("Freedom and Responsibility in the Christian Family"), a banquet, and a play.[21]

Hispanic women's conferences continued throughout the 1980s and 1990s in various locations, often attracting more than two hundred women for a long weekend at a camp or hotel. Maria Bustos served as coordinator for the first several conferences, but soon that role rotated among a group of talented women, many of whom were or would become significant leaders in congregations and in the denomination. Seferina De León, who coordinated the 1982 conference and had notable musical as well as leadership gifts, would in 2004 become the first Hispanic woman ordained by Indiana-Michigan Conference. Marta Hernández, who coordinated several conferences, has since worked as a church planter, pastor, and facilitator of Spanish-language church leadership training in Oregon and Iowa. Maria Magdalena De León, coordinator of the 1990 conference, served in numerous wider leadership roles and was a bridge for many Hispanic Mennonites to the work of the denomination.[22]

The women celebrated the twenty-fifth anniversary of the first conference at their 1999 gathering, coordinated by Juanita Nuñez. Nuñez's

Past coordinators of Hispanic women's conferences (left to right): Esther Hinojosa, Maria Magdalena De León, Marta Hernández, Maria Tijerina, Seferina De León, Elizabeth Perez, and Maria Bustos.

"Reporte de la Coordinatora" gives a glimpse into the significance of the conferences in promoting spiritual growth and leadership for individual women. Nuñez writes that she first attended the conference in 1990, during which she shared part of her testimony and requested prayer for her husband's salvation. At the 1992 conference she reported the good news that this prayer had been answered. For the 1994 conference, she was asked to prepare a meditation on the conference theme, "Ten cuidado de ti misma" ("Take Care of Yourself"), for one of the evenings. At the next conference in 1997, Nuñez shared part of a presentation on being an Anabaptist woman that she had given in another context. At the conference banquet, she was elected as the coordinator for the 1999 gathering. Nuñez's report mentions the name of each coordinator of the previous conferences she attended; the coordinators were obviously instrumental in calling forth her participation and leadership. Nuñez currently pastors a church in Florida with her husband and has served as moderator of Iglesia Menonita Hispana and on the Mennonite Church USA General Board.[23]

As with the denominational or area conference women's retreats and activities, Hispanic Mennonite women's conferences provided both inspiration in faith and opportunities for leadership development. The Hispanic gatherings also had some characteristics that differentiated them from typical WMSC retreats. By the late 1990s, organizers of the Latina retreats announced colors selections ahead of time, and attendees dressed in those colors for a formal Saturday night banquet. Music had always been an important component of the event, with special musicians chosen with as much care as speakers. Music also provided a way to represent the cultural variety of the Spanish speakers in attendance, with songs from

A promotional flier for the 1999 conference celebrating twenty-five years since the first Hispanic Mennonite women's event. Designed by Maria Tijerina.

Caribbean, Mexican, and Central American traditions, along with a mixture that many younger people enjoyed.[24] Worship displayed the charismatic flavor of many Latino Mennonite churches; a 1999 document summarizing the conferences mentions that women got up before dawn to pray, resulting in healings, prophecy, singing in tongues, and other gifts of the Spirit.[25]

Maria Tijerina remembers how significant the conferences were for her when she started attending them in the mid-1970s. At that time she was a young mother of four whose husband was studying to become a pastor, and her own mother had recently died of cancer. "I was so tired," Tijerina said in a 2015 interview, recalling that the conferences helped her see that "there was more to me than a pastor's wife."[26] Tijerina became involved in organizing publicity for the gatherings and coordinated the 1984 conference. More recently, she served as the Hispanic organization's representative to the Mennonite Women USA board.

Elizabeth Perez, who coordinated the 1980 conference, remembers her surprise when she was chosen for the role. "I didn't even realize I had gifts, you know!" she said in a 2015 interview. The mentorship of Maria Bustos helped draw out Perez's leadership ability, which she uses today in her congregation in Sarasota, Florida. For Perez, the important part of the early conferences was not so much their content but simply that they existed at a time when Latina Mennonites did not have many opportunities for significant involvement in their congregations. "Just to have a conference [of] all women, this was very exciting," she said.[27]

The Hispanic Mennonite women's conferences of the 1970s and 1980s show Latina Mennonites engaging with the feminist movement in a nuanced way. Instead of pushing for more inclusion of women in church leadership—as many white feminists at the time were doing—they demonstrated their skills as preachers, Bible interpreters, and musicians in a separate space.[28] As Felipe Hinojosa discusses, most Latina Mennonites rejected the politics of the feminist movement, but they were still sympathetic to some of the changes it called for in terms of greater access to leadership and the utilization of women's full potential.[29] Though Latina Mennonite leaders, including Maria Bustos, generally did not question the role of men as head of the household, Steve Bustos recalls that his mother, Maria, "really was a champion for women in leadership."[30] The people around her did not necessarily realize this at the time, because she was the type of person who simply engaged in everything. "For her it wasn't just about women; it was about, 'This is what you do because you're a follower of Christ,' " Steve Bustos said.[31]

Hispanic Mennonite women's conferences, separate from both male-led Latino churches and white-led denominational women's organizations, flourished as they helped Latinas embrace their full identities as Spanish speakers, as women, and most importantly, as followers of Christ.

Black Mennonite Women's Retreats

While Hispanic women's conferences have continued to the present day with strong participation, black Mennonite women's gatherings were smaller and had less longevity. There is also much less documentation of these events; just a few announcements and evaluations from some of the retreats are preserved in the Mennonite Church USA Archives.[32] But the little information that does exist hints at important conversations and profound moments for participants related to their personal lives and the navigation of their place within the denomination.

Black Mennonite women did not organize themselves into a separate conference with its own regional groupings and constitution, as Latina Mennonites did, and there was less communication with and financial support from the WMSC. It appears that the costs of the retreats (above women's registration fees) were covered by the African American Mennonite Association, though the WMSC did sometimes contribute funds to enable women to attend other AAMA gatherings.

The first black Mennonite women's retreat, or "fellowship conference," was held in 1977 and coordinated by Frances Jackson. The theme was "Challenges Facing Black Women in the Mennonite Church." The retreat likely provided space for black women to lament the barriers they faced in the church and in society—which not all attendees fully appreciated. One attendee wrote on her evaluation form that there was "too much complaining and groaning." Another said, "It's not so much what others do to me, but how do I as a Christian react to them?" While several women noted that they were expecting more explicitly spiritual content from speakers, at least one person had a different view. She wrote, "I felt as though it was a cop-out for women to keep going back to 'getting right with God.' We have to move on beyond that and get right with each other to get something done!!" A major highlight for participants at the first black women's gathering was simply getting together. "I enjoy hearing and knowing that others are sharing some of the same frustrations that I'm having," one person wrote on her evaluation. "The exchange with other black women about common concerns . . . was very valuable to me," said another. One person commented that she was "very young in the Lord" and had never been to a conference like this before. She found it very "spiritually uplifting," adding, "I didn't know that there could be so much love shown in a meeting like this."[33]

Frances Jackson speaking at the 1977 Black Mennonite Women retreat. Wilma Ann Bailey is seated in the foreground.

The comment about wanting to "get something done" shows a more outwardly focused mentality, perhaps one more in line with the service element of the dual purpose of Mennonite women's gatherings. For some, the main attraction of women's gatherings was and is a desire to participate in productive work, whether that comes through material aid for mission or through planning social justice initiatives. But African American and Hispanic Mennonite women started to officially gather during a time of increased attention to spirituality in Mennonite contexts and during an era of identity politics in wider society. In these contexts, some saw a need for developing and strengthening a sense of personal growth and sisterhood within their ranks. Black and Hispanic women's retreats, perhaps more than area conference Mennonite women's events, engaged women who were at different places on their spiritual journey and were sometimes facing severe challenges. The sisterhood and spirituality elements of the gatherings were a kind of service as well, one directed not at people in faraway lands but to members of their own circle.

The second retreat for black Mennonite women was held in Halifax, Pennsylvania, in 1979. Attendees included about seventy-five women from eleven states. The September 1979 *Voice* was dedicated to the event, which WMSC editor Vel Shearer attended. Comments were printed from participants who came from Hampton, Virginia; Bronx, New York; New Haven, Connecticut; Southfield, Michigan; Los Angeles, California; and Saint Anne, Illinois. Though not everyone expressed unequivocal praise (one person commented that, as a single woman, she could not relate to the testimonies), most people celebrated the fellowship and spiritual aspects of the gathering. Rose Covington said, "The testimonies and the spiritual singing were most helpful in my spiritual growth." Fannie Hardy noted, "All the women made me feel that I could say what I felt. . . . This meeting was like a new rebirth experience for me."[34]

The *Voice* issue contained several articles drawing on input from speakers at the 1979 retreat. Their content suggests that there was serious and hopeful engagement with issues faced by black Mennonite women. Rosemarie Harding contributed a four-page article drawn from her conference address, titled "Loving and Accepting Myself." She wrote about leading, with her husband, Vincent, an interracial

"Mennonite House" in Atlanta, sponsored by Mennonite Central Committee, in the early 1960s.[35] Harding reflected on the powerful experience of traveling as a representative of MCC and Mennonites while white members of the unit did more of the behind-the-scenes work. (The Hardings left the Mennonite church more than a decade before the 1979 retreat because of frustrations about the denomination's reluctance to embrace the civil rights movement.) In another *Voice* article, Shearer recorded some of Wilma Ann Bailey's Sunday morning address, including the quotation that starts this chapter. Bailey had served in several pastoral and scholarly roles at Mennonite and other religious institutions and would eventually be named a professor emerita at Christian Theological Seminary (Indianapolis, Ind.). She described black Mennonite women as "a small group, gifted, diverse, faithful, and intelligent. We can worship, celebrate, love, forgive, survive against unbelievable odds and be creative in dealing with our unique problems as Christian black women in a society which has stacked the deck against us."[36] Bailey's eloquent words surely stirred the spirits of attendees, inspiring some and challenging others. Shearer reflected, "It was in facing again some of the evils of a white-dominated world that I, as a white, saw what you [black Mennonite women] must give to the Mennonite Church. Through your suffering God has forged in you a depth of understanding of forgiveness we as white Mennonites will never know. We need your wisdom."[37]

The third gathering of black Mennonite women, in 1981, was hosted at a retreat center in Indiana. The theme was "The Be-attitudes of Being a Woman." In the promotional flyer, coordinator Shirley Seals promised a "discussion of who we are in relationship to the image of God as Black Mennonite Women who live at the end of the twentieth century in the United States of America."[38] Resource persons included Carliss McGhee, a Mennonite woman active in civic affairs in Los Angeles; Angie Williams, a Mennonite Media/Choice Books employee and vice president of the WMSC; Florence Grimes, a member of a Mennonite church in Norristown, Pennsylvania; and James B. White, a professor of urban sociology from Grand Rapids, Michigan. Evaluation forms asked participants to list the most meaningful aspect of the conference. Most comments mentioned fellowship and support. One person enjoyed "being with all the beautiful sisters in Christ." Another respondent coined an appropriate phrase when she wrote about "getting togethering with the ladies to give testimony." People also noted the spiritual aspects of the retreat: devotion and worship, the testimony service, a teaching about meditating on God's Word. Other evaluation comments perhaps indicated a generational divide, which was becoming common in church women's activities in many contexts. One person mentioned that "some of the younger women aren't as friendly . . . and that put a damper on things." Several people said that they would have liked to see more young people attend, or more people in general. One person highlighted the variety of people involved in leading the event. "I was blessed seeing so much talent in a small group," she said. While attendance at the black Mennonite women retreats was relatively small, participants came from across the United States and sometimes brought perspectives from other parts of the world; Rose Covington remembers being inspired by women from Jamaican and African contexts.[39]

Black Mennonite women's retreats emerged and developed in a time of increased focus on racial and gender identity among Mennonites, in evangelical circles, and in society in general. In chapter 10 of his book *Moral Minority*, David Swartz discusses the fragmenting of the evangelical left (which some Mennonites connected with) and the rise of "identity politics" in the 1960s and beyond. Fueled by the racism members of the National Black Evangelical Association experienced in mostly white Christian contexts and by the Black Power movement in wider society, the organization turned toward a more separatist mentality.[40] A move toward autonomy was happening in Mennonite circles as well. At a time when Mennonite women's organizations were being criticized for their separate nature, black women, like Latinas, seemed to find value and power in separate gatherings that explored and reinforced their sense of identity. During the 1980s, almost all the fifty or so black and "integrated" Mennonite congregations were led by male pastors (African American or Anglo), even though the majority of attendees at many of these churches were women.[41] But at the retreats, black women were speakers and preachers, seminar facilitators, logistical administrators, and music and worship leaders.

The late 1970s and early 1980s were also a time of increased attention to celebrating black identity. Black History Month was officially established in the United States in 1976, and the hugely popular 1977 television adaptation of Alex Haley's *Roots* brought a personalized story of slavery to wide audience. In *Moral Minority*, Swartz writes that black evangelical women in this era, "while sympathetic to the feminist cause, often found race a more salient category than gender."[42] Angie Williams's perspective notwithstanding (see chapter 3), many black Mennonite women wanted to talk about race and the impact of racism on their lives and faith journeys. During the 1970s and 1980s, this conversation was unlikely to happen in a woman-centered way in black Mennonite spaces or in any way in gatherings of mostly white Mennonite women. So separate retreats, although never attended by large numbers of black women, provided valuable sharing spaces for those who participated and perhaps, to some extent, for others who simply knew they were happening.

Joy Lovett coordinated the black Mennonite women's retreat in 1983. Lovett was the denomination's most prominent African American female leader at the time. She served on the AAMA staff and as associate general secretary of the MC. The 1983 gathering, like the ones before it, stressed connection to the everyday lives of African American women. An announcement in the *Gospel Herald* read: "Participants will be led to consider who God would have them become as they continue to change, to grow, and to struggle with being human and woman. The program will also deal with some of the very real day-to-day difficulties women face in life situations."[43] The featured speaker was Goldie Ivory, a social worker and educator who had taught at Goshen College. A recording of the event contains heartfelt, free-flowing singing as well as Ivory's lecture-style presentations. About forty attendees heard historical examples of strong women from the Bible (Deborah, the daughters of Zelophehad), black history (Harriet Tubman, Ida B. Wells), and contemporary America. "Your ancestral roots go deeper than Africa," Ivory told the women, encouraging them to connect with the biblical stories. She also spoke against the "tunnel vision" of white feminists who wanted to only talk about sexism and deal with racism later.[44]

Ivory's presentations connected with the identity politics of her day. She advocated for a self-love and empowerment that not all attendees at the 1983 retreat appreciated without reservation. One person wrote on her evaluation form: "Goldie's ideas on submission were indeed radical if not un-biblical," though she also noted, "I did appreciate her positive up-lifting of self." Another person wrote that while she enjoyed the speaker very much, she would probably prefer someone who, "rather than focusing so much on culture and roots," would spend more time "expounding the Word to us!" Several attendees reacted positively to the speaker's input, however, and the overwhelming sense from the evaluations was appreciation for the time of connection and spiritual renewal. Many mentioned singing and fellowship as most significant, enjoying the chance for "mingling with the sisters and gleaning from them." As in other years, not all participants came from Mennonite churches, and not all were African American. One attendee wrote, "I am white with biracial and black daughters. My dear black sisters have been so accepting and helpful in my understanding them a bit more. Individual sisters have taken time to share, encourage, and pray with me—a very special experience!"[45]

The next retreat was not held until 1987. The coordinators were three women from Michigan: Bernice Scott, Patricia Genwright, and Ann Jones. (Scott and Jones, a mother and daughter, had been involved with their congregational WMSC group at Ninth Street Mennonite Church in Saginaw, Michigan, for several decades.[46]) The theme was "Black Women: Focus on the Family" with guest speaker Catherine Meeks, a distinguished sociology professor. Seminars explored topics such as "Male Leadership and the Black Woman," "Relating to Teenage Pregnancies, "Black Women in the Working World," and "Dealing with Our Children and Drugs."[47] The worship leader was Addie Banks, who copastored a Mennonite church in New York City.

Another retreat was held in 1990, coordinated by Rose Covington. Thirty-nine people attended, including two WMSC representatives. WMSC executive committee minutes show that plans were made for another "AAMA women's retreat" in 1994, though there is no mention of it in later sources.[48] Covington thinks that she may have coordinated another retreat in 1996, and Cora Brown may have organized several gatherings for black Mennonite women after that.[49] Banks continued to participate in the retreats and remembers speaking at one in Akron, Pennsylvania, in 2005 or 2006.[50] While participation in black Mennonite women's retreats waned in the 1990s and beyond, some older black women continued to regularly attend annual women's retreats in their area conferences. One of those retreats revived a focus on

African Americans when "Black Mennonite Women ROCK" was chosen as the theme for Central District Conference's 2014 retreat (more on this in chapter 11).

Women who attended the black Mennonite women's retreats and were also familiar with white Mennonite contexts noted that the African American gatherings had a more intense spiritual focus and expression. Covington described the black women's retreats as "dynamite," saying, "We were empowered; the Holy Spirit was always with us."[51] Mertis Odom, a member of a GCMC church in Markham, Illinois, always attended her area conference's retreats but also went to the AAMA retreats. She described the conference retreats as having more "fun stuff," like quilting and craft activities. Black women's retreats were "more spiritual" and included more singing and sharing.[52]

Addie Banks, whose church was started by mission workers from Lancaster Conference, vividly remembers attending her first area conference retreat, probably in 1978. "I was the only woman at the conference who had a little black head covering. It was a sea of white head coverings—I'd never seen anything like it," she said.[53] By the late 1970s, the wearing of prayer coverings was declining in the MC, though perhaps most slowly in Lancaster Conference. While most women wore a small white cap made of organdy, rayon, or nylon net, a few wore smaller black lace doilies.[54] Banks's choice of head covering marked her as different from the mostly white retreat participants, as did her skin color. But her donning of the symbol was not necessarily (or not only) an imposition of a patriarchal religious culture; Tobin Miller Shearer points out that some African American Mennonite women wore coverings to "claim belonging in a church that frequently denied them full status."[55]

Banks's first Mennonite women's retreat prompted reflection on her status in the denomination beyond her outward appearance. The speaker at the retreat was a church planter from Baltimore who told a story about someone Banks knew. It was a mission story; the person Banks knew was the "missionized person." The experience made Banks think about the way her story would be told. "It was my first awareness that I had come into a church that was culturally and ethnically different," she said. But despite her discomfort, Banks was inspired by the retreat and came back to her congregation with an enthusiasm for getting more women engaged. "I started becoming much more conscious of my role as a woman in the church," she said.[56]

In contrast to mostly white Mennonite women's events, Banks said that black women's retreats were "a much more interactive, dynamic experience."[57] Banks describes herself as an idealist, and she was most interested in getting people of diverse backgrounds together, as she has done with RAW (Radical Anabaptist Women), an intercultural group she cofounded for mentoring female ministers in New York City. But she saw also the need for gathering with her African American sisters. "Our context was different, so we discussed different issues," she said. "Or when the same issues were discussed, it was from a different perspective."[58] Banks developed her leadership gifts at the African American women's retreats as well as in her congregation and community. In the late 1990s, she started a nonprofit organization focused on conflict resolution; in 2011, she became the first African American woman ordained by Lancaster Conference.[59]

Radical Anabaptist Women mentors and mentees, March 10, 2012, in Manhattan. Front-row honorees (left to right): Sara Mateo Deo, Melody M. Pannell, Keyla Cortez Vanegas, Hyacinth Stevens, and Nancy Maldonado; back-row mentors (left to right): Sandra Perez, Ruth Yoder, Sylvia Shirk, and Addie Banks.

Like black Mennonite women, Latina Mennonites have observed differences between their gatherings and events planned and attended mostly by white Mennonites. Maria Tijerina mentioned the many "prayer warriors" who attend Hispanic women's conferences and the special times of laying hands on people for prayer and proclamation.[60] She noted that gatherings with mostly Anglo Mennonite women are much quieter. "I discern complete sincerity and integrity," she said, "but sometimes I think they just want to bust out and they're not!"[61] Separate gatherings planned, led, and largely attended by black or Hispanic women gave Mennonite women of color space not only to discuss topics of special relevance but also to express and affirm their unique spirituality.

The retreats of the 1970s and beyond did for black and Hispanic Mennonite women much of what the denominational women's organizations did for (mostly) white Mennonite women. The retreats embodied the dual purpose of Mennonite women's organizations: service and sisterhood. A document from the 1980s lists one goal of the black women's retreats: "To challenge Black Women to personal growth and development *and* to greater commitment in carrying out God's mission in the world" (emphasis mine).[62] A goal of the original Latina organization was to "encourage spiritual commitment *and* service" (emphasis mine).[63] Black and Hispanic retreats nurtured and empowered participants, creating a sense of sisterhood that was especially valuable in a denomination in which they were marginalized because of gender in their congregations and because of ethnicity in their denomination. These retreats also embodied the more outward or service purpose of Mennonite women's gatherings, though with a more spiritual rather than material focus. Both the black and Hispanic retreats were spaces for evangelism and ministry, as leaders called for commitments or recommitments to Christ and "prayer warriors" ministered to women dealing with difficult circumstances. These gatherings may have also contributed to the shift in Mennonite women's activities toward the need for service and ministry among people in their own congregations and communities rather than in faraway lands (see the interlude "A Mission to Themselves").

Interaction among and between the various cultural groups in the denomination, including groups besides African Americans and Latinas, would continue to be a topic of conversation for the MC women's organization and denomination. This topic will be discussed in later chapters, but we first return to pick up the story of the GCMC women's organization in the 1970s and 1980s.

6
Women in Mission

> We are involved in the total mission of the church, the broad application of the teachings of Jesus as they relate to the whole person. With this in mind you will readily understand why the WMA executive council is recommending "Women in Mission" as the name for our organization. It suggests that not only groups but individual members should be personally involved in the mission of the church.
> —Naomi Lehman[1]

A formational story for the MC women's organization—a narrative that has shaped its sense of purpose and identity—is clearly the story of its early organizer, Clara Eby Steiner, and the "takeover" by the denominational mission board of the organization she formed. The GCMC women's organization does not have such a dramatic early story, but it did have a crucial moment that influenced the direction and perception of the organization for years to come. The action of the women's organization in securing female representatives on the leadership boards of the GCMC in the 1970s has served as an important reference point and as a catalyst for future activity in the organization and in the denomination overall.

Representation on Commissions

By 1973, the GCMC women's organization, then known as the Women's Missionary Association (WMA), had representatives on each of the denomination's three commissions (the Commissions on Overseas

Ministries, Home Ministries, and Education). However, these representatives were considered unofficial members and did not have voting privileges, except for the Commission on Home Ministries, which had two members from the women's organization and involved them as regular commission members. When the WMA executive secretary wrote to the GCMC General Board requesting a review of the status of the women's group representatives, the board referred the matter to the denomination's Constitution Committee. This committee replied with a recommendation to continue current practice, saying that the members appointed by the women's organization should not have votes, as they were a "special interest group." Perhaps wanting to avoid further discussion of the matter, the Commissions of Overseas Ministries and Education dropped their WMA representatives.[2]

In February 1974, GCMC commissions and boards were gathered for their annual meeting, a time when the leaders of the women's organization gathered as well. Gladys Goering, who had recently begun as executive secretary of the women's organization, went before the GCMC General Board with two other women to deliver a statement on behalf of the WMA that argued for voting representation within denominational bodies. Elsie Flaming, who at that time was president of the Ontario women's organization, remembers sitting in a side room with other women and praying together while their leaders spoke to the board. "They went to this meeting with a lot of apprehension," Flaming said in a 2015 interview, pausing with emotion at the poignant memory. "And they came back and they were just beaming, that they had been accepted."[3]

Goering's statement outlined several reasons why the women's organization should be granted voting representatives in the structure of the denomination. First, the organization had 10,692 members, two-fifths of whom were Canadian, a bond that helped unite the binational GCMC. Second, women's groups were significant contributors to the denomination, giving well over half a million dollars annually to projects at various levels. Third, being part of the commissions would enable the women to be more informed about the denomination and its programs. The fourth point mentioned that, ideally, the percentage of women elected to commissions would be much higher, but that this was not likely to happen soon.[4] Finally, as the women's organization was in the process of reassessing its future direction, being part of the commissions could be a real help. "To be shut out will say something to us also," the statement noted.[5]

The General Board unanimously granted the request, and the Mennonite Biblical Seminary board also made changes to accommodate a representative from the women's organization. Naomi Lehman, board president of the women's organization, recalled the "gratefulness and celebration" that followed the General Board's decision.[6] "We experienced the joy of being full-fledged partners in the mission of the church, accepted for ourselves as well as for the financial and material aid contributions we have made for so many years," she wrote in the magazine of the women's organization.[7]

Attaining representation on the denomination's commissions fit the dual purpose of women's groups: serving others and empowering the participants themselves. The women saw that they had much to offer to the commissions, as indeed they had already been offering in their material and financial contributions. They also had much to gain from the closer collaboration, both for their organization and for themselves personally. A 1977 memo from Goering shared reflections from the appointed women members three years into the arrangement. The seminary board member reported on the encouragement she felt and the sense that "in some way I completed the missing part of the picture" and added, "Personally, I have learned a great deal about carrying responsibility and making administrative decisions."[8] Goering concluded the memo by saying that the past three years "have added a feeling of self worth to our organization and greater understanding of our function and potential" in the denomination.[9] The women were beginning to see that the service they could provide the denomination came not just through their material handiwork or behind-the-scenes actions but also through their leadership gifts. And in some ways, venturing into new realms of leadership only increased the need for a sisterhood of other women with whom these new leaders could share their doubts, fears, and triumphs.

The women did not become competent contributors to the male-dominated meetings overnight. Jeannie Zehr sat in on some of the commission meetings in her role as editor for the women's organization. She remembers that the women representatives would often just sit there, not asking questions or saying anything. "I thought, oh, we're there, but we're not really there," she said.[10] Zehr enjoyed watching the women develop their acumen and become more involved, especially as other women joined the meetings.[11] By 1987, women were being elected to all the commissions and serving as chairpersons of committees.[12] One commission had a woman executive secretary, and the GCMC had a woman president, Florence Driedger—the first woman in the top position of a Mennonite denomination.

New Identity

The desire for the women's organization to push for appointees to the denomination's commissions came out of discussions at the Consultation on the Role of Women, a gathering initiated by the Commission on Home Ministries in 1973. Another recommendation from that gathering was a name change for the women's organization. With the affirmation of members at the triennial assembly in 1974, the organization adopted the name Women in Mission. Goering explained that the new name "has the broader concept that all Christian women are in mission, women with work to do for God and church, 'sent out.' "[13] In a way, the women's organization presaged the "missional" concept that would become popular in Mennonite Church USA several decades later. Women were no longer seeing themselves as simply supporting missionaries; rather, they were beginning to see themselves as missionaries and their everyday work as mission oriented. This shift in understanding again highlights the dual service and sisterhood purpose of women's groups, but in a different way than in previous eras. Women were beginning to realize that people in their own congregation and communities needed service and encouragement to fully grasp God's liberation and salvation. While women's organization members brought the service-mission concept closer to home, they also extended the sisterhood concept, looking for ways to connect more directly with "sisters" on other continents and in other organizations.

A 1974 self-study gathered information from 522 GCMC congregational women's groups in Canada and the United States. Given the choices of "strong," "average," or "weak," most respondents (58 percent) rated their congregational group as average (37 percent said their groups were strong and 5 percent felt they were weak). Just over half

Women in Mission leaders, 1978. Front row (left to right): Lois Deckert, Joan Wiebe, Naomi Wollman, Naomi Lehman, Lora Oyer, and Elsie Flaming. Middle row (left to right): unidentified, Joyce Shutt, Anita Froese, Norma Wiens, Nina Roupp, Jeannie Zehr, and Kay Ann Franzen. Back row (left to right): Margot Fregoth, Helen Friesen, Margaret Ewert, Jeanette Schmidt, Marilyn Mace, and Anne Neufeld. The cross-stitch reads "We are Women in Mission like our counterparts in Scripture. We serve with vigor and enthusiasm, with courtesy and kindness, with love and compassion, making Christ known throughout the world."

the respondents said their group put a strong emphasis on "handwork," while 20 percent put a strong emphasis on "study and program." Out of several phrases describing the function of groups, the one chosen most frequently was "material aid contributor" (180 groups), followed by "fellowship" (139 groups). Third and fourth were "financial contributor to the G.C. [denomination]" (105 groups) and "financial contributor to the district/province" (90 groups). This survey shows the strong service and social functions of local women's groups. It also shows that while the denominational organization's leadership was exploring new horizons of leadership, influence, and empowerment, the primary focus for many women continued to be their material and financial contributions.[14]

During the 1970s and 1980s, many women's groups in GCMC churches continued to sew, quilt, roll bandages, and make layettes (sets of clothing for babies), often directly supporting missionaries from their congregations. They also gave time and money to countless projects in their congregations and communities. Most groups near a GCMC higher education institution included it in their giving and supported it with material items. Other activities included cleanup days at homes for the aged, helping with blood drives, serving as hosts for visiting choirs, assisting families during a hospitalization, and volunteering at church-sponsored nursery schools. "Catering meals," Goering notes, "is on the list of numerous [congregational women's] societies as a function performed when it is convenient and often when it is not."[15] Goering points out that the *organization* of church women's societies is especially important.[16] While in many congregations the activities listed above were covered in an ad hoc way, congregations with an established women's group had (and in many cases still have) a source of immediate help. Many women's groups also had "programs" as part of their regular meetings or as special events. A program might take

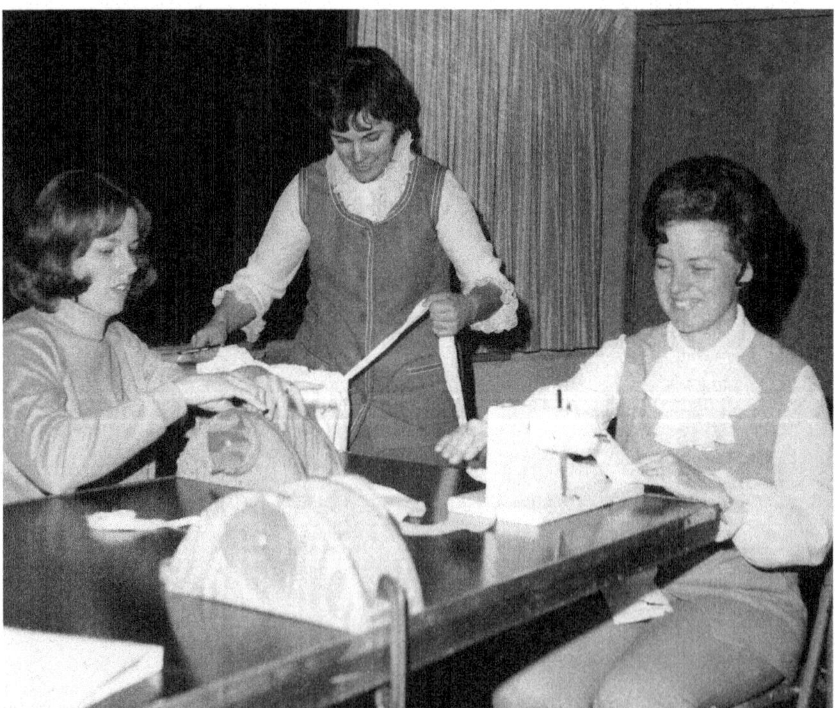

Women from Salem-Zion Mennonite Church (Freeman, S.Dak.) rolling bandages. (Left to right) Mavis Ortman, Renee Hartman, and Rosella Schwartz.

the form of a reflection on a biblical text with sharing and singing, a holiday-themed meal, a mother-daughter banquet with a special reading, an exploration of an overseas mission context, or a ritual celebrating the history of the group and installing new officers.[17] While more Mennonite women were beginning to work outside the home and becoming less involved with church women's group activities, those who were involved had plenty to keep them busy.

Promoting retreats was not as great a priority for Women in Mission as it was for the WMSC during this time, but some GCMC women did begin having retreats in their areas. Phyllis Baumgartner recalls seeing an article in a Christian magazine in the 1960s about retreats and feeling inspired to organize one for Central District Conference women at their new camp, Camp Friedenswald. Baumgartner, who had five children, worked to organize the retreat with another woman, who had even more children than she did. "It was so good to just have a little free time to read and meditate, to be with other moms who were struggling," Baumgartner said.[18] The Central District Conference women's retreat became an anticipated annual event for women from a variety of backgrounds and locations, including Ivorie Lowe. Lowe served on the denomination's Commission of Home Ministries and remembers having "such turmoil" one year because the commission meeting was the same weekend as the retreat.[19] For Lowe, the retreats were meaningful because they provided an opportunity to "sit down and talk with or listen to women who were organizing something other than what I was involved in."[20] As a school administrator, mother, and active congregation member, Lowe enjoyed hearing how other women balanced their concerns and commitments.

The proliferation and popularity of retreats show a shift from the service focus of Mennonite women's groups to more of a sisterhood function. Women also performed service to each other as they supported attendees dealing with difficult life circumstances. Area conference retreats, which were often attended by the same core groups of women, enabled participants to form bonds of sisterhood in a more organized and intentional way than had happened somewhat inadvertently during the sewing and service activities of previous years.

Women from the Conference of Mennonites in Canada connected with Women in Mission but also gathered in their own yearly meetings starting in 1952. The gatherings, held in conjunction with the annual assembly of the Conference of Mennonites in Canada, usually included an afternoon business meeting and an evening mission program. Esther Patkau writes that the largest meeting was at the 1974 assembly in Steinbach, Manitoba, when 575 women gathered for the evening mission program.[21] By the mid-1970s, the evening presentations at these gatherings were often less focused on international mission and more about domestic social concerns and the role of women in the church. The address in 1974 was on "Mennonite Pioneer Women," highlighting inspiring women in the past and present.[22] In 1975, the program included informal presentations by missionaries but also presentations on local projects, including Meals on Wheels, Friendship Coffee Hours, Ladies Time Out, Community Self-Help stores, and a Big Sister program.[23] Presenters also spoke about work with the aged and passing on the faith to one's children.[24] A year after the name change to Women in Mission, it appears that the Canadian women had fully embraced the idea that all women could be doing "mission" in their home contexts.

International Connections

International connections remained important for Women in Mission, however—not only through missionaries but also through women's organization members themselves. In 1971, two GCMC women took part in a small delegation of women to Zaire (now the Democratic Republic of the Congo) sent by the Women's Auxiliary of the Congo Inland Mission Board.[25] Participants noted how important it seemed that a group of women had come specially to connect with women in that country.[26] In 1977, Women in Mission sent two representatives to the All-India Mennonite Women's Conference. When they returned, these women traveled around the United States and Canada sharing about their experience with the women who had supported them. In 1978, a twenty-four-member women's choir from Taiwan came to North America, primarily to attend the Mennonite World Conference assembly in Wichita, Kansas. Women in Mission arranged for the choir to make more than thirty additional appearances in five provinces and eight states, taking care of most of their lodging, food, and travel needs.[27] This visit led to personal connections with women from a part of the world where the GCMC had several missionaries and to a reciprocal trip by two Women in Mission leaders, who visited women's groups and missionaries in Taiwan, Japan, and Hong Kong in 1981.

These international visits made women aware of the desire for leadership training felt by Mennonite-related women around the world. While a program supporting international exchanges had been part of Women in Mission's budget since 1974, a new fund for education and professional training for international women began in 1979, called the Women's World Outreach fund. The fund was designated for international women's travel to future Mennonite World Conference gatherings and for leadership training and seminars in various countries. By the mid-1980s, the fund had been used to enable wives (and sometimes children) of international church leaders to accompany their husbands when they came to study in the United States and to take some classes themselves, as well to aid some attendees of a Hispanic Mennonite women's conference.[28]

The Women's World Outreach fund was important for its contributors as well as its recipients. In discussing the initial efforts to provide these international scholarships, Lora Oyer (Women in Mission board president) said, "Our emphasis was to try to get women to go beyond needlework and lift their horizons."[29] Writing about Protestant women's organizations in general, Rosemary Skinner Keller discusses the way that joining efforts for international support helped women form a sense of community within a denomination.[30] She writes that "raising money to support women in far-flung foreign countries was a way of bringing together women in remote reaches throughout the United States to serve a larger common purpose."[31] (Women in Mission of course included contributors from Canada as well.) Working together to support women studying in international locations, as well as female North American seminary students, surely helped some Women in Mission members feel connected not only to the women they were supporting but also to others who contributed to the fund across the continent and denomination.

Lora Oyer provided leadership for the first international scholarships for Mennonite women.

The Women's World Outreach fund is first on a list of "projects of special interest" in a Women in Mission brochure from around 1980. Other special projects included a personal growth fund for pastors' wives and women in church vocations, publications, a Bible society, and the Missionary Pension Fund. However, the bulk of the organization's contributions went not to their own projects but to aspects of the denomination. Financial goals for 1980 included $109,000 for the Commission on Overseas Mission, $33,000 for the Commission on Home Ministries, $12,000 for the Commission on Education, and $9,000 for Associated Mennonite Biblical Seminarys. The brochure listed the purpose of Women in Mission: "To help its ten thousand members in approximately 440 groups become effectively involved in the total mission of the church." Goals listed for the 1980s included commitments to: foster spiritual growth among members; strengthen relationships with women abroad; assist women in developing their gifts; relate to the hurting and lonely; strengthen family and marriage relationships; unite efforts to improve television through advocacy; encourage communication among societies, districts, and various cultures; and continue financial support of local, district, and denominational ministries.

This list of goals reveals a shift in the women's organization. While the organization's goals in 1929 all had to do with promotion of mission, fifty years later the words *mission* and *service* do not appear in the goals list. Rather, the goals show a concern for bettering the society and denomination of which the women were a part. A statement from the brochure sums up the interwoven aim of the organization: "Bible study, prayer, and fellowship are blended with a desire to meet the physical, spiritual, education, and emotional needs of those near and far."[32] Meeting needs of others (in other words, service) was still obviously a concern for the women's organization. But its stated goals now fully embraced the sisterhood function of the groups, perhaps even eclipsing its foundational service purpose. The 1980s financial contributions of Women in Mission still show a significant commitment to international mission and ministry. But the emerging focus on relationships, spiritual growth, developing gifts, and encouraging communication also promoted connections between group members and to their more immediate contexts.

Publications

One way that Women in Mission fostered a sense of connection among women in and beyond the denomination was through its magazine, *Window to Mission*. The organization had discontinued its previous magazine, *Missions Today*, in September 1973. Women had indicated a continued desire for their own publication, so Women in Mission leadership met with denominational leaders in 1974 to discuss options for a new magazine. Goering recalled that the organization met some resistance, with leaders wondering what women wanted that they did not get in *The Mennonite* (the GCMC periodical). Goering reflected that the women felt a need for something less formal and more personalized. They weren't just looking for news items, but something that would "provide a bond of mutual interests."[33] In the end, the first issue of *Window to Mission*, edited by Muriel Stackley and with a compact format and a coordinated color scheme, appeared in April 1974 as a quarterly insert in *The Mennonite*. The publication of the women's organization now potentially reached the sixteen thousand recipients of the denominational magazine. Jeannie Zehr, Women in Mission editor from 1975 to 1984, recalled being surprised at how many men said they read the magazine cover to cover.[34]

Window to Mission was full of readable stories, including reflections from missionaries and service workers, interviews with seminary women supported by the organization, and a regular biographical profile called "A Woman in Mission." The magazine also carried poetry and articles on relevant topics ranging from singleness to evangelism to nuclear fuel. A large part of each magazine was devoted to a program resource guide, which could be used for group meetings or personal devotions throughout the year. While the annual guide was based on a biblical passage, each year surveyed a variety of topics and usually included a focus on an international location, a North American cultural context, social issues, and church-related concerns. For example, the 1974 guide, using the theme "The Earth Is the Lord's" (Psalm 24), contained resources on Uruguay, Bible study methods, families, dealing with crises, "Indianness" (perspectives of Native Americans), sexuality and the church, and the value of life.

Although the tone of the resource guide was largely inspirational and informative, it did not necessarily shy away from the hot-button issues of the day, perhaps especially in its earlier years. One segment of the 1979–80 guide was called "No Simple Answers: Let's Look at Abortion."[35] It explored why women might choose abortion and advocated that women use the GCMC's separate Abortion Packet to study the issue. Because of the magazine's inclusion in *The Mennonite*, it reached the attention of many beyond the women's group, including a man who voiced his concerns in a letter printed in a subsequent issue of *The Mennonite* with the title "Abortion Fallacies in *Window to Mission* Insert."[36] The resources also reached an anonymous woman whose lengthy letter to Women in Mission was printed in the April–May 1980 magazine. "I am a Christian and I recently had an abortion," the woman wrote. "It was the most difficult decision I've had to make."[37] The writer encouraged continued conversation about the topic. She concluded, "I thank you for having an article on abortion in a Christian magazine. . . . I'm glad people are really trying to help others in areas which 'people just don't talk about' or admit to."[38] *Window to Mission* also printed a short response letter from Pearl Bartel, who had contributed to the GCMC's Abortion Packet, indicating her care for the woman and her story.[39] While there had been discussion about abortion in other GCMC spaces, the anonymous reader's letter reveals the potential for a special kind of ministry that came with having such a conversation in the pages of a women's magazine.

Besides reaching out to women who were struggling or simply providing a bit of inspirational reading material, *Window to Mission* gave women writers the chance to develop and use their gifts. "*Window to Mission* was one place where women were able to try out their writing and artistic skills and talents," Jeannie Zehr reflected in an article celebrating the magazine's fifteenth anniversary. "It was exciting to see new writers and artists test their wings here and then go on to contribute to other publications."[40] Bek Linsenmeyer, who edited the magazine in the 1990s, expressed a similar view, noting that it provided an opportunity for writers who might never have something published elsewhere.[41] Linsenmeyer, Zehr, and Lois Deckert (editor from 1985 to 1992) all also commented on the opportunities that emerged for them thanks to the very part-time editor position. Linsenmeyer was asked to speak to so many women's groups that she decided to cut back to one Sunday commitment per month. "That gave me experience," said Linsenmeyer, who went on to serve in a variety of nonprofit and pastoral leadership roles.[42] Deckert especially enjoyed using her creativity to help lead women's retreats and speak to different groups, including for women of other denominations.[43] Zehr wrote that her time as *Window to Mission* editor "opened up many windows and doors" in her own life.[44] She enjoyed developing connections with women across the denomination, including speaking at retreats for Canadian women. "That was a very enriching experience for me," she said. "It was terrifying at first, but it was a good way to get in touch with where women were in all the various congregations, what they were thinking and needing."[45] Zehr used this knowledge in her later work as a staff member for the Commission on Overseas Ministries.

Women in Mission also commissioned several books used across (and beyond) the denomination. *I Heard Good News Today* by Cornelia Lehn, published in 1983, was geared to children and told inspiring stories of missionaries and Christians around the world. Sponsorship of the book fit with the organization's longtime interest in mission promotion and education. In 1980, venerable women's organization leader Gladys Goering wrote *Women in Search of Mission*, a history of Women in Mission and its predecessor organizations. Goering recounted key events and programs of the past and posed questions about the future. At the close of the book, she pointed out that it was easier to see the contributions of women's groups when one could simply count the garments they sewed and the money they sent. "How does one measure personal growth, moral backing, the representation of women and women's concerns to the church, support of conference, leadership training, the worth of international relationships, and acts of service and kindness in congregation and community?" she asked.[46] Women in Mission was still holding on to its identity of mission and service, but Goering's work made it clear how much the role of the organization had expanded and broadened over the years.

Gladys Goering, author of Women in Search of Mission.

Collaboration

Women in Mission collaborated with the denomination's commissions on many projects in the late twentieth century. These collaborations were doubtlessly facilitated by having Women in Mission members on each of the commission boards. In the early 1970s, the women's organization teamed with the Commissions on Home Ministries and Education to pay the salary of Herta Funk, who was hired to work on the issue of women's and men's roles. One creative collaboration drew on the sewing skills of women in the congregations. A new children's Sunday school curriculum in the mid-1970s required one thousand "Oliver" puppets, which women's groups sewed. Margaret Ewert commented that the puppets "created so much enthusiasm for the Commission on Education that the other commissions are looking on in envy wondering what they could do to create interest in their programs."[47] Joan Wiebe, coordinator of Women in Mission from 1977 to 1986, recalled collaborating with the commissions on efforts related to "parenting for peace and justice," which included presenting seminars and distributing peace kits. "That was something that I really enjoyed," Wiebe said, noting that earlier women in her role had not had similar opporunities to collaborate with male church leaders.[48] (Wiebe remembers being the only woman who attended the regular meeting of the denomination's commission leaders during her time.) In the 1980s, Women in Mission supported the *Neighbors Near and Far* children's curriculum, which explored different cultures in North America and around the world.

Another collaborative effort with the commissions came through sponsoring learning tours—one connecting with work of the Commission on Overseas Mission and one with the Commission on Home Ministries. A 1988 learning tour to South America took place under the direction of Sara Regier, the first Women in Mission coordinator with significant experience as a missionary herself. Ten women were chosen from across the denomination to travel in pairs, each to a different country. Regier recalled that it was very energizing for women to actually be in the mission field; it brought insight and vitality to those women and to the organization as whole.[49] Marlene Bogard, who almost twenty years later would be hired as executive director of Mennonite Women USA, was one of the women chosen to go. She was amazed by the fruits of the mission work she saw in Colombia and the way people there were living as disciples in challenging circumstances.[50]

When the learning tour participants returned, they were expected to travel around sharing about what they had observed. "That experience shaped me into wanting to continue work in the church, shaped me as a more confident leader as I talked to people, and certainly gave me a heart for missions," Bogard said.[51] By August 1988, the women had given approximately 155 presentations in various locations. One Alberta woman who heard a presentation wrote to the Women in Mission office with her appreciation: "We live so far away from the conference hub and seldom see or get to know any COM [Commission on Overseas Mission] workers. This type of tour gives opportunity for more people to see COM in action. It forms that connectedness."[52] In an article about the learning tour, Regier commented that most tours of mission projects focused on church offices and buildings, but this one focused on the people. "If there is a reason for WM [Women in Mission] to exist it will be for us to keep pushing out the boundaries," she said.[53] Along with encouraging people in the countries the women visited and informing North American participants, the tour perhaps served a third purpose: it affirmed the existence of a women's organization that, in the late 1980s, was struggling to maintain the vitality it had enjoyed in the past.

Another learning tour in 1991 took participants to different mission locations within Canada and the United States. Five pairs of women visited either Washington, D.C., Chicago, Toronto, Winnipeg, or Arizona, interacting mostly with Hispanic and Native people. Two women connected with a young Chinese Mennonite church in Toronto and observed the compassionate work of volunteers at the Welcome Inn in Hamilton, Ontario. A woman who worshiped in a Spanish-speaking Mennonite church in Chicago pondered what it must be like to come to a new country and be unfamiliar with the language and culture. An article about the learning tour in *The Mennonite* reported that "Earlene Clark, a social worker from Philadelphia, and Mary Litwiller, a farmer from Wellman, Iowa, learned almost as much about each other as about the Hopi people they met in Arizona." Clark said that her interaction with Litwiller over their ten days together was "the closest relationship I've had with a white woman." Clark found some similarities between her African American heritage and the challenges facing the Hopi people, and Litwiller temporarily experienced what it was like to be a racial minority. The participants in this learning tour also traveled to share their experiences with congregations and women's groups, helping to strengthen the connection between congregation members and the missionaries and projects they were supporting.[54]

The church's understanding of mission was changing drastically, though, both within the women's organizations and in their related denominations. By the 1970s there was increased awareness that North America was part of a globalized world and that North American Mennonites were part of a globalized church. The methods and the very premise of spreading the "good news" of Christianity from the West to the rest of the world was being questioned and critiqued from many quarters. And the sense of the mission of women's organizations themselves was also shifting as the organizations more fully embraced the sisterhood and service functions of their work. We now consider how changing views of mission in general affected women's organizations in particular.

"A Mission to Themselves"

Mennonite understandings of mission went through a major shift in the mid-twentieth century.[1] As local populations assumed leadership of many missions institutions, North American missionaries reconsidered their role in the international missionary endeavor. At the same time, North American Mennonites were sensing a need to better proclaim and embody the saving gospel of Jesus Christ in their own countries and even their own congregations. In the context of these trends, Mennonite women's organizations shifted to a more local and even internal sense of mission. For example, when the leaders of Women in Mission gathered to set their goals for the 1980s, the prevailing desire they articulated was to be a supportive group for their members. The organization's leaders wanted to affirm women who were happy with their existing roles and to encourage those who were exercising gifts in domains previously unavailable to women in the church. To better relate to all women in the denomination, they outlined several areas of focus, including personal strengthening, spiritual growth, gifts discernment, and addressing the breakdown of family traditions. "They were, in effect, calling for a mission to themselves," writes Gladys Goering.[2]

* * * * *

Women in Mission's more inward focus was a striking—though not sudden—shift for an organization that had begun with the purpose of supporting missionaries and promoting interest in mission in the denomination. Each of the four points in the GCMC women's organization 1929 purpose statement included the word *mission* or *missionary*. But something happened when women gathered together to engage in tasks they could have done in their own homes. Women shared concerns and prayed for each other. They gave their opinions on matters in the church and community. They led devotionals and gave "talks." Women who attended for the main purpose of helping others also found a source of personal support and spiritual uplift in their gatherings, which in some contexts happened as often as once a week. Women's groups provided a place for their members to exercise not only tasks like sewing and preparing food but also skills such as speaking in public, managing finances, and chairing committees. The groups were places women came not only to support missionaries but also to minister to each other and to receive encouragement themselves.

By the 1970s and 1980s, the GCMC women's organization had begun to embrace and articulate this more member-focused approach. As mentioned in chapter 6, Women in Mission's goals for the 1980s were not (primarily) about supporting externally focused workers and aid projects. Rather, the goals show a concern for bettering the society and denomination that women members were part of themselves. In some ways, this was a shift from the strictly service orientation of the past to a more explicit focus on sisterhood. It was perhaps also a redefinition of the idea of service, as women realized the opportunity their groups provided for them to serve and support each other as they faced the challenges of a demanding world. This shift was also due to practical realities. Goering notes that sewing assignments from the denominational mission organizations decreased sharply in the mid-twentieth century.[3] In 1962, Hilda Janzen, a GCMC women's group leader said, "As the mission work shifts from dependent churches to the indigenous so must our work change to keep in step with progress."[4] For some women, this was a difficult shift to accept. "They no longer want what we do," one woman lamented.[5]

The MC women's organization also shifted the way it articulated its mission—and its connection to missions—over the years. As chapter 1 relates, the organization was a subcommittee of the Mennonite Board of Missions for part of its existence. But when the WMSC listed ten goals in its 1975 handbook, none of them included the words *mission*, *missionary*, or *service*. (See chapter 4 for a list of the organization's goals.) Many local groups continued to maintain close connections with missionaries and engaged in material work for Mennonite Central Committee projects and relief sales. However, like those of the GCMC group, the goals of the MC women's organization show a shift from primarily supporting missionaries and mission projects to seeing its members as doing gospel work themselves. There was also a new articulation in both organizations about the importance of experiencing personal renewal. Barbara Reber (WMSC director) expressed this greater attention to personal needs during her report to the 1979 MC delegate assembly. "It is as important to drink from the well as it is to give a cup of cold water in His name," she said.[6]

For generations, Mennonite women's groups had chosen verses like Galatians 6:9 for their theme: "Let us not become weary in doing good, for at the proper time we will reap a harvest if we do not give up" (NIV).[7] The admonition to serve others and tangibly live out one's faith has always been strong in Mennonite contexts. But as activities like silent retreats and small group Bible studies became popular in the 1970s, Mennonite women also started referring to other sorts of biblical passages. A late 1970s WMSC devotional guide that promoted intrapersonal development and spiritual friendships cited verses like Ephesians 3:4: "If you will read what I have written, you can learn about my understanding of the secret of Christ" (GNT) and Philemon 1:6: "My prayer is that our fellowship with you as believers will bring about a deeper understanding of every blessing which we have in our life in union with Christ" (GNT). Perhaps the most appropriate biblical passage for late twentieth-century women's groups was the story of Mary and Martha (Luke 10:38-42), in which Jesus commends Mary's attentive listening over Martha's busy preparations. While there was an increased interest in spirituality and faith sharing in broader Mennonite circles during the 1970s (see chapter 4), women's groups often led the way, drawing on their existing structure to create spaces for women to attend to their spiritual lives as well as the physical needs of others.

A shift in the goals of women's organizations was not just happening in Mennonite contexts. In fact, the move from a solely external focus probably happened earlier in many other denominations. In her discussion of Presbyterian women's organizations, Joan LaFollette writes that by 1943, many groups within the denomination had started to "move away from being strictly missionary societies to being more inclusive societies, with broader activities of study and service."[8] LaFollette notes that this shift happened "partly in response to the church's broadening definition of mission," as well as in an effort to attract younger women who were not participating in the organizations as their mothers and grandmothers had.[9] In the mid-twentieth century, many Christian groups were starting to recognize some of the problematic aspects of international mission and at the same time were sensing the need to become more relevant to their own North American contexts.

As Wilbert Shenk writes in his history of Mennonite-related mission work, the 1970s were a time of an emerging global reality.[10] During that decade, the insights of contextual theology were introduced to mission theory, thereby replacing the understanding that mission was about taking an external idea and planting it into another culture.[11] Authority was shifted from the outside agent to the local context, while continuing to recognize that all local churches were part of the universal church.[12] The 1980s saw the smallest number of new Mennonite-related mission initiatives started since 1940; Shenk cites agency reorganization and financial difficulties for this phenomenon, but surely changing perceptions of mission work in general also contributed.[13] Mennonite women's groups, whether consciously or not, contributed to these changing perceptions and priorities.

While members of local Mennonite women's groups may not have noticed much of a shift in their understanding or activities in the late 1970s and beyond, some returning missionaries did. In a compilation of the history of Canadian Women in Mission, Esther Patkau records the reflections of one missionary who joined a local women's group for a prayer retreat in 1977: "I found a fellowship which was very deep and a spiritual maturity in the participants which is hard to find anywhere. I came away, however, with a question, 'Is it out of date to pray for missions?' This question has not yet been answered. . . . I have concluded that while, in general, the spiritual life of the church has greatly improved, our concerns are immediate concerns: me, my family, my church, my friends, etc."[14] This unnamed missionary both applauded a deeper spirituality and lamented a narrower focus in the Mennonite women she observed.

On the one hand, it can seem selfish (a trait certainly frowned upon in Mennonite women) to focus on concerns only within one's own sphere. On the other hand, by drawing the focus in to their own contexts—by proclaiming "a mission to themselves"—Mennonite women in the 1970s and 1980s were in some cases uncovering serious concerns that had been ignored for years. Mennonite women also saw themselves as capable of at least starting to address these concerns. The shift in understandings of mission in the 1970s and 1980s was not only about globalization and decline. Looking at this shift through the lens of Mennonite women's organizations reveals that it was also a time of revitalization and expansion of women's gifts in service and care in and beyond their communities.[15]

One concern that emerged during this time of shifting mission priorities was the topic of violence against women, including domestic violence and sexual abuse. In an article about women of Anabaptist traditions in the *Encyclopedia of Women and Religion in North America*, Marlene Epp notes the irony that most peace churches did not include violence against women in their theological work until quite late in the twentieth century.[16] It took efforts from grassroots networks of women to convince church leaders of the importance of this issue.[17] While these networks of women were mostly outside the denominational women's organizations, the turn to more local concerns within the organizations helped open spaces for conversation. Chapter 4 mentions the attention Vel Shearer gave to domestic violence in the WMSC's magazine in the mid-1980s and describes one response she received. Sara Regier, coordinator of Women in Mission in the late 1980s, remembers that there was beginning to be a strong awareness of inappropriate sexual behavior in the church during her time with organization. "I think every district I went to, I heard stories," she said in a 2014 interview.[18] Regier met many women who expressed the sentiment, "If I say something, nobody will listen."[19] While neither the MC nor the GCMC women's organizations started specific programs to address domestic violence or sexual abuse, the attention they gave these issues in their magazines and program resource guides were small steps toward cultivating a greater attention among church members.

Of course, giving attention to personal and social issues does not preclude an interest in international mission, and the magazines of both women's organizations continued to carry reflections from missionaries and relief workers. But the role of Mennonite women's organizations was undoubtedly changing. Lois Deckert, who was involved with Women in Mission during the 1970s and 1980s, reflected on the changing role of the GCMC women's organization in a 2014 interview. She commented that some older missionaries felt abandoned by the women's group, whose "mission outlook had changed and broadened."[20] Deckert, who grew up as the child of missionaries in India, said that some of her missionary friends saw her as a deserter. "But mission to me was much more than some place overseas," she said.[21] Patkau mentions that Canadian Women in Mission sponsored six women to attend a Calling-Caring Ministries seminar in 1988.[22] "Individually and corporately Women in Mission were changing from not only supporting missions, but also doing mission," she writes.[23]

Marian Hostetler directed the MC women's organization (WMSC) from 1987 to 1996, bringing connections from her work in Africa with the mission board and Mennonite Central Committee. Hostetler remembers having regular contact with returned missionaries, who would come to the MC offices in Elkhart and be sent to her for help with material needs such as bedding.[24] But the WMSC's most significant activity during Hostetler's time continued to be promoting retreats, where women in area conferences and congregations gathered to listen for God's leading and to connect with each other.

When the MC and GCMC women's organizations merged in 1997, reference to mission or missionaries was omitted from the new organization's name in favor of a more general title: Mennonite Women. However, Mennonite Women's leaders bolstered the organization's somewhat tenuous identity by engaging in projects of aid and service (more on this in chapter 8). After the organization split along national lines in 2003, Mennonite Women USA found a new avenue for caring and connection through its Sister Care seminars. These seminars, originated by Rhoda Keener, are discussed in chapter 10. Here it is worth noting that Sister Care was initially promoted with the tagline "Equipping women for caring ministry." But as the seminars were further developed by Keener with Carolyn Holderread Heggen and Ruth Lapp Guengerich, they took on more of a self-healing component. "Our own wholeness is what precipitates being an effective caring person," Keener said in a 2014 interview. "And so we start with ourselves."[25] Keener remembers a comment from one of the first meetings she had with women leaders after she began as Mennonite Women director in 2001. When Keener asked what the organization should be doing, Gracie Torres replied: "The most important thing is that women know that they have worth."[26] Keener and Heggen have seen this statement validated in the many places they have presented Sister Care.

* * * * *

Today's Sister Care seminars are a prime example of Goering's "mission to themselves" comment from 1980—in both the "selves" and the "mission" sense. The seminars begin with a focus on the individual wounds and blessings of women and give participants tools for extending Jesus' message of comfort and wholeness to others. In a way, Sister Care's proliferation in settings around the world has brought the Mennonite women's organization full circle, returning it to significant international engagement. Mennonite Women USA's current mission statement is "to empower women and women's groups as we nurture our life in Christ through studying the Bible, using our gifts, hearing each other, and engaging in mission and service."[27] The statement's first three activities describe more of an inward, or sisterhood, focus. But the statement includes the words *mission* and *service*, articulating that these outwardly directed activities are still important components of the organization.

POR LA FE
1 COR. 13:13
DEL 3-6 DE 1984
HARRISONBURG
VIRGINIA
SPANISH MENONITE
EMC
LANCASTER
PA.
MAYO 3-6 1984
CONFERENCIA
F.H. 84 3-6 MAYO
HARRISONBURG, VIR.
ESPERANZA
CONFERENCIA FEMENIL
AMOR

7
Decline and New Vision

> I see my role as president of WMSC as a minister—a servant to God and to you, the women of the Mennonite Church. . . . We must together develop a vision that will carry us into the future, for if we fail to expand the vision, we risk losing a vital part of the Mennonite Church.
> —Terri Plank Brenneman[1]

The final decades of the twentieth century brought new challenges for Mennonite women's organizations. In previous years, these organizations had seemed to be thriving and necessary components of most congregations and area conferences. Changes in the church, in society, and in the interests and commitments of individuals prompted the groups to confront new realities and frame a vision that could carry them into a new era.

In his 2000 text, *Bowling Alone: The Collapse and Revival of American Community*, Robert Putnam argues that in the late twentieth century, Americans became increasingly disconnected from family, friends, neighbors, and social structures in general.[2] Putnam cites surveys that suggest that active involvement in all sorts of clubs and organizations drastically declined from the 1970s into the 1990s. For example, in 1975 and 1976, Americans attended an average of twelve club meetings per year, but in 1999, they attended only five club meetings per year, a 58 percent drop.[3] Putnam's data also covers church-related organizations. He writes that in the late 1950s, about one in every four Americans were members of church-related groups (that is, beyond being members of the church itself).[4] By the late 1980s and 1990s, such affiliations had dropped to one in seven or eight.[5] One study found that between 1974 and 1996, church-related group membership decreased by at least 20 percent.[6] While Putnam's research focuses on the United States, similar trends were likely present in Canada, and these trends certainly affected women's groups, including Mennonite ones.

An Era of Decline

In her chapter in *Beyond Establishment: Protestant Identity in a Post-Protestant Age*, Barbara Brown Zikmund outlines the situation in the 1980s for Protestant women's organizations. Many local organizations continued to function as they always had, but overall, women's organizations had decreased in size and influence. Some congregations had done away with specific women's organizations in favor of study courses or special events. "Younger women are more critical of the church and more demanding," Zikmund wrote in 1993. "When they choose to get involved, they refuse to be limited by the entanglements of an organization." While many older women across denominations continued to see their church's women's group as a significant outlet for service and social interaction, many younger women began to see it as yet another claim on their already limited time and resources.[7]

Mennonite women's organizations faced many of the same realities. Gloria Neufeld Redekop's study of Canadian Mennonite women's groups concludes that the 1970s and 1980s were "an era of decline for Mennonite women's societies."[8] As in other eras, women cited busyness as a major reason for not participating, but Redekop notes that women now had additional involvements such as moms' groups, mixed-gender Bible studies, and roles in the larger church.[9] Sara Regier, coordinator of Women in Mission in the late 1980s, noticed a difference between generations as she heard from groups as part of the organization's self-evaluation. One group of women in their seventies who were heavily involved in the organization said, "We're burning the candle at both ends and we love it."[10] But Regier heard younger women expressing the feeling of burning the candle at both ends and *not* liking it. With jobs, families, and other responsibilities, many younger women were not prioritizing the congregational sewing circle or women's meeting. Phyllis Wiebe described the evaluation results of Canadian Women in Mission groups this way: "If there was one message that came out loud and clear, it is: 'our group is getting smaller . . . enthusiasm is dying . . . the younger women won't come.' "[11] Wiebe continued, "That was the reason for the survey. So what is the answer?"[12] There was no easy answer. But women's organization leaders sensed that the time for Mennonite women's organizations was not over yet, even amid continuing questions from those outside the groups and sometimes even from the leaders themselves.

Marian Hostetler began serving as executive secretary of the WMSC in 1987. When someone told her about the position, she remembers thinking that she was not sure she even believed in the WMSC. Was a separate organization really what the church should promote for women? A woman pastor questioned why Hostetler would want to be involved with the organization and told her, "Well, maybe you can bring it to a peaceful end." Hostetler said, "It's almost like her statement made me think more about it." Hostetler was aware of the long history of the organization, including its strong support for missionaries. "I knew it had to change," she said, "but it just didn't seem to me as though we were going to, poof, end it like that." In her role as denominational WMSC director, Hostetler received reports of the work of congregational and regional or district groups. "It just *overwhelms* you when you think of all the stuff that was happening and also the good relationships that were happening," she said.[13]

Anita Froese had a similar experience as president of the Canadian Women in Mission board. Amid her questions about the organization, the annual reports would come in. She would read about myriad community and church activities, the support for mission, and the extra dollars for congregations and the denomination as a result of the women's work. "I remain convinced that Women in Mission have a role to fulfill in the future of our total kingdom work," she concluded.[14]

Widening the Circle

One way the WMSC and Women in Mission found new energy and direction was through meeting together. Like their respective denominations, the organizations had functioned quite separately in previous years. But in the 1980s, the larger MC and GCMC denominations started exploring the possibility of integration, prompted at least partially by the decreased membership and funding both were facing. The denominations held joint assemblies in 1983 at Bethlehem, Pennsylvania, and in 1989 at Normal, Illinois. At the 1989 assembly, Women in Mission and the WMSC held separate business meetings but had a joint rally with a parade of banners from each district, a celebrative litany, and an exchange of brochures.[15] Later that year, the executive committees of the two organizations met and decided to prepare a joint devotional guide, combining the publications each organization had been producing in various forms for decades. The resulting guide, designed for use in 1990–91, was titled *Widening the Circle through Prayer*. (This publication, which continues to be published annually, would later be called the Bible Study Guide.)

The idea of "widening the circle" brought the excitement of new partnerships and relationships, but it also may have seemed like a necessity for the shrinking women's organizations. In 1980, Women in Mission estimated it had 10,000 members in 440 groups.[16] In 1991, it reported 7,000 members in 350 units.[17] In 1995, the numbers were 6,500 women in 300 groups.[18] While the 1995 budget had been

Women in Mission staff members (left to right) Doris Schmidt, Susan Jantzen, and Bek Linsenmeyer reviewing the 1992–93 joint resource packet, Carrying God's Light.

lowered from previous years, the coordinator still had to announce that it looked as if the organization would not have enough undesignated funds to meet expenses. "This has occurred before in the history of WM but not for several decades," she noted.[19] The numbers for WMSC participation are a bit harder to track, since it did not have as much of a focus on dues-paying membership. (WMSC counted four hundred local groups in 1995.[20]) But it is not hard to find references to the organization's dwindling finances. Notes from a 1993 executive committee meeting end with: "Finances—are declining."[21] The recorder added, "As I recall, we dismissed rather abruptly and very tired and frustrated."[22] A 1996 treasurer's report in *Voice* noted that receipts were $96,593, while disbursements were $99,809.[23] The report continued, "Because we started this year $1,926 in the red, we are now $5,142 in the red as the year ends. This is very serious."[24]

In the 1990s, women from the denominational to the congregational levels wondered about the continued functionality of their groups and how to make them appeal to younger generations. In a 1993 issue of *Voice*, Marian Hostetler reported that her most frequently asked question was, "Do you have suggestions about how to get more women out to our monthly meetings?"[25] A vigorous conversation about the WMSC's purpose emerged in the pages of its magazine, with articles with titles such as "Have We Lost Sight of Our Goals?" (1991) and "WMSC: Dead or Alive?" (1993). Susan Gingerich and Ruth Lapp Guengerich, who served in WMSC leadership during the 1990s, remember sitting together at one executive committee meeting and asking, "Is it time to bury WMSC?"[26] Still, the organization continued several projects, including its scholarship fund. During 1994 and 1995, scholarships were granted to seventeen undergraduate women at Mennonite colleges and four graduate students, for a total of $20,400.[27]

While WMSC leadership asked its members several times about cutting back on the scholarship fund, women continued to insist on its importance.[28] In 1990, Women in Mission hired Susan Jantzen, a younger mother whose husband had grown up in a missionary family, as its director. Jantzen did not want to spend a lot of energy talking about why women's groups were declining. "There was nothing interesting to me about that," she said, "and it felt like a lot of negativity that would never yield anything."[29] Under Jantzen's leadership, the organization strove to develop new connections between congregational groups and missionaries, continued financial support of international women studying theology, and developed new collaborations with GCMC commissions. One such collaboration was cosponsoring a "church visitation couple" to meet with congregations across the denomination. Phyllis Schultz met with a variety of Women in Mission groups in this role. Schultz's summaries of her visits show that while the denominational organization's leadership may have been downplaying the viability question, it was very much on the mind of local groups. Schultz's 1991 report stated, "There was the ongoing concern over including the younger ladies in the WM groups, with declining membership a real worry to many."[30] She added, "I encouraged them to look at the things these younger ladies are doing as mission also."[31] Schultz's encouragement was in line with the organization's broadening vision of mission—though that vision did not necessarily translate into vibrant congregational women's groups.

The atmosphere in church and society had changed dramatically since the "golden era" of Mennonite women's organizations in the mid-twentieth century. The women's movement of the 1960s and 1970s had helped to provide new opportunities for women and new respect for women's endeavors—which sometimes drew them away from the women's organization. Somewhat ironically, male church leaders now often spoke about the value of the women's organizations. In 1981, the moderator of the Conference of Mennonites in Canada called the women's societies the "deacons of our church and conference."[32] He continued, "Your service is the glue that puts stability into our church social functions, and your support of Mission and Service activities at home and abroad is the leaven around which so much of our congregational mission is built."[33] In a 1985 *Gospel Herald* article, Alice W. Lapp wrote that Boyd Nelson, a former MC mission board administrator, "credits WMSC with doing more to promote new ideas, introduce new literature, develop retreats, spread information, and show sensitivity to the feelings of people than any other organization."[34]A 1990 WMSC self-study provided an opportunity for male leaders to apologize for the actions of their predecessors. Marian Hostetler recalled that when the study, which included notes about the organization's history, was presented to the MC General Board, they "unanimously agreed to acknowledge the hurt, and repent of the injustice, caused in the 1920s when the male leadership of the church formed a new women's organization without prior counsel with the existing Woman's Missionary Society."[35] In later communication with Ruth Lapp Guengerich, Paul Gingrich (head of the mission board) restated the apology, noting that "women were in the forefront of the great mission expansion and outreach in those early years but didn't get much credit or recognition and I'm sorry for this oversight."[36] Yet despite these statements of support, Mennonite women's organizations did not grow in numbers or influence during the 1970s and 1980s, but rather declined.[37] Many reasons for this decline have already been mentioned. It may also be that for some older women, the women's organizations were changing too much, while for some younger women, they were not changing enough.

Third-Wave Feminism

The late 1980s and the 1990s were marked by a fragmentation of women's interests, in comparison to the more focused agenda of the second-wave feminism of the 1960s and 1970s. In the 1980s there was a significant backlash against the women's liberation movement; by the early 1990s, scholars were noting a trend among women and men toward questioning feminism and a tendency in the media to portray women's problems as stemming from too much feminism.[38] Third-wave feminism, a categorization some scholars started using in the early 1990s, sought to address this backlash and the critique that second-wave feminism had focused primarily on the concerns of white, middle-class, heterosexual women. Third-wave feminism brought attention to issues of power and overlapping identities, including race, class, sexual orientation, and social location, and it sought to include men in the conversation about gender and discrimination. These were concerns that, for the most part, Mennonite women's organizations were not addressing. Mennonite women engaged with feminist thinking in the 1980s and 1990s tended to find more support in academic settings or grassroots groups than in the established women's organizations.

However, there were some aspects of third-wave feminism that fit well with the projects and concerns of Mennonite women's organizations. As Leslie Heywood notes in *The Women's Movement Today*, third-wave feminism has been aware of its place in the globalized world and has sought to engage with women's movements and issues of women's rights around the world.[39] In the 1980s and beyond, Mennonite women's organizations that had always had international connections through missionaries began connecting more directly with women in international locations themselves. Missionaries, mission agencies, and other groups such as Mennonite World Conference became not just entities to support but also mediators that helped those involved in the women's organizations promote the uplift of women around the world, primarily through providing funds for education.

The concerns of third-wave feminism were much broader than simply granting women access to traditionally male roles and spaces. Perhaps in the spirit of this different focus of feminism, in the early 1990s, Women in Mission discontinued its practice of appointing female representatives to the denomination's commissions. Susan Jantzen remembers that she was somewhat reprimanded for this action by some women leaders, who told her, "Don't give that kind of power away." But Jantzen saw the appointments as awkward when women were now being elected to the commissions through the same process as men. "It was very clear that the time and the function had shifted enough that [it] was now a problem rather than a solution," she said, also acknowledging her gratitude for those who had done the hard work of securing female representation in the first place. The women's organization no longer seemed like such a necessary entity for women to have their voices heard in the larger denomination.[40]

The Value of the Women's Organization

Sometimes even the leaders of the women's organizations were ambivalent about the value of the organizations, though they often had a different view after a few years of working with the organization. Terri Plank Brenneman became involved with the women's organization as a way to participate in wider church leadership; she accepted the presidency of the Pacific Southwest Conference WMSC because that position had a seat on the conference board. Attending a conference women's retreat out of a sense of duty, Brenneman was inspired by the multicultural expressions of faith, the speaker's message, and the powerful history of the church mothers and grandmothers. "I realized that I was experiencing a spiritual awakening as a result of women role models," she wrote.[41] When Brenneman later became a member of the MC General Board, she noticed that many female board members and denominational leaders had been or were currently involved with the WMSC. "Something had been occurring in the church that had not been explicitly stated as a goal of WMSC—the identification and on-the-job training of women leaders for the wider church," she wrote. Brenneman served as the denominational WMSC board president from 1991 to 1995, defining the organization's function as "women supporting women to use our gifts in service."[42]

Two glimpses into congregational and regional contexts give a sense of the continuing function of women's organizations and the conversation about them that was taking place in the mid-1990s. In an editorial in the 1996 newsletter of the Ohio Conference, Siegrid K. Richer voiced a feeling of disconnection and the inability of the WMSC to speak to her needs. "Where are the Mennonite women who successfully balance home, career, congregational responsibilities, and personal spiritual discernment?" she asked. "I do not find them at WMSC."[43] The article prompted several responses that were printed in the next newsletter, including an article by Zelma Kauffman describing the WMSC group at Lockport Mennonite Church (Stryker, Ohio). She described their most recent meeting, where forty-four women and twelve children gathered to quilt, knot comforters, make bibs for a local nursing home, do crafts for future bazaars, cut and roll bandages, participate in a devotional, and fellowship around lunch.[44] Kauffman praised the preparation of the group's leaders, some of whom took a day off from their jobs to prepare for the meeting. "If WMSC dies, who will organize school kits . . . meet the needs of rest homes . . . crisis pregnancy centers, food banks, fire and flood disasters?" she asked.[45] Kauffman described the group as a place her congregation provided to help women connect with God and each other. "Attending meetings and sharing in service projects shows that you care about your own spiritual welfare and about your sisters in Christ," she wrote.[46] These two articles and several related letters show that many women were longing for something meaningful from the women's organization. The question was whether they would find it.

Also in 1996, the forty-ninth annual conference of Alberta Women in Mission gathered in Taber, Alberta. The event included sharing from congregational women's groups. A leader from the Taber Friendship Circle reported her group had twenty members ranging in age from thirty-two to eighty-three. Two members of the Bergthal Women in Mission group reflected on its function as something of a support group for young mothers; one year its entire leadership was pregnant. The group developed into a service arm of the congregation, providing for children, youth, families, and seniors. Members had also served on committees of the wider conference. "WM provides a lifeline to their faith," the conference's report noted. Another woman spoke about a women's group in Tofield that formed in the 1930s even before a congregation was founded there. This group, eventually called the Tofield Senior Ladies' Aid, had dwindled to four members by 1990 and had its last meeting in 1996. These three Alberta groups show the continued significance of women's societies for some but also the struggle to sustain involvement. The notes from the conference record that there were "no nominees at this time for President-Elect or for Secretary-Treasurer" of the provincial organization.[47]

Integration Conversations

Discussion of the identity and viability of Mennonite women's organizations came to the fore as the WMSC and Women in Mission took steps toward a merger. When a vote at the 1995 joint denominational assembly affirmed eventual integration of the MC and GCMC denominations, the women's organizations took it as their cue to move ahead with their integration process. What followed were many meetings, conversations, drafted documents, and musings about possibilities. There was excitement about what might lie ahead, lament at what would be lost, and confusion and uncertainty about new structures, budgets, and ways of operating.

One source of debate was "racial/ethnic" representation on the executive committee of the new women's organization. The WMSC executive committee had included Maria Bustos as a representative of the Hispanic Mennonite women's organization in some of the committee meetings starting in 1975. By 1987, they had also invited a representative from the African American Mennonite Association to join them. At a 1987 executive committee meeting, Joy Lovett gave a "Black Concerns Report" noting that black congregations were mostly

WMSC and Women in Mission executive committees at a joint meeting in at Community Mennonite Church in Markham, Illinois, in October 1996. Front row, seated (left to right): Ruby Harder, Erna Goerzen, Elizabeth Klassen, and Terri Plank Brenneman. Back row, standing (left to right): Lara Hall Blosser, Susan Gingerich, Pat Swartzendruber, Kathy Shantz, Louise Auernheimer, Doris Schmidt, Joy Hess, Susan Jantzen, Bek Linsenmeyer, and Rose Covington. Not pictured: Seferina De León, Jeanne Rempel, and Eve MacMaster.

made up of women.[48] After this report, the committee discussed the fact that during the past few years they had invited the Hispanic representative to one meeting per year, but that did not seem adequate. So they decided to include Lovett and the Hispanic representative (at that time, Esther Hinojosa) in all future executive committee meetings.[49] In 1991, the committee invited United Native Ministries (later called Native Mennonite Ministries), the other organized MC cultural group, to also send a representative; Vernie Lee began attending meetings in 1992, though she stopped in 1994 because of full-time employment by her tribe.[50] In the following years there would be sporadic Native representation and more regular Hispanic and African American representation on the WMSC's executive committee, with women chosen by their respective cultural groups.

Women in Mission had a much smaller executive structure, and the GCMC also did not have organized cultural associations as the MC did. At an October 1996 meeting of the two organizations to discuss integration details, some Women in Mission leaders pushed for a lean executive committee with no requirements for specific ethnic representation. When the African American and Hispanic WMSC representatives present (Rose Covington and Seferina De León) voiced concern about this arrangement, some Canadian Women in Mission members responded that ethnic diversity in their context was broader than African American and Hispanic individuals.[51] What about Indonesian, Vietnamese, and Hmong Mennonites, for example? They were also concerned that having slotted "ethnic" representatives would feel like tokenism; women of different ethnicities should naturally be part of those elected to positions. Covington and De León agreed but thought this was unlikely to happen, perhaps because they had already experienced a sidelining of their voices. In a previous WMSC meeting, they had been asked to leave the room while the rest of the committee took a vote about some matter—an incident both women recalled in interviews twenty years later. Covington, who had experience standing her ground as a black Mennonite woman in other mostly white denominational contexts, remembered, "I would not allow that happen. I'm a professional social worker; that didn't work for me."[52] De León commented that the women on the board were all nice people. "But we felt like they were being prejudiced against us," she said.[53]

At the October 1996 joint meeting, De León again expressed frustration at the marginalization of her voice, even though she represented about seven hundred Hispanic Mennonite women and had been asked to participate. "Now what you tell us [is] okay you're here, but we can't use you, we just want you to sit over there and don't say too much," she said.[54] After a time of prayer and a decision to table the conversation until the next day, the women ultimately decided to invite full executive committee participation from each organized racial/ethnic group.[55] In her editorial in the next issue of *Window to Mission*, Bek Linsenmeyer reflected on how the group had wrestled with the financial costs of having a bigger executive committee that included cultural representatives. She felt convicted about her own silence during the conversation and noted her appreciation for the courageous words of the Hispanic representative. "I want our organization to not make excuses but to make sacrifices," Linsenmeyer wrote. "I am thankful God used our sisters to hold us accountable."[56] WMSC leaders also seemed to take seriously their commitment to better incorporate women of color into the identity of the organization. When the WMSC chose a representative for the 1997 Mennonite World Conference in India, they appointed De León, with Covington as a backup.[57] Covington ended up attending the conference and developing some significant cross-cultural connections of her own. She fondly remembers hearing Elizabeth Soto (Albrecht) give one the of major addresses, as well as sharing about her own experience as an African American, leading breakout groups to empower women, and later hosting an Indian woman in her own home.[58]

WMSC notes from the October 1996 meeting of the two women's organizations end with a reflection from the (anonymous) recorder. The recorder noted that the gathered women "felt two opposing things"—completely overwhelmed and full of a sense of God's saving grace. "We decided to move forward in confidence even though we didn't know where we were going," she wrote. "That was exciting."[59] The women leaders had been the most successful when they continued to openly share their stories, supporting each other and reminding themselves of God's faithfulness. The work ahead placed them in a long tradition of inter-Mennonite (and ecumenical) efforts in Mennonite women's organizations.

"We Moved Our Two Tables to Make It One"

At the 1995 joint MC and GCMC assembly in Wichita, Kansas, delegates voted in favor of a process to integrate the two denominations. In the exhibit hall, the tables for the two women's organizations were set up near each other, with a pole and some cloth in between. Marian Hostetler, WSMC coordinator, recalled that when the women heard the results of the vote, "we did something that we felt really good about. . . . We moved our two tables to make it one table."[1] The denominational women's organizations, which had been meeting together sporadically for several years, celebrated the vote as affirmation to move ahead with creating a new merged entity.

A November 1997 *Gospel Herald* article about the merged women's organization bore the title "Integration Groundbreakers."[2] The article noted that the new group, called Mennonite Women, had become the second Mennonite organization to complete the integration process (after Associated Mennonite Biblical Seminary). There were certainly difficulties in merging the two organizations, with their different budgets, structures, and ways of relating to their constituents. But the women involved felt excitement—and a bit of pride—at their pioneering integration work. "It just felt good to us and to God and everybody the way we came through that," said Susan Gingerich, who was involved with the WMSC in the 1990s and served as the WMSC's representative to the MC General Board.[3] She felt the organization set an example that integration could be done "in a congenial way."[4] Pauline Toews, who was part of the Mennonite Women board, also thought that the women's organizations could set the tone for others in the integration process. "That's a mission [women's groups] have," Toews said, noting that she thinks women generally find it easy to work together.[5]

* * * * *

Are women really better at working together than men? The assumption, or at least suggestion, that they are has been part of the conversation around women in the church for generations and continues to the present day. In a February 2016 letter titled "Would Women Split?" posted on the *Mennonite World Review* website, a male writer suggested that if women had been more represented in the Lancaster Conference voting process, that conference would not have decided to leave Mennonite Church USA in late 2015.[6] Whether or not this is true (at least two female commenters disagreed with parts of the writer's letter), the letter articulates a common perception that if women were more in control, there would be less division.[7] The anthropological and psychological facets of this idea are outside the scope of this study, if they are even possible to prove. However, the history of church women does show an ecumenical—and in the case of Mennonites, an inter-Mennonite and inter-Anabaptist—impulse, or at least ideal.

In an essay titled "Women's Organizations: Centers of Denominational Loyalty and Expressions of Christian Unity," Barbara Brown Zikmund writes that Protestant women's organizations in general are clearly connected to their denominations.[8] Yet, she says, they "refuse to be limited by many of the confessional, cultural, and racial divisions that separate Protestant denominations" in the United States.[9] In their introduction to *Women and Twentieth-Century Protestantism*, Margaret Bendroth and Virginia Brereton express a similar view. They claim that Protestant women have been less influenced by theological distinctions and doctrinal controversies than their male counterparts, including the fundamentalist-modernist debates of the 1920s (which affected Mennonites as well). "Often not having as much stake in Protestant hierarchies, [women] were inclined to address social and political ills with more boldness than their brothers," they write. "And they tended to be ecumenists and cooperators."[10]

Mennonite men did forge significant inter-Mennonite and ecumenical partnerships through the creation of organizations like Mennonite Central Committee for relief work and Civilian Public Service (CPS) as an alternate to military service. But these endeavors had their share of detractors among (male) Mennonite leaders concerned about their doctrinal purity. Paul Toews writes that Mennonites later looked back on the CPS program as a "great ecumenical event."[11] Yet all the Mennonites groups except for the GCMC challenged the cooperative basis of CPS.[12] "Mistrust and even suspicion between Mennonite groups was common in the early 1940s and beyond," Toews says.[13] There also has been serious hesitation from many Mennonite leaders about working with Christian groups not committed to pacifism. While the GCMC joined the National Council of Churches after World War II, the MC did not, and today Mennonite Church USA is not an official member of the large ecumenical organization (though individual MC USA members have participated in the National Council of Churches and the denomination is part of a broader group called Christian Churches Together). In general, ecumenism has often been regarded with skepticism by Mennonite leaders.

But many early Mennonite women's groups crossed denominational lines, and the history of Mennonite women's organizations shows a desire for collaboration and congeniality. Elaine Sommers Rich records that early local MC women's groups met with Church of the Brethren women in Maryland and with Presbyterians in Ontario and were influenced by Lutheran and United Brethren sisters in Indiana. "Perhaps it is time to reclaim our ecumenical heritage," Rich wrote in 1983.[14] Early sewing circles in Canada sometimes brought GCMC and Mennonite Brethren women together, such as in Gem, Alberta, and Springstein, Manitoba.[15] In areas where Mennonite populations were less concentrated, Mennonite women's groups often connected with other denominations and ecumenical groups. Brian Froese's book *California Mennonites* covers Mennonite Brethren, GCMC, MC, and other related groups in the state. Froese writes that through sewing circles and women's societies, Mennonite women in California "openly, creatively, and actively associated with a range of evangelical and mainstream organizations."[16] For example, in the late 1950s, the women's society at Immanuel Mennonite Church (a GCMC congregation in Downey, California) joined the Women's Auxiliary of the National Association of Evangelicals and the United Church Women of Downey.[17] Froese argues that the women in their organizations shaped Mennonite identity in the context of social outreach and mission activity and helped give California Mennonites a more outward, broader focus.[18]

A significant partnership at the denominational level began among women from the GCMC, Central Conference Mennonite Church, and Defenseless Mennonites in 1941. The leaders of the women's organizations of the three denominations felt a need for closer collaboration and met to form the United Mennonite Women's Service Committee. The new organization wanted to especially focus on mission among migrant workers, something that none of their denominations nor Mennonite Central Committee was doing. The women extended their collaboration beyond Mennonite circles by choosing to partner with the Home Missions Council, a New York–based group of men's and women's mission boards from a variety of denominations. The women worked with the Home Missions Council for the next twelve years, appointing some female Mennonite mission workers among migrants and supporting many workers from other traditions. After some unfruitful conversations with GCMC leadership about their interest in migrant work, one member of the GCMC women's organization commented: "So perhaps we are to pioneer in participating in this interdenominational missionary work."[19]

Collaboration among Mennonite-related women's missions groups happened in regional contexts as well, often in the form of annual events. One such event was the Indiana All-Mennonite Women's Missionary Rally, which started in 1937. Indiana women from the GCMC and Defenseless Mennonites (later known as the Evangelical Mennonite Church) met for the first gathering; several years later, MC women and some Ohio societies joined. The first meeting, held in Topeka, Indiana, drew 127 women.[20] There were several worship services and musical performances led by different women; each society gave a report; returning and outgoing missionaries shared with the group; and Harold S. Bender brought the evening address on "The Mennonites of Brazil and Paraguay." A document summarizing the event notes that "many worthwhile ideas were exchanged."[21] In subsequent years the rallies consistently drew more than two hundred people—sometimes more than three hundred. A program for the fiftieth anniversary rally in 1987 notes the denominational affiliation of each participant and committee member, with roughly equal participation from GCMC, MC, and Evangelical Mennonite women.[22] By this time the addresses were not just about specific mission projects or areas but rather were centered on a biblical theme ("Christ the Same Yesterday, Today, and Forever"), and all the speakers were women.[23]

The 2002 Indiana rally picked up on the "missional" concept emerging in Mennonite and other Christian circles. Featured speakers shared about mission in their everyday roles as a counselor, a leader of a Moms in Touch group at a jail, a neonatal nurse, and an informal teacher of homemaking skills. But the gathering drew only sixty women and the nominating committee was not able to fill the slate for the next year. During a sharing time, people recalled the rally's history. Some felt it had served its purpose, while others hated for it to end. Sarah J. Yoder, that year's recording secretary, noted, "The Rally has offered a special fellowship where women have made friends and been blessed. We were challenged to remember all the work that is still to be done overseas." Yoder's comments highlight the sisterhood (fellowship) and service (mission) of women's gatherings. Yoder also noted a third function of the Indiana meeting, writing that if it discontinued, "we will lose an avenue for inter-Mennonite cooperation." The women did vote to make the 2003 gathering their last one. But their sixty-seven years of cooperation certainly inspired attendees not only with new ideas for mission support but also with relationships across denominational lines.[24]

A regional inter-Mennonite endeavor that continues to today is Kansas Friends of Mennonite Central Committee, formerly called Kansas All-Mennonite Women. This organization involves women from Mennonite Brethren, Conservative Mennonite, Amish, and other traditions, as well as women from GCMC and MC backgrounds. Originally, women had gathered to hear a mission-related speaker, but by the year 2000, attendance at the event had dwindled. The organization took another approach and began holding a "comforter blitz." Several hundred people attend the two- or three-day event held in a large gymnasium in Yoder, Kansas. Carol Peters, current president of the organization, described a scene with dozens of frames set up with comforters to knot, nine or ten sewing machines whirring, women in one corner working on comforter batting, and others stitching on a large hand-sewn quilt.[25] Women in Amish dress and bonnets work with teenagers in jeans and ponytails around colorful swaths of fabric. In 2015, the blitz produced 204 comforters for Mennonite Central Committee to deliver around the world.[26] An MCC representative has come to talk about those who receive the blankets, who sometimes call the comforters themselves "Mennonites."[27] "Look at the impression given by people getting blankets in Syria and Jordan rather than by giving a sermon," said Peters in a 2015 interview. "And it's women's hands that did that."[28] Since MCC is an inter-Mennonite organization, its endeavors provide an opportunity for women and men from various denominations to work together. As traditional church-based Mennonite women's groups have declined, some women who still want to engage in tangible service have found meaningful outlets through MCC programs. At MCC material resource centers across Canada and the United States, women and men sort through donations, knot comforters and stitch quilts, and repurpose old fabric into new creations. Some material resource centers developed programs that address the needs of people in their own communities, such as a grocery distribution program run by several of the centers in Pennsylvania.[29]

MCC thrift stores, which started in the 1970s, have also been significant places for women (and, to a lesser degree, men) to serve and connect with others. Today there are more than one hundred MCC shops in Canada and the United States. In the 2014–15 fiscal year they brought in $16 million for MCC's work.[30] In her history of Canadian Women in Mission, Esther Patkau notes that as women from various careers and congregations worked together at MCC stores, they also developed friendships and supported one another.[31] Large stores like the Et Cetera Shop in Newton, Kansas, utilize hundreds of volunteers. One of these volunteers, Lela Mae Sawatzky (also a former secretary for the GCMC women's organization) described the shop as "a place of inter-Mennonite and community cooperation."[32] MCC stores continue to engage many women who have been involved with congregational women's

Rhoda Charles (left) and Kathleen Roth at a PREP event in Hesston, Kansas.

organizations in the past. (In fact, one weekday afternoon in 2015, I tried to call two former women's groups leaders in different parts of the United States for my work on this project, and both of their husbands told me they were volunteering at the local MCC shop!)

Collaboration between different groups provides positive experiences in what can feel like a divisive denominational climate. In Pennsylvania, Lancaster Conference and Atlantic Coast Conference share similar geography and, until recently, were part of the same denomination (Mennonite Church USA). But the two groups have different histories and theological commitments. Several years ago, the presidents of the women's organizations of the conferences, Rhoda Charles and Kathleen Roth, met while traveling to a Mennonite Women event. They brainstormed all the way there and back about ways to work together and soon started an annual "Chatter, Chow, and Cheerful Service" event at the local MCC material resource center. Women and girls of all ages get to know each other as they work, talk, and eat together. For lunch, women bring a pint of either chicken or vegetable soup to combine into two large pots. "We thought the women were going to unite these two groups into one!" said Charles. "We were so visionary." While unification did not happen, the joint gatherings continue, as do the relationships. "Well, we developed a lifelong friendship," said Roth, speaking about the fruit of their collaboration.[33]

* * * * *

The merging of the GCMC and MC denominational women's organizations, which was completed in 1997, required a new sort of collaboration between women from different countries and with different histories, cultural backgrounds, and theological views. While the organization existed as a binational entity for only a few years, the decisions and conversations that leaders had during this period would shape the direction of Mennonite women's groups far into the future.

GOD'S TABLE

PART III: 1997–2017

Now as they went on their way, he entered a certain village, where a woman named Martha welcomed him into her home. She had a sister named Mary, who sat at the Lord's feet and listened to what he was saying. But Martha was distracted by her many tasks; so she came to him and asked, "Lord, do you not care that my sister has left me to do all the work by myself? Tell her then to help me." But the Lord answered her, "Martha, Martha, you are worried and distracted by many things; there is need of only one thing. Mary has chosen the better part, which will not be taken away from her."

—Luke 10:38-42

8
Mennonite Women

> Mennonite Women has come through the complex journey of integration. The more urgent tasks of communication and organization have been tended to. Now, fundamental questions come into focus more clearly. How shall we lead women of the Mennonite congregations?
> —Susan Jantzen[1]

After much discussion between leaders of the MC and GCMC women's organizations and the collection of mail-in ballots from their constituents, by the summer of 1997 the two groups were ready to merge and announce their new name: Mennonite Women. A special GCMC assembly in Winnipeg and the biennial MC assembly in Orlando provided opportunities for women's group members to gather and mark the transition. In Winnipeg, about 275 GCMC women gathered for a banquet and a time of singing, remembrances, and prayers. An article about the event notes that "a few tears were quietly shed as women said goodbye to Women in Mission, an organization with a history of some eighty years." Several weeks later in Orlando, WMSC members gathered at a dinner delegate meeting and a women's breakfast to honor the eighty-six-year history of their organization and to hear updates about what was next. "We celebrate the growing, thriving, changing sisterhood to the glory of God and the enrichment of the church," they read together in a litany.[2]

The new organization's name was not wholeheartedly embraced by all members. Some lamented that the title no longer included the word *mission* or *missionary*, an integral element of both organizations since their inception.[3] Some women did not like that the new name had the word *Mennonite* in it, which they feared might create a barrier for local groups that regularly invited women from other denominations into their activities. "While it's a terribly uncreative name, we knew that there was a Mennonite Men organization, and we decided it would be that simple," said Ruth Lapp Guengerich, who, as a WMSC board member, contributed to discussions about the name.[4] Susan Jantzen, who was coordinator of Women in Mission, saw the new name as exemplifying women's attitudes at the time. "The feeling was, 'We'll be who we are,' " she said. "Whoever's on board with this, we'll just see what we can do together."[5]

Support and Outreach

The co-coordinators of the new organization, Jantzen and Lara Hall Blosser, were explicit about holding the sisterhood and service foci together. In the first issue of the organization's new magazine, Jantzen described Mennonite Women's dual "active and rooted" nature—active in working together for the community and world and rooted in gathering as women dependent on God.[6] Less than a year into the existence of the new organization, Jantzen and Blosser wrote an article titled "Is Mennonite Women for Support or Outreach?"[7] They noted that both priorities were present in the organization's purpose statement: "Mennonite Women encourages women to: nurture their life in Christ, study the Bible, utilize their gifts; hear each other; and engage in mission and service."[8] The co-coordinators acknowledged that most of the organization's budget went to the support side to fund publications, staff, and resourcing functions. But they understood that their members strongly valued service and mission, and they promised to regularly publicize stories, service project ideas, and lists of denominational and MCC endeavors for groups to fund. Women were encouraged to contribute directly to other church agencies.

In the past, some women's organizations participants had wondered if their groups were simply fundraisers for denominational projects. Now, Mennonite Women's budget went mainly to its own initiatives. The decision to let local groups choose their own projects helped provide some autonomy in the structure of an organization that brought together two denominations and two countries.[9] It perhaps also revealed a lack of cohesion between the traditional service and sisterhood priorities of the women's organizations. At this point early in its existence, at least judging from its financial goals, Mennonite Women was giving more attention to caring for its own constituents than to substantial service projects or mission support. A November 1997 newsletter article explained that contributions to Mennonite Women covered the organization's International Women's Fund, annual Bible Study Guide, board costs, and staff salaries.[10] In the late 1990s, participation in congregational women's groups that automatically connected to the denominational organization continued to dwindle, and the denominations in general continued to diversify. Mennonite Women leadership faced a significant challenge in effectively ministering to its own members, let alone engaging in costly or labor-intensive outreach efforts. A 1999 survey by the organization shows the wide variety of interests among Mennonite women. Different respondents said they would like a women's group that would reach out to those less fortunate, gather for in-depth Bible study, have a younger girls' group, do projects for service and fun, hire a babysitter, not serve food at weddings, encourage healing in women, or do creative worship with dance and inclusive liturgy.[11]

Mennonite Women attempted to connect with this variety of women through its new magazine. As at previous points in the history of the women's organizations, there was serious conversation about whether Mennonite women needed a separate publication. Cathleen Hockman-Wert, whom the organization hired as a part-time editor, outlined in her application for the job why a Mennonite women's publication should exist. In today's world, she wrote, it was not so necessary to have a space simply for women's concerns to be heard; nor did it seem feasible to promote a "women's perspective" on controversial issues.[12] Rather, she said, "we need a figurative room of our own to do what women have always done among themselves. . . . In our personal lives, we look to other Mennonite women for wisdom, inspiration, practical advice, and encouragement; a magazine by and for Mennonite women can provide the same benefits."[13] Hockman-Wert, who had worked for the *Gospel Herald* and had recently received a master's degree in journalism, brought a new level of professionalism and experience to the communication platforms of the women's organization. She hoped the magazine could help connect individual women to the denominational organization and even provide a sense of community to women who did not meet regularly with a congregation.[14]

The magazine took the name *Timbrel* in reference to the instrument of praise played by Miriam as she led the Israelites in song, as recounted in Exodus 15:20. It was a somewhat different publication from previous magazines of the women's organizations. For example, rather than publish reading lists of mostly inspirational and nonfiction texts, it ran a book club with comments from readers on a recommended novel (including somewhat controversial picks such as *The Poisonwood Bible* and *Harry Potter and the Sorcerer's Stone*). It included contemporary versions of psalms by women and new versions of biblical stories written from specific international contexts. Stories of individual Mennonite women were the most well-received item, according to a reader survey a little over a year into publication of the new magazine.[15] The organization's leaders had little sense of how or even if the magazine would be viable, but they were encouraged by displays of interest from constituents, such as the purchase of some five hundred subscriptions by College Mennonite Church (Goshen, Ind.) for its congregation.[16] While *Timbrel* has never been fully sustained by its subscription base, it continues to be a venue for some women to learn about the denominational organization and find reflections that connect with their life experiences.

Denominational Reorganization

As Mennonite Women began, it also had to navigate its place in the wider denominations, which were in an integration process that would not be complete until 2002. Susan Gingerich served as the women's organization representative to the MC General Board, first for the WMSC and then for Mennonite Women. The women's organization had a seat on the General Board as an "associate group" of the MC, a status it shared with the organized "racial/ethnic" groups (African American, Hispanic, and Native). Gingerich remembers attending her first General Board meeting, at which she planned to simply listen and learn. "We were at the point of making recommendations of people across the United States to go on to the various agency boards," she said. "And all

I was hearing were male names. I spoke up and said that I think we also need to consider having female representation."[17]

Like Joyce Shutt several decades earlier (see introduction), Gingerich felt the need to advocate for women's representation—though rather than receive affirmation from a male leader, as Shutt did, Gingerich was told by a female pastor that the focus should just be on gifts and not gender.[18] This exchange shows the tension between different ways women preferred to work for greater representation in the church. Some women saw the importance of giving special consideration to women to ensure their continued leadership roles as the church grew into the future. Other women, including some of those who had fought for the recognition of their gifts as pastors and denominational leaders, seemed concerned with keeping the focus on their qualifications rather than their gender.

In talks about the structure of the new denomination's Executive Board, plans seemed to move toward having a totally elected board with no specific considerations for gender or cultural diversity. Gingerich remembers sitting at a table with Leslie Francisco from the African American Mennonite Association (AAMA) and other associate group representatives and feeling as if they were all being pushed to the side together. "At that point Leslie was advocating for women, and I was advocating for Hispanics and AAMA," she said. "Nobody else was advocating for us, so we did it for each other."[19] In the end, the women's organization, the men's organization, and the cultural associations became "constituency groups" of the new denomination, with representatives at the annual Constituency Leaders Council advisory meetings. While Mennonite Women would not receive a seat on the Executive Board, the plan was for the board to be half women and half men.[20] In a 1999 *Timbrel* article, Gingerich wrote, "We have reached a milestone: women's representation on the churchwide board is comparable to the actual gender composition of the church."[21] The current bylaws of Mennonite Church USA, last revised in 2013, do not specify a gender requirement for the Executive Board, though the board does consider gender representation in the nomination process.[22] The bylaws do specify one representative from each "recognized Racial/Ethnic group," which includes African American, Hispanic, Native, and Asian networks.[23] In recent years, at least half the members of the Executive Board have been women, and at least a third have been people of color.[24]

Beyond the Sewing Circle

In its first few years, Mennonite Women spent much of its time on internal maintenance and connecting with its members, some of whom felt confused or even left behind by all the changes in the organization. One important externally focused activity, however, was the International Women's Fund. This fund, which built on the existing Women's World Outreach fund administered by the GCMC women's group, provided financial support for theological and church leadership training for women around the world, either in the United States or in their own contexts. In the 2000s, seven to thirteen small grants were given each year, with some students receiving scholarships for multiple years. Recipients were enrolled in programs ranging from a pastoral training certificate to graduate studies in conflict resolution to a doctoral program focused on international feminism. Paula Brunk Kuhns, who served on the Mennonite Women board, said that one of her favorite parts of her involvement with the organization was the connections she felt with women around the world who were supported by the fund. "We personally adopted some of those women to hold in prayer," she said. "I found that very meaningful."[25]

In 2000, Mennonite Women's co-coordinators resigned because of increasing demands in their families (for Susan Jantzen) and their studies (for Lara Hall Blosser). The board hired Rhoda Keener as the new executive director. Keener remembers "confessing" during the interview that she did not sew. "That might be good," she recalled one of the search committee members saying. "The perception and the reality of what Mennonite Women is doing needs to shift."[26] Keener remembers that she felt as if she had to make a connection to sewing when she spoke to traditional women's groups; she would often tell a story about trying to make a skirt for her daughter that ended up with pockets on the outside rather than inside! "There are many ways to sew, and I probably sew with words," she would say, and then continue with her presentation.[27] Even in the twenty-first century, sewing was a marker of the denominational Mennonite women's organization and of many congregational Mennonite women's groups. But that identity had been changing, and Keener's background took the organization in a new and ultimately fruitful direction.

Before accepting the role with Mennonite Women, Keener had worked in education and as a mental health professional. As had some women's group leaders before her, Keener encountered confusion about why a professional woman would get involved with what seemed, to some, to be a marginal, dying organization. A male church leader even suggested to her that there should be "an honorable burial" for the women's organization. "That made me mad—well, it raised my stubbornness," she said. Keener believed the church needed a place where women's needs could be addressed, and she saw the women's organization as a structure where this was happening for some participants.[28]

Still, Keener knew that things needed to change. When she started with Mennonite Women, 97 percent of its funding came from sewing circles and other organized congregational women's groups. But those groups were fading away. Keener recalled, "Every year we'd get letters from sewing circles saying things like, 'There are three of us left, and we're all in our nineties, so we're going to disband. God bless you.' And I would know that their faithful giving would also stop." In some areas, regional structures, which had served as connection points and financial funnels for women to the denominational organization, were also disintegrating for lack of volunteers for leadership positions. Though fundraising was not part of Keener's job description, she soon realized that it would be necessary. She also saw that there needed to be new focus and energy among those involved with the organization. At a PREP (Preparing, Resourcing, Encouraging, Praising) retreat for regional women's organization leaders in 2001, women from all twenty-one area conferences were invited, but participants were from only ten or twelve of those conferences. The event's theme was "What Is Our Mission?" and Keener got the sense that women were wondering if the organization even had a mission. Keener herself wondered about the organization's purpose as she started applying for grants and sending out appeals for funding. "What are we doing that is worthy for women to send us money?" she asked herself. "What are we really doing for women in the church?"[29]

Keener sensed that the organization needed a new ministry for women to unite around and support. And so, with the help of the board, she came up with the idea for Sister-Link. Under the Sister-Link framework, Mennonite Women, often in partnership with other Mennonite agencies, would facilitate an international or cross-cultural relationship between two groups of women. This new initiative united the sisterhood and service functions of Mennonite women's organizations that had existed in a sometimes-uneasy interplay for decades. In the early days of the organizations, the focus was almost exclusively on service; with the attention to personal retreats and fellowship groups in the 1970s and 1980s, the emphasis had swung more toward sisterhood. Under Keener's leadership, the organization began to explore sisterhood *as* service, seeking projects that would not repeat unhelpful patterns of past missionary activity but would connect women to each other while meeting a need.

One of the first Sister-Link programs connected women in several Florida churches with women in the Caucasus Mountain region in Russia, where Alice and Phil Shenk were serving with Mennonite Mission Network. The Florida women sent packages for Alice Shenk to distribute to new mothers; the packages included a receiving blanket, an infant outfit, vitamins, socks, and a picture of the giver with a note of congratulations and love.[30] Alice Shenk helped the recipients reciprocate with their own photos and greetings. Another Sister-Link happened when women from Pennsylvania, with leadership from Flo Harnish, supported an MCC project for people living with HIV/AIDS in South Africa. Keener, Harnish, and several others who had helped with fundraising visited the project site when they traveled to Africa for Mennonite World Conference in 2003.

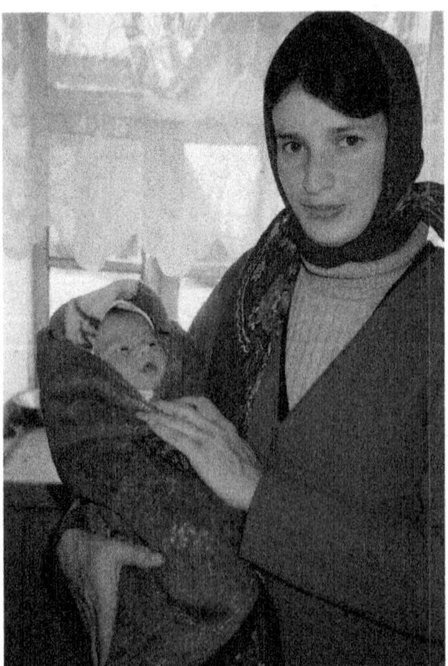

A mother and baby from a southern Muslim republic of Russia.

Sister-Links happened closer to home as well. Cora Brown (co-pastor at Church Without Walls in Elkhart, Ind.) expressed interest in

Esther Hinojosa (left) and Marilyn Hartman participated in a Sister-Link prayer partnership.

the program after hearing about it at an Indiana-Michigan Conference women's gathering led by Thelma Martin. Soon a partnership began between Brown's mostly African American, urban congregation and Martin's mostly white, rural one not far away (Yellow Creek Mennonite in Goshen, Ind.). Women from Yellow Creek helped with the Elkhart church's homelessness prevention program, and women from Church Without Walls helped the Goshen group quilt and knot comforters.[31] Another U.S.-based project involved setting up prayer partnerships between Hispanic women in South Central Conference churches and Anglo women in Western District Conference congregations.

Some Sister-Links were more successful than others. But the projects gave participants a new opportunity for more direct service and a sense of the value of a denominational women's organization in coordinating such efforts. Sister-Links also brought wider publicity to Mennonite Women. In the early 2000s, news about Sister-Link projects —and Mennonite Women's role in them—appeared in *Mennonite Weekly Review*, *The Mennonite*, several area conference newsletters, the annual report of Mennonite Mission Network, and some local newspapers. A 2003 *Mennonite Weekly Review* article highlighted several Sister-Links and quoted Keener extensively. "Women are naturally relationally-oriented," Keener said in the article. "So Sister-Link is a way of connecting our mission with who we are. It takes women's strengths and uses them to help grow the church."[32] Sister-Links helped extend the women's organization, giving it a sense of vitality that would be further developed through other programs in the coming years.

Loss of Canada

While Sister-Links helped to revitalize the women's organization in the early 2000s, many women also felt a significant loss when the wider denominations decided to merge but also divide along national lines. The MC, GCMC, and Conference of Mennonites in Canada (which had congregations with both MC and GCMC ties) had been working on a merger since the 1980s, and some area conferences had already been functioning as integrated bodies. At a 1995 joint meeting in Wichita, Kansas, the delegates approved moving ahead with a merger. After much conversation and consultation, at another joint assembly in 1999 in Saint Louis, delegates adopted recommendations that led to the formation of two separate entities, Mennonite Church Canada and Mennonite Church USA. Mennonite Church Canada held its first sessions in 2000, and Mennonite Church USA officially incorporated in early 2002.

Canadian women had retained the name Canadian Women in Mission for their branch of the joint Mennonite Women organization. With the transformation of the denominations, the Canadian group would now relate separately to the new Canadian body. For many women, this was a disappointment after all the work they had done to form a cohesive joint organization and because of the relationships they had developed. It also posed a financial concern for Mennonite Women leaders, since Canadian women provided about one-third of the organization's funding. Elizabeth Klassen, a women's group leader from Ontario, had been on the Mennonite Women board from its beginning. She felt that Canadian church leaders had not included the women's organization in the discussion leading up to their decision, but now suddenly wanted them to join the new denomination. "I was just really annoyed, when they decided," Klassen recalled. "We were really on a direction, as a binational group," she said, though she noted that not all Canadian women felt as she did.[33]

Rhoda Keener did not have as much history or emotional connection to the Canadian-U.S. relationship as those who had toiled through the integration process. In Keener's meetings with Canadian women, she got the sense that most of them were interested in being a national group connected closely with their denomination.[34] In July 2002, Keener traveled to a Mennonite Church Canada meeting in Saskatoon, Saskatchewan, to meet with the Canadian women's organization members. She and Canadian Women in Mission president Lorna Rogalski lit a candle to symbolize the continuing relationship between the two groups and read a litany, blessing each other as they relinquished their official organizational ties. The two groups continued to work together on *Timbrel* and the annual Bible Study Guide. Though *Timbrel* became a U.S. magazine in 2007, the Bible Study Guide collaboration continues to the present.

Mennonite Women's Bible Study Guide was a new iteration of the devotional guides and program resource packets that the women's organizations had been producing jointly since the early 1990s and separately long before that. The annual Bible Study Guides explored stories of women in the Bible, a specific book of the Bible, or a theme, such as a two-part series in the late 1990s titled Servanthood/Sisterhood. As with other publications of the women's organization, the project has promoted the voices of prominent and emerging women in the denominations. The guides continue to sell well and are appreciated by many women as an Anabaptist alternative to some of the more popular materials available for Christian women.[35]

Mennonite Women's relatively short existence—from 1997 to 2002—was characterized by transition, continuing questions, and some hints of new vitality. But as in previous eras of the women's organizations, it seems that the most significant aspect for the women involved was the relationships they formed. People like Doris Schmidt, who served as administrative assistant for the first few years of Mennonite Women (and with Women in Mission before that), were crucial in managing details and in providing timely bits of encouragement, constructive criticism, and humor. Schmidt fondly remembers the staff members she worked with, as well as times of navigating cramped quarters at the office in Newton, Kansas.[36] Schmidt, who grew up in the small community of Freeman, South Dakota, said that learning to know other cultures was one of the most interesting parts of her work with the women's organization, especially as the merged organization brought her into contact with women from Hispanic, African American, and other backgrounds.[37]

Advances in technology made it possible for Jantzen and Blosser to jointly coordinate the organization from different states, though they had to navigate the challenges of relating to each other mostly through email and conference calls. Their communication reveals an attempt to support each other during somewhat turbulent times in their own lives as well as their efforts to effectively lead the new organization. Keener, who worked from her home in Pennsylvania, relished opportunities for one-on-one conversations with board members who lived closer to her or whom she encountered at retreats.[38] At times, relationships outside the organization were important as well. Overwhelmed with the financial and logistical demands of the organization when she started, Keener found significant support from several women in the denominational office in Newton as well as from Jim Gingerich, the director of Mennonite Men.[39]

Despite the organization's struggles, being involved in its leadership turned out to be a worthwhile commitment for many who took on the role. Paula Brunk Kuhns remembers that when she received the phone call inviting her to join the Mennonite Women board, the caller told her, "If you're ever interested in serving on a board at the denominational level, this is the one, because we have a lot of fun!"[40] She found this comment to be true, and also felt that her board appointment was a good "jumping-in point" for other denominational work and connections.[41] Elizabeth Klassen said she felt "a real loss" after her time on the Mennonite Women board, even though she had plenty of other things to fill her time. "I missed the meetings, I missed the relationships, the connection with some really dynamic women," she said, describing her board service as an enriching and energizing experience.[42] The Mennonite women's organization continued to enrich and energize its participants in North America as well as, increasingly, women around the world. The next chapters follow the story of Mennonite Women USA, its domestic and international Sister Care seminars, and the continued activities of local and regional Mennonite women's groups in the United States.

9
Mennonite Women USA

> We are simply trying to create new circles for women to do the same things that they always have—which is to care about God, each other, and themselves.
> —Rhoda Keener[1]

The spirit of those involved with early Mennonite women's groups lived on in the new women's organization of Mennonite Church USA, which officially adopted the name Mennonite Women USA (MW USA) in February 2003. The new organization continued the legacy of missionary support that early participants had held so dear. As previous chapters relate, in the 1930s the GCMC women's association asked its members to contribute "two cents a week and a prayer" for missionary pensions. Women gave faithfully over the years and even (in "a rare display of independence") rejected a proposal from the mission board and their own executive council to roll the fund over to the mission board budget in 1952.[2] In the intervening years the Missionary Pension Fund had been largely forgotten, with the mission board continuing to use the interest and letting the principal accrue.

Soon after the formation of the new denomination and its new mission agency (Mennonite Mission Network), the fund, which had grown to $95,717.60, was brought to the attention of the women's organization.[3] Mission Network asked to have the money released for its use, but MW USA board member Nancy Sauder recalled the history of the fund's accrual. "We need to honor those women and keep this money," she said.[4] After transferring the percentage to Canadian Women in Mission that belonged to it, the MW USA board chose to restrict use of the fund's interest to activities that met its original purpose: caring for unmet needs of missionaries. Today, the annual interest (about $2,900 in recent years) is used for physical and mental health leaves and funeral travel expenses for mission workers.[5]

One mission worker couple wrote to MW USA expressing appreciation for use of the fund. Their spiritual director had encouraged them to take some time away together for recentering and prayer. A few days later, they received a Mission Network newsletter saying there were funds available for workers wanting to do spiritual retreats. The couple indicated their interest, and they were able to use the money for a three-day retreat where they had a "life-giving time" praying, discussing, and enjoying God's creation together. "It was exactly what we needed, and we could really relax knowing that the expenses were covered," they wrote. "Thank you again so much for . . . Mennonite Women's generosity and for this great gift!" In a way, the women who saved their Sunday egg money so many years ago were still supporting otherwise unmet needs of missionaries.[6]

New Sister-Link Partnerships

MW USA continued not only financially supporting missionaries but also working more directly with women in various global contexts through its International Women's Fund and Sister-Link projects. One of the most significant Sister-Links arose after the 2003 Mennonite World Conference assembly in Zimbabwe. This gathering introduced attendees to the efforts of Mennonite-related African women theologians who had been influenced by the work of prominent Ghanaian theologian Mercy Oduyoye and had begun networking in 2001.[7] At the Zimbabwe assembly, English- and French-speaking African women, aided by translation from Sylvia Shirk, met and elected seven leaders for an organization of African Anabaptist Women Theologians (AAWT).[8] When this group met again in Kenya in 2004, they stated a clear objective: by the year 2009, at least twenty women would be trained in theology across Mennonite and Brethren in Christ churches in Africa.[9]

MW USA leadership thought the African women's dream was worth supporting, though they knew it would take a substantial commitment.

So they sought to collaborate with the AAWT using their Sister-Link framework and also partnered with Mennonite World Conference's Global Gift Sharing program. One component of this Sister-Link was providing scholarships for women identified by the African network, mostly with funds external to MW USA's existing International Women's Fund. Cathleen Hockman-Wert and Susan Jantzen, former women's organization staff members, led the scholarship fundraising effort as volunteers. MW USA also committed to walking with the African women as they developed the vision and structure of their organization. Finally, MW USA appointed Shirk to facilitate prayer partner relationships between the AAWT leaders (from Democratic Republic of Congo, Kenya, Tanzania, Zambia, and Zimbabwe) and female pastors and theologians in the United States and Canada.[10]

The AAWT Sister-Link engaged many women. MW USA solicited funds from individuals, calling the group of North American donors Les Amies (French for "female friends"). The final list of donors included five women's groups and more than one hundred individuals, from college students to prominent female church leaders.[11] In the end, the AAWT Sister-Link supported nine different women with scholarships, usually for multiple years, for a total of nearly $38,000.[12] Rhoda Keener and Rebecca Osiro, the AAWT secretary, had mutually supportive conversations as they shared the joys and challenges of guiding a women's organization. While not all the prayer partners connected well because of the challenges of international communication, some, such as Shirk and Sidonie Swana, developed significant friendships. Shirk and Swana, like several of the partners, met each other and exchanged gifts at the 2009 Mennonite World Conference assembly in Paraguay, which marked the closure of the Sister-Link.[13] Mary Schertz, an

Mary Schertz (left) and Rebecca Osiro participated in a Sister-Link connecting African and North American women theologians.

Associated Mennonite Biblical Seminary professor, was paired with Osiro, who also received a scholarship to aid her graduate work. In Paraguay, Schertz and Osiro conversed about biblical Greek, Schertz's specialty, and Christian-Islamic relations, Osiro's area of expertise.[14]

During this Sister-Link, Osiro became (in 2008) the first woman ordained as a pastor in the Kenyan Mennonite Church. An article in the Les Amies newsletter reports on the dramatic events surrounding the ordination. Osiro was summoned before seven bishops, who deliberated at length about ordaining a woman. Eventually, the decision was left up to the bishop of the Nairobi diocese, who affirmed the wishes of Osiro's community, congregation, and family for her to be ordained. "Sometimes I felt overwhelmed by the discussions," Osiro said. "However, I had to stand my position for the sake of other women."[15] Sidonie Swana was also one of the first women ordained as a pastor in her denomination, Communauté Mennonite au Congo (Mennonite Church of Congo) in 2013.[16]

The AAWT Sister-Link, like most cross-cultural endeavors, was not easy. It was difficult for the African women to gather and communicate and sometimes to decide who should receive scholarships. There were not as many scholarships awarded as both they and MW USA had hoped. The challenges of the African context intruded via limits placed on women's roles, the displacement of participants because of conflict, and even the tragic death of one scholarship recipient. But the Sister-Link ultimately yielded inspiration for the women involved on both sides. Shirk based her doctoral dissertation on the project, concluding that, despite the real challenges, the relationships "created a space for liberating independence that offers ongoing benefits for all those who participated."[17] Like some other Sister-Link projects, it also provided positive publicity for MW USA. James Krabill, a Mennonite Mission Network executive, commented that Sister-Link "is an enormous gift to the global church family and one we have not even begun to maximize to its fullest potential."[18] The culmination of the AAWT partnership was featured in *The Mennonite*'s November 2009 cover story.

Other, smaller-scale Sister-Links also occurred during this time. Around 2003, a connection formed between women at Weavers Mennonite Church in Harrisonburg, Virginia, and a Mennonite church in Arusha, Tanzania. Edith Shenk Kuhns, a Mission Network worker in East Africa and a former pastor at Weavers, helped facilitate an exchange of emails, prayer requests, and small gifts. The Tanzanian women sent batik fabric that the Virginia women crafted into a quilt, which they sold to aid the ministries of the Arusha church. Yvonne Martin, a member of the quilt committee at Weavers, noted that both inexperienced and experienced quilters were eager to contribute to the project. "Really, our interaction with the African quilt has pulled our entire congregation together," she said.[19]

Another Sister-Link paired female students in a 2003 Goshen College cross-cultural communication course with Tanzanian women who attended an AIDS support group run by Mennonite Central Committee.[20] Some of the students bonded significantly with their email pen pals and

Women at Weavers Mennonite Church display the quilt being created from a Sister Link gift of African fabrics. (Left to right) Gladys Driver, Yvonne Martin, Jan Kauffman, and Brownie Driver.

Tanzanian Sister-Link group. (Left to right) Hellen Bradburn, Ines Ngadada, Margaret Lymo, Mary Muhochi, Miriam Makgmbo, and Gemima Nyafanga.

organized a benefit concert at the college to raise money for the support group. Starting in 2004, a group of women in Franklin Conference (Pa.) marketed the work of Kekchi weavers who were part of a co-op in Guatemala. A year into the partnership, three Franklin Conference women sent letters to the women, and the Franklin group was delighted to receive twenty-five letters in response that gave them a glimpse into the women's difficult yet hope-filled lives.[21] In 2005, women at Cedar Street Mennonite Church (Chambersburg, Pa.) provided a loan to Gambian women through a development association run by Denise and Gary Williamson, who were in the Gambia with Eastern Mennonite Missions. The Gambian women made soap and dyed fabric and repaid the loan for reinvestment with another group. One woman from Cedar Street visited the groups, carrying pictures and notes from the Pennsylvania women and bringing back photos and a nutritious powdered drink mix as a gift from the Gambian women. "I marveled at how one Sister-Link project sparked this extraordinary friendship between Mennonite women and Muslim women in two very different cultures," said Denise Williamson.[22]

Two significant U.S.-based Sister-Links also developed. Hurricane Katrina, which struck in 2005, affected everyone in Gulf States Mennonite Conference in some way. Elaine Maust, copastor of Jubilee Mennonite Church (Meridian, Miss.) received a prayer shawl at an event in which people shared their stories of loss from the storm. She reflected on what a powerful experience it was and wished that every woman in the conference could be given a prayer shawl. Maust contacted the president of the conference women's organization (Karen Yoder), who contacted the board chair of MW USA (Elaine Good), and a prayer shawl Sister-Link was born. "It just went crazy," Maust said. "We started getting shawls from random old ladies in Texas who weren't even Mennonite but heard what we were doing."[23] Good collected shawls from women in fourteen states and drove with her husband from Pennsylvania to Mississippi in a car packed full of shawls.[24] At the conference women's retreat, ninety women received shawls for themselves as well as extras to give to friends; 170 total shawls were distributed during an emotional time of prayer and sharing.[25] While the event was meaningful for the women who had suffered from the storm, Maust pointed out it also "gave good-hearted people something useful to do."[26] Women across the country who felt overwhelmed by the news of the disaster could knit or crochet while they prayed, giving both material and spiritual support.

The Housewarmer Project, which started under the Sister-Link framework, continues to connect the tangible gifts of women to people who have experienced tragedy. After Hurricane Charley in 2004, Rebecca Sommers (who would later serve as MW USA board chair after Elaine Good) traveled to a Mennonite Disaster Service site in Florida. At a house blessing held upon completion of work on a home, Sommers presented the new owners with a quilted wall hanging she had made.[27] She realized that MW USA could facilitate similar offerings at other project sites. Since many Mennonite Disaster Service clients were single mothers, the project also fit with Sister-Link's goal to connect women to each other. Different volunteers have coordinated the project for more than a decade, providing quilting instructions to crafters and funneling finished products to appropriate locations. A 2015 article reported that MW USA had sent nearly 250 wall hangings for presentation at house blessings,[28] with additional pieces coming from people not affiliated with the organization. Saundra Gale reflected on the looks of joy and gratitude she saw when she presented the gifts as a Mennonite Disaster Service volunteer in 2008. "A needle is just as powerful as a hammer," she concluded.[29] For quilters who are unable to attend a congregational sewing group or no longer have one to attend, the Housewarmer Project is a way they can continue using their skills in service to others. The Housewarmer Project is a particular example of how Sister-Links combined the service and sisterhood aspects of the women's organization. Even if they never met each other, those giving and receiving the wall hangings could feel connected by pictures and notes passed through volunteers.

Developing an Organization in a Postmodern Age

Through its Sister-Link projects, MW USA's important role in connecting women and their gifts was becoming more obvious. But the organization still had to raise the money needed to sustain itself and further its mission. The May–June 2004 *Timbrel* announced that while women had contributed $10,000 more to the organization in that fiscal year than in the previous one, it was still $11,000 short of its budget.[30] The board approved hiring an organizational consultant, and Keener began meeting with Rebekah Basinger, a consultant who worked primarily with faith-based nonprofits. Basinger challenged Keener to see fundraising as a spiritual act and to move MW USA from an organization dependent on contributions from congregational women's groups to one that focused on gifts from individuals.[31] Together they developed the "Lydia Circle" designation for individuals who give $500 or more per year. Keener cultivated relationships with well over one hundred "Lydias" in her travels across the country, and "Lydia Teas" to thank donors are now a regular event at Mennonite Church USA assemblies.[32] MW USA also started an endowment, funded by individuals and estate gifts.[33] By 2008, individual and group giving to the organization was about equal, a huge shift from the 3 percent individual giving rate when Keener started as director in 2001.[34] In 2011, MW USA hired Ruth Lapp Guengerich as a coexecutive director. With Guengerich focusing on program and administration, Keener could give more time to financial development (and the burgeoning Sister Care program). By 2014, individual giving to MW USA had surpassed group giving by more than $30,000.[35]

Ofelia García (left) sharing with Lydia Circle members at a tea in San Jose, Calif., while Linda Shelly (center) translates.

MW USA, like most nonprofits, is still dependent on somewhat unpredictable grants and donations. But its financial situation—and the perception of the organization in general—has become more stable and positive than in the early years of the merged organization, when many wondered if it was worth continuing. Guengerich said she felt recognized and affirmed when she represented MW USA at the denomination's Constituency Leadership Council (CLC) in 2011 and beyond. "When we go to CLC, we are treated as equals," she said in a 2014 interview. "We are not an auxiliary fringe group anymore."[36] Many congregational and area conference women's groups continue to struggle with low attendance and a lack of volunteers for leadership positions, and there still is a perception among some younger women that MW USA is an organization for one's mother or grandmother. But the denominational organization has a strong presence in the denomination. In a January 2015 interview, Rebekah Basinger said that when she tells other Mennonite agencies about working with Keener, they say that MW USA is a bright spot in the denomination. "I've worked

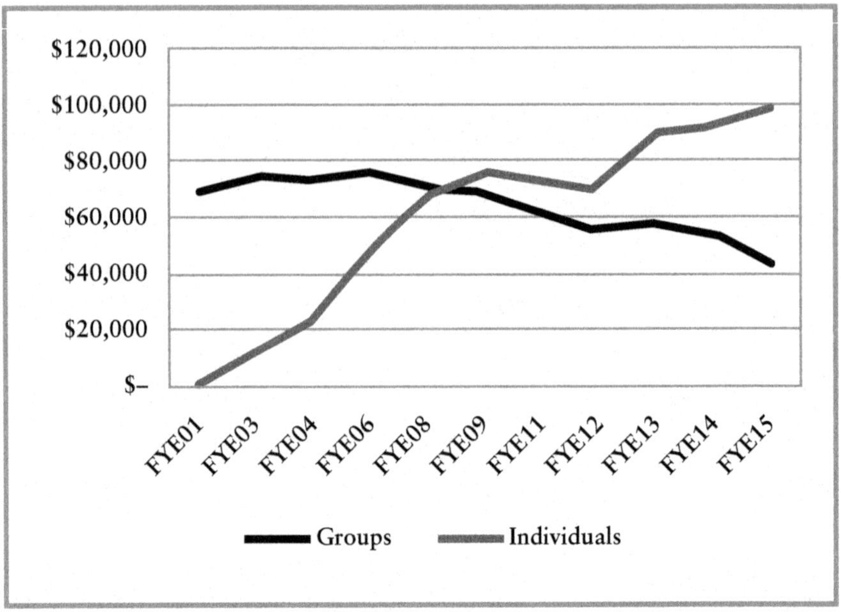

Individual giving to Mennonite Women USA increased from 2001 to 2015, while giving from groups decreased.

with other denominations, and I certainly do not hear that about their women's organization," she said.[37]

Mennonite Women USA's relative vitality is worth pondering in a climate of decreasing denominational loyalty and religious interest in general. As Diana Butler Bass discusses in *Christianity after Religion*, many people are finding conventional religion less satisfying, are attending church less regularly, and are looking for new expressions of spiritual community.[38] In *The Great Emergence*, Phyllis Tickle memorably describes the current era as part of a "rummage sale" that happens in Christianity every five hundred years—the last one being the Protestant Reformation.[39] During these so-called rummage sales, institutional structures are shaken and sometimes shattered so that new growth can occur.[40]

In this time of crumbling institutions and new religious experiments, why has a hundred-year-old church-based women's organization survived and even thrived? MW USA's continued existence is at least partially due to the development of Sister Care and that program's flexibility in addressing the concerns of women from diverse cultural backgrounds, ages, and theological perspectives (chapter 10 discusses

Sister Care in more detail). But more generally, perhaps MW USA is a bright spot in a denomination with an uncertain future because it has managed to clearly integrate the dual aspects of its identity (service and sisterhood) and to provide opportunities for a variety of women to feel at home.

Both Tickle and Bass describe how "emergent" Christians reverse the traditional religious pattern of "believe, behave, belong" and instead focus first on belonging and then behaving and believing.[41] Bass uses knitting as an example of this reversal. "In knitting, the process is exactly the reverse of that in church," she writes. "Belonging to a knitting group leads to behaving as a knitter, which leads to believing things about knitting."[42] Maybe Mennonite women's groups, without necessarily realizing it, are poised to continue to thrive as new expressions of Christianity emerge. Women's groups have always stressed belonging (the sisterhood of talking and studying together) and behaving (quilting and doing service projects) as much if not more than believing. They may be able to serve as spaces where the increasing number of "spiritual but not religious" North Americans can come together and work together, even while holding and exploring a variety of beliefs. While most current participants in Mennonite women's groups are older and have somewhat traditional Christian beliefs, the connections fostered by their gatherings could, perhaps, position them to survive and thrive in the atmosphere of emergent Christianity.

Tickle discusses how "emergents," who are thoroughly postmodern, are not afraid of paradox. Postmodern people see the limits of logic and all human thinking; they tend to distrust overarching metanarrative but embrace narrative. "Narrative speaks to the heart in order that the heart, so tutored, may direct and inform the mind," Tickle writes.[43] Mennonite women's organizations have always created space for stories, from the informal sharing that arose as women worked in sewing circles to the profiles of women that filled the pages of its publications starting in the mid-twentieth century. Carolyn Holderread Heggen picked up on the importance of story as she reflected on the continued thriving of MW USA in 2016. She noted that the denomination has been stuck on contentious discussions about human sexuality, in which people tend to speak in terms of thoughts and opinions that easily divide people into opposing camps.[44] "Mennonite Women, through our periodical, women's gatherings (whether in a Bible study or around a quilting frame), Sister-Link networking, and the worldwide ministry of Sister Care, has provided a way for women to share their stories with each other," Heggen said. "Stories help us see similarities and touch hearts, thus uniting and energizing people."[45]

Connections Near and Far

Connections with others are certainly what motivate and inspire the women who are most committed to the organization. Evie Hertzler began serving on MW USA's board in 2005. A couple of years later, she was diagnosed with Lou Gehrig's disease. While her physical health deteriorated, she continued to participate in board meetings, speaking by typing into a machine. When Hertzler died in 2008, Keener attended the funeral, where Hertzler's husband gave her an envelope with a $10,000 contribution. "Evie was so proud to be a part of Mennonite Women USA," the accompanying letter said. "We are grateful for this gift of remembrance that will live on."[46] Hertzler's legacy was not just monetary. Before her death, she had urged Twila King Yoder, an administrator at Eastern Mennonite University, to be the next East Coast representative

Twila King Yoder (left) and Evie Hertzler.

on the MW USA board. "What a gift that has been to me!" Yoder wrote in a 2015 blog post.[47] Yoder, who is also a "Lydia" donor, reflected on the growth of the organization during her two board terms, which she described as "eight fruitful and meaningful years that have blessed me in so many ways."[48]

MW USA's editors have been especially important in maintaining and promoting the organization. Hockman-Wert developed the vision for *Timbrel*, which helped set a wider vision for the organization in general. Laurie Oswald Robinson was hired as MW USA editor in 2005. Before, during, and after her time with the organization, she wrote many articles for other Mennonite publications, highlighting women and women's issues for the denomination. In 2008 she was succeeded by Patricia Burdette. Burdette brought to the magazine an ecumenical background and a concern for hearing a variety of voices. In an editorial, she described *Timbrel* as an indigenous talking circle, in which each person can see and hear everyone else, creating "a safe place for all Mennonite women to gather and converse."[49] MW USA hired Claire DeBerg as editor in 2013, whose job title soon changed to the more accurate "communications manager." DeBerg's responsibilities went beyond editing *Timbrel* and other print publications to developing the organization's website, blog, Facebook page, Twitter feed, YouTube channel, and other forums. She stressed *Timbrel*'s tagline, "Women in Conversation Together with God," seeing the magazine as a bridge where the voices of women across the denomination could come together.[50] Dawn Araujo-Hawkins, who succeeded DeBerg as communications manager in 2016, has viewed the magazine and Mennonite Women USA's other communication platforms as spaces to connect with a wide variety of women across the denomination. She saw continued value in *Timbrel* as a platform for Mennonite women's prophetic voices, saying that print media "has the ability to speak truth to power in a way that isn't always possible in the Internet age."[51] Berni Kaufman has been another valuable part of the MW USA staff, serving as the organization's executive assistant since 2004. Kaufman is often the first point of contact for individuals wanting to communicate with the organization and has helped MW USA grow for more than a decade.

Beyond its publications, MW USA seeks to connect with women in the denomination through activities at biennial Mennonite Church

Elaine Good, board chair of MW USA, sharing with the Constituency Leadership Council about the quilt project for Atlanta.

USA assemblies. At the 2003 assembly in Atlanta, a large quilt (eight by eighteen feet) incorporating beautifully designed wall hangings made by women in all twenty-one area conferences was displayed onstage. Elaine Good, MW USA board president, organized the project, which used fabric pieces from worship at the previous assembly and connected the squares as a colorful sign of unity for the first official gathering of the integrated denomination. At the 2005 assembly, MW USA sponsored a seminar led by Brenda Martin Hurst called "Women Addressing Pornography." Approximately seventy-five women attended, and they shared personal stories and concrete steps to address the issue in congregations, area conferences, and the denomination.[52] Four years later, MW USA held another seminar on pornography, this time in partnership with Mennonite Men. MW USA leaders have also facilitated other seminars, such as one for spouses of pastors led by Guengerich at multiple assemblies. In 2009, the organization brought a resolution against human trafficking to the delegate body. Keener presented the statement, which was affirmed by the delegates and generated conversation about further education and action on the issue.[53] MW USA dinners at each assembly gather women who are interested in the organization or simply want to connect with other women in the denomination.

MW USA also continued to run PREP (Preparing, Resourcing, Encouraging, Praising) events for regional leaders and Women in Conversation retreats, two programs started during the organization's Mennonite Women era. PREP, first held every year and then every eighteen months in various locations, introduced area conference women's organization leaders to MW USA projects, gathered input about new directions for the organization, and provided resources and opportunities for networking. Women in Conversation retreats happened every two years in Kansas and Pennsylvania, cosponsored by Laurelville Mennonite Retreat Center. The retreats provided space for participants to connect with each other, pamper themselves a bit, and hear input from a female Mennonite pastor or scholar. Susan Gingerich vividly remembers an early Women in Conversation gathering she attended where Brenda Martin Hurst spoke about sexuality.[54] Gingerich was "astounded" at the open conversations that ensued among women from a variety of ages about their sexual experience. This and subsequent retreats helped Gingerich "understand the continued need for women to get together for maybe no reason other than to talk and to support each other."[55]

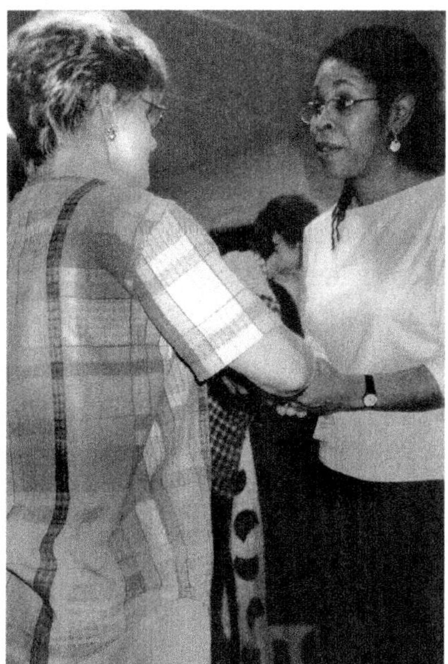

Regina Shands Stoltzfus (right) blessing a participant at the 2002 Women in Conversation retreat.

Women in Conversation events also provided a platform for women who were emerging as leaders or who had done significant work in the church but perhaps had not received as much exposure as many male leaders. Keener was a workshop copresenter at Women in Conversation the year before she was hired as executive director of Mennonite

Women. Regina Shands Stoltzfus was one of the speakers in 2002, the year she started teaching at Goshen College. She continued to be involved with MW USA, serving as a board member from the Great Lakes region. (Stoltzfus has also helped shape the denomination's Women in Leadership Project, and in 2016, her significant antiracism work earned her Indiana's highest civil rights award.) June Alliman Yoder, a long-time seminary professor, presented at the 2006 retreat with her daughter Mandy Yoder Schrock, an Indianapolis pastor. Carolyn Holderread Heggen, an expert on trauma healing and a MW USA board member, spoke in 2008. The next three retreats featured younger female pastors who were emerging as significant voices in the denomination: Megan Ramer, Meghan Good, and Jennifer Davis Sensenig. Feedback from the retreats shows overwhelmingly positive evaluations from participants, but also a concern about dwindling attendance.[56] With area conference women's retreats a priority for many, two regular MW USA-sponsored gatherings seemed unsustainable. Women in Conversation was discontinued after 2014, and MW USA has plans for a new regular event that incorporates elements of both the Women in Conversation and PREP events.

Women in Church Leadership

Promoting women leaders, both through its own events and in the wider denomination, has been a priority for MW USA, even though many female denominational leaders and pastors are not involved with the organization. After Lancaster Conference leaders decided not to ordain women as pastors in 2007, a letter signed by MW USA's entire board and staff (fifteen people in all) was printed in *Mennonite Weekly Review* and *The Mennonite*. The letter expressed sadness at the decision, stating, "We affirm that women are called by God to share their gifts with the church and the world, without restriction due to gender."[57] After the statement appeared, Keener received an email from a male Lancaster Conference leader saying that it seemed "a bit 'in your face'" and did not "build bridges."[58] She also received an email from a female Lancaster leader who expressed thanks for the letter.[59] These exchanges show that people in the denomination were interested in the perspective of the women's organization and that there was still need for an organized voice promoting women's leadership.

In 2009, MW USA invited its board members and a diverse group of female church leaders to a strategic planning retreat for the organization. At this meeting, participants observed that it seemed fewer women were serving in leadership roles in the denomination than had in previous recent years. They urged MW USA to speak out for increasing the number of women in leadership. This concern eventually led to the creation of a Women in Leadership Audit, housed under the Executive Board of Mennonite Church USA and conducted by Joanna Shenk. The audit revealed a complex picture of the denomination, with an increase in the number of women in full-time pastoral ministry but nevertheless a large disparity between the number of active male and female pastors. While women had consistently been filling more positions on church boards, there had not been a similar increase in directors of Mennonite agencies and board presidents. Interestingly, the pages that reported this information in *The Mennonite* also included a sidebar (by Shenk) that briefly recounted the story of Clara Eby Steiner's work to create the Mennonite Woman's Missionary Society and how it was "banned" by

Maria Magadalena (left) and Hatoko Inoue participating in strategic planning for Mennonite Women USA in 2009.

the (old) Mennonite Church. Though the early women's organization was not explicitly concerned with women in church leadership, there clearly has been a continued connection between traditional women's organizations and expanding roles for women in their denominations.[60]

Mennonite Women USA also continued its support of international women studying theology through its International Women's Fund (IWF). In 2011, MW USA increased its annual funding for this program to $10,000. International mission workers noticed the impact of the organization's commitment to women leaders. Speaking from his experience with congregations in Africa, Tim Lind said the fact that an Anabaptist agency had dedicated itself to supporting women's theological studies imbued value to the women pursuing those studies in the eyes of (male) church leaders in their countries.[61] Linda Shelly, Mennonite Mission Network director for Latin America, said, "IWF scholarships are particularly effective because they are given by women to women. That relationship gives special meaning for recipients. It's a more personal and warm connection."[62] The connections that developed between scholarship recipients and MW USA helped pave the way for future collaborative efforts, such as many of the international Sister Care seminars (which are discussed further in chapter 10).

The International Women's Fund also gave North American women concerned about the circumstances of women worldwide a place to direct their support. "When I see the prayer list of International Women's Fund students, I am heartened," said Elizabeth Goering, a Kansas woman who recently decided to include MW USA in her estate planning.[63] "I know that education is about the only salvation for women, the only way for them to get out from under the yoke," she said.[64] At the 2015 denominational assembly, MW USA donors heard firsthand from Latina leaders who worked with IWF recipients. Alix Lozano, herself an IWF recipient, shared that when she started as director of the Mennonite seminary in Colombia, almost all the students preparing themselves for ministry were men. But thanks in part to IWF scholarships, enrollment of women being trained for ministry has grown to slightly over 50 percent.[65] Olga Piedrasanta spoke about teaching IWF recipients at the Anabaptist seminary in Guatemala. "These women who were afraid to speak now have this new awakening within themselves," she said. "And some have fulfilled their dreams of being ordained as

International Women's Fund recipients who participated in the Guatemala Sister Care seminar in 2013. Front row (left to right): Yanette Palacios, Guatemala; Albania Molina, Honduras; and Ofelia García, Mexico. Back row (left to right): Rosario Rosales, Honduras; and Elizabeth Vado, Nicaragua.

pastors."[66] These testimonies were met with a standing ovation from the North American listeners.

Mennonite Women USA's activities in the early twenty-first century show a continuation of the dual purpose of Mennonite women's organizations. MW USA found new ways to serve and connect with others far away through its Sister-Link projects and expanding International Women's Fund. The organization also focused on ministering to women and cultivating sisterhood within the denomination through stories shared in its publications, seminars led at assemblies, and public support for women in congregational leadership. One major endeavor that sought to enhance women's care for themselves and others was Sister Care, which would become MW USA's most active and visible program.

10
Sister Care

> [Sister Care] has been like a spark that has taken off throughout all of Latin America—because it's touching a felt need within us women. We've learned to listen to each other, to share our most secret feelings. And by now we don't have any idea how many times this program has multiplied itself in the different countries.
> —Olga Piedrasanta[1]

The October 2012 Sister Care event in Cuttack, India, featured the story of "Meena," an Indian woman given a fictional name for the event. Meena's story was read in Hindi and English to the 325 women gathered in conjunction with the All-India Mennonite Women's Conference.[2] Meena was the wife of a well respected pastor. Each weekend he became overwhelmed with the stress of the upcoming Sunday and would berate Meena's chapati cooking, lecture her on being more submissive, and eventually end up beating her with his hands or a stick. After the story was read, the group was asked how women of the church might help Meena. "Pray for her," some suggested, or "Get an older woman to teach her how to make better chapatis."[3] Others mentioned that Meena should be nice to her husband and forgive him. Rhoda Keener and Carolyn Holderread Heggen, who were leading the seminar, were struck that none of the women said the husband's behavior was sinful or that he should be held accountable for his actions.[4] Heggen and Keener guided the group through several Scripture passages, highlighting God's concern for all people and Jesus' liberating interactions with women, and naming violence against women as sin.[5]

Participants in a Sister Care small group talking together at the All-India Mennonite Women Conference in Orissa.

After the seminar, women came up to the leaders to privately share their stories with them. "I am Meena," one woman said, with tears streaming down her face. "I have been Meena for a long time."[6] Another said, "You speak beautiful words. I have never heard that it is a sin for a Christian husband to beat his wife."[7] Later, Keener and Heggen traveled to area churches with Twila Miller, a former Mennonite Central Committee worker, and Cynthia Peacock, a leader among Indian Mennonite women. They heard many more stories of "Meenas," either from women who faced similar circumstances themselves or knew friends or family members who did. Since the seminar, Peacock has continued to talk with women—and to talk about the importance of hearing women—as she works in different congregations.[8] She has witnessed more women wanting to share their stories and even talking with male church leaders about creating space for women to support each other.[9] "The impact of the Sister Care workshop . . . has been tremendous," Peacock said almost a year after the event. "I see changes in thought, attitude, and courageous steps by women to be seen as valuable creations of God."[10] Sister Care in India, and its legacy in Peacock's continued ministry, is a striking example of a combination of sisterhood and service, or even sisterhood *as* service. The program, a ministry of Mennonite Women USA, has provided space for meaningful sharing among women, which has led women to explore new avenues of service and ministry to each other.

Sister Care's Start

Sister Care grew out of Keener's work as a mental health therapist and her desire for women to experience healing in the church, something she had needed in her own life. Carolyn Holderread Heggen, who joined Keener as a Sister Care presenter in 2010, had done extensive work with others around trauma healing, sexual abuse, and other related topics. "Carolyn and I carry a passion that is born out of our own healing journeys; for both of us this work is something that often goes beyond words," Keener said in a 2014 interview. In some ways, Sister Care was a natural continuation of MW USA's Sister-Link concept, which connected women to each other and provided opportunities for service and ministry with some element of mutuality. Like the Sister-Link projects, Sister Care became a fitting expression of the dual service and sisterhood purpose of Mennonite women's organizations.[11]

An early step toward the creation of Sister Care came in 2003, when rather than have women's groups send in the regular annual reports of their activities, Keener asked them to write about the needs of women in their congregations. "They came back with pages and pages of very real needs," Keener remembered. The surveys mentioned concerns about connecting with other women, gender and the church, mental health, and the life stages of women. Keener kept these topics in mind as she continued her work as director of MW USA. In 2006, she attended a Women in Ministry conference at Bluffton University, where the speaker discussed caring for women's mental health within faith communities. Keener realized she wanted to seriously engage with this topic. But should MW USA start a program, or were the increasing number of female pastors in the denomination already addressing this concern? Keener sought advice from friends and MW USA board members. Mary Swartley, an educator and church leader, pointed out that even if female pastors were addressing women's mental health,

Keener could at least start working with the many congregations without women in ministerial roles. Cora Brown, a pastor and MW USA board member, told Keener that she felt like she couldn't do it all as the leader of a congregation. "I need women to be doing this," Keener recalls Brown telling her.

Rhoda Keener decided to start in Franklin Conference, her home area. After consulting with local (male) pastors, she gathered women's group leaders and pastors' wives from several congregations. Keener shared research from Al Dueck's study of several Anabaptist-related congregations, which found that given the choice of a professional, their pastor, a deacon, or a friend in the congregation, 91 percent of people chose to talk with a friend when they had a struggle.[12] Keener's goal was to equip women for caring ministry in the church. She met with the group of Franklin Conference women for nine months, developing ideas as she continued conversations about her vision with the MW USA board. After a visit with Barb Borntrager (president of Mennonite Women of Virginia), Keener began to make plans for a pilot "Sister Care" weekend retreat. Ninety women attended the February 2008 event in Harrisonburg, Virginia, where participants role-played effective and ineffective listening skills, learned from Keener about setting boundaries in caring relationships, and heard Rebecca Sommers (MW USA board chair) share about her journey with depression.[13] Keener remembers one woman saying, "I've been in this church for thirty-five years and this is the most helpful thing that I've attended."

Despite the positive response, Keener was unsure about Sister Care's place in MW USA and how it—and the women's organization in general—might develop in the future. She was also feeling discouraged about her own direction. She held a second Sister Care weekend in her area but designed it as a shorter time with part of the input on raising children, and many attendees were disappointed that they did not experience the full seminar. But when MW USA held a strategic planning meeting in March 2009, the vision statement that emerged fit perfectly with Keener's hopes for Sister Care. She felt encouraged to continue and held several more weekend seminars, sometimes with help from Ruth Lapp Guengerich (MW USA board chair). At this point each seminar was different, with Keener assembling materials that she thought would be relevant for each group. When 185 women attended an October 2009 Sister Care seminar in Harrisburg, Pennsylvania, Keener realized the program was perhaps bigger than she knew how to handle. So she arranged for a multiple-day meeting with Guengerich and Heggen (MW USA West Coast representative), two women involved with MW USA who had been supportive of the program and could help her develop it.

At their meeting, Keener presented her materials, thinking that the other women would look over them and suggest some areas for further development. Instead, they began to reenvision the entire seminar, building on Keener's basic concern for helping women work on their own healing and provide a healing presence for others. The three women considered what women in congregations most needed and what could realistically be covered in a weekend seminar format. They came up with the four topics that would shape the Sister Care program: claiming our identity as God's beloved, caring for self and others, compassionate listening, and transforming loss and grief. Heggen, who had experience in manual writing, took the lead on developing a clear structure, and the three women authored a sixty-four-page manual.

In October 2010, Heggen and Keener copresented three Sister Care seminars in the Pacific Northwest. "I was absolutely blown away by the response of the women," Heggen recalled in a 2015 interview. "It was just magic to see the materials that we'd worked with for so long actually come alive with real women participants."[14] Heggen expressed interest in becoming a regular copresenter, and Keener felt a returning energy for her work. The board approved an arrangement for Keener and Guengerich to share the MW USA director role, while Keener would lead Sister Care, with Heggen copresenting.

Keener described the involvement of Heggen, who has a PhD in counseling psychology and a history of working on serious issues in the church, as "a quantum leap for Mennonite Women USA."[15] Keener, who had lived in rural Indiana and Pennsylvania and developed relationships with the sewing circles during her years with the organization, had connections to traditional Mennonite women; Heggen, with her West Coast context and work experience around issues of trauma and abuse, had connections to women who had not necessarily been involved with the women's organization in the past. Their coleadership helped bring different kinds of Mennonite women together to attend

Sister Care seminars. After numerous requests for a coed seminar, in 2012 the Sister Care program expanded to include men for the first time at a Compassionate Care event in Portland, Oregon. Heggen and Keener have encouraged men to develop a similar program (and Heggen has offered to be a consultant), but as of early 2017, this has not yet occurred. Also in 2012, the manual was translated and contextualized into Spanish by Wanda Gonzalez Coleman.

Sister Care International

Carolyn Holderread Heggen also brought international connections (and fluency in Spanish) to the Sister Care ministry. Having grown up in Puerto Rico and worked with Mennonite Central Committee in Asia, Heggen was engaged in mentoring relationships with women around the world. When these women asked what Heggan was working on, she told them about Sister Care. "And I just kept hearing over and over, we need something like that in our context," she said.[16] Heggen's connections and Keener's relationships with International Women's Fund

Rhoda Keener, Olga Piedrasanta, and Carolyn Holderread Heggen (left to right) of Sister Care.

recipients led to the first international Sister Care seminars, held in India and Nepal in the fall of 2012.

The real international flourishing of Sister Care, though, started with a seminar held in Guatemala in February 2013, which about sixty female leaders from across Central America attended. The local organizer for the event was Olga Piedrasanta, who had worked with Heggen previously. "That seminar was such a blessing," Piedrasanta recalled in 2015. "It was like when it's raining, having been a drought, and then the rain falls down and you feel the blessing, and the possibility of all that can happen."[17] Gloria Chacón, who attended from Costa Rica, described the deep thinking that happened in a context of profound emotion. "The training took place amid powerful stories of pain," she said. "It was a healing space for many of us."[18] More than eight hundred copies of the Spanish manual, titled *Cuidándonos entre mujeres* (*Caring between Women*) were distributed for women to use in their contexts. Phyllis Groff, an Eastern Mennonite Missions worker who attended the seminar with two Kekchi indigenous women, was inspired to translate the manual into Kekchi and later distributed three hundred manuals to Kekchi Christians.[19]

At the Guatemala gathering, the women also celebrated the ten-year anniversary of the Movimiento Teólogas Anabautistas Latinoamericanas (MTAL, or the Movement of Latin American Anabaptist Women Theologians). Going forward, Sister Care in Latin America would be closely linked with this network, many of whose members also received support from MW USA's International Women's Fund. A report of the MTAL celebration notes that conversations centered around plans for reproducing the Sister Care workshop "to spread Jesus' liberating message for women."[20]

The key to the spread of Sister Care in Latin America has been its ownership by Latina leaders. This ownership happened sooner than Heggen and Keener may have originally envisioned. Initial plans were for Heggen and another North American woman to lead a second Latin American Sister Care in Chihuahua, Mexico. But the murder of a female Mennonite pastor in the area in late 2012 gave them pause about entering the area as outsiders. So Ofelia García, a Mexican Mennonite pastor, was trained and commissioned as a Sister Care leader at the Guatemala seminar, along with Piedrasanta, and the two women presented the

Participants in a mask exercise in the 2013 Sister Care event in Chihuahua, Mexico.

seminar in Chihuahua in May 2013. That seminar became a space for women to process their grief over lost loved ones—including, for some, their murdered pastor. García and Piedrasanta developed a poignant new exercise for the event in which participants wore masks as they shared about the "masks" they hid behind. Then, one by one, women removed their masks and were affirmed by the group.[21] The mask activity has since been used in other Sister Care seminars.

Ofelia García's creativity and passion for the Sister Care material led her to adapt it for further use in various contexts. She developed a coed children's Sunday school curriculum called *Caring for Each Other in Love* with concrete activities to help children process strong emotions. She also used the Sister Care material in her regular meetings with Mexican women married to Mennonites from Germanic colonies in the region. García trained Anna Giesbrecht, a woman of German descent living in Mexico, who then took Sister Care to a group of Low German–speaking women in rural Chihuahua. In a 2015 interview, Giesbrecht described guiding the women through the material in twelve weekly sessions.[22] She recalled a significant moment related to the group's exploration of the biblical passage where Tamar (King David's daughter) is sexually abused by her brother. A woman came up to her after the discussion, expressing surprise that this was in the Bible. "The same thing happened to me with my brother," she told Giesbrecht. "Well, we cried," said Giesbrecht. "We cried a lot. And I believe there was much healing."[23] García attended the group's closing ceremony. She observed a transformation in Giesbrecht and the women she had worked with, some of whom were playing their musical instruments for the first time in years. "It is incredible to hear what the Lord is doing and the way this workshop has brought them a new outlook," García wrote in an email to Heggen and Keener.[24] Since her first experience leading Sister Care, Giesbrecht has guided 120 more women through the materials, and at their "graduation" ceremony, 240 friends and family celebrated with them.[25]

Mennonite Women USA held another international Sister Care seminar in Colombia in August 2013. It was led by Heggen and Elizabeth Soto Albrecht, a seminary professor of Puerto Rican heritage who had worked in Colombia with Mennonite Central Committee. As with the Guatemala seminar, female leaders from surrounding countries were especially invited, and the gathering doubled as a meeting of MTAL participants from the Andean region.

Soto Albrecht remembered one woman in particular, a Colombian leader who came to the seminar in a very vulnerable physical and mental state. One of the biblical passages explored during the seminar was the story of the four friends who lower their companion through the roof to Jesus (Mark 2:1–12)—in this context, they called the friends the four *amigas*. During a time set aside for prayers for healing, four women who were taking care of the Colombian church leader brought her forward for prayer, and she collapsed into the arms of the leaders. "All of the sudden, what this sister represented for us was all our pains, when churches sometimes use us and abuse us, when we overgive ourselves and we burn out," Soto Albrecht said.[26] As the group prayed for the woman, they could see and feel her liberation. By the time they were finished, she was standing and smiling. "So the narrative of the four amigas came out," Soto Albrecht said. "When we take care of each other, God is there, present."[27] Soto Albrecht's comment captures the integration of service and sisterhood evident at so many Sister Care events. No longer was the Mennonite women's organization solely concerned with serving others or with nurturing sisterhood

Women dramatizing the story of the four friends carrying their friend to Jesus.

in a somewhat closed group. Instead, serving one another as sisters has become a crucial component of Sister Care and of the emerging identity of MW USA.

One of the local organizers of the Colombia seminar was Alix Lozano, director of the Mennonite seminary in Bogotá. At a 2015 gathering of MW USA supporters, Lozano spoke about how Sister Care had developed in her country. Since it was difficult for women to gather for a weekend retreat, churches adapted the material to share on four consecutive Saturdays or in monthly gatherings. In Lozano's church in Bogotá, a group of about sixty women had been meeting bimonthly, drawing in women of other denominations who heard what they were doing and wanted to join. As the group approached the end of the Sister Care materials, they felt the need to continue the process and explore themes particularly relevant to the Colombian context, especially the theme of reconciliation as the country entered a long-awaited peace process. "So Carolyn and Rhoda and others, we're going to go beyond the manual, and we hope that you don't call it to our attention later!" Lozano said with a laugh during a presentation for MW USA.[28]

A November 2013 Sister Care seminar in Bolivia led by Heggen and Keener also drew female church and community leaders, this time from the Southern Cone region. The Bolivian Mennonite women found it meaningful to simply gather together, something they had not done before.[29] At the seminar, they decided to form a women's organization and plan more regular meetings. In March 2014, Sister Care was held in Puerto Rico, a special time for presenters Heggen and Soto Albrecht with their personal connections to the island. Seventy-two women from eight of the ten Puerto Rican Mennonite churches attended the seminar, organized by Eileen Rolón and Mim Godshall. The Puerto Rican women spoke with gratitude about having Mennonite resources written specifically for women. "I really like how Sister Care combines theology and psychology in a practical way," one participant said. "I've not seen that done so well before."[30]Along with the international seminars, Keener and Heggen continued to lead Sister Care in the United States. When 199 women attended a November 2013 seminar in Lancaster, Pennsylvania, it marked both the largest U.S. event and the fact that the seminar had now been held in all twenty-one area conferences of the denomination.[31] MW USA also sought to expand and adapt Sister Care for different groups of women within North America. In 2014, seminars were held specifically for Hmong Mennonite women in Minneapolis and at the Native Mennonite Ministries assembly in Winnipeg.

The Hmong and Native seminars faced particular challenges in participation and communication, yet they proved meaningful. Heggen remembered that at the Hmong gathering, some women shared things they said they had never spoken about before. At this seminar in particular, Heggen saw the value Sister Care provided in having a format for structured sharing, outside leaders to help manage the grief that emerged, and a healing ceremony to bring some resolution.[32] A closing ritual—in which women anoint their own faces with water to represent their tears and compassion for their own suffering, then anoint a partner with water representing Jesus' living water—is an important component of each Sister Care seminar and was especially meaningful for the Hmong women. Carol Roth, a MW USA board member representing Native Mennonite Ministries, attended part of the Winnipeg

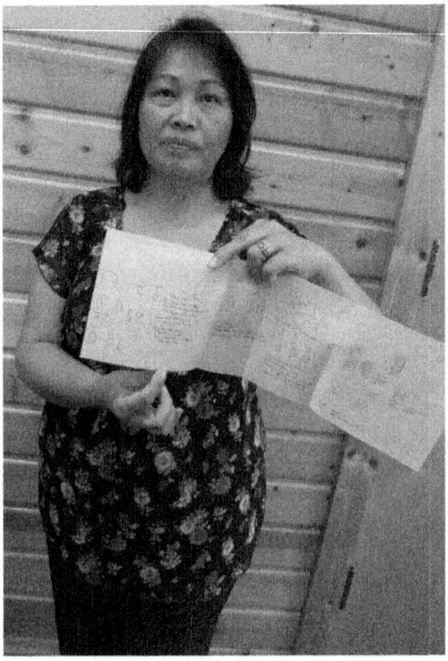

Memee Yang, coordinator of the Hmong Mennonite women in the United States, sharing her life story with the group.

seminar and an earlier Sister Care in Gulf States Mennonite Conference. She sometimes refers to the Sister Care materials when Native women have questions for her, since some of them have attended the seminar as well. Roth recalled once hearing someone say that it doesn't just take a village to raise a child; it takes a *healthy* village to raise a child. "That's where Sister Care comes in," she said, referring to the program's focus on self-healing. "I have to be healthy to raise the rest of the village."[33]

Heggen and Keener led additional international Sister Care seminars in Paraguay and Argentina in August 2014, Trinidad in November 2014, and Brazil in January 2015 (with the manual translated into Portuguese). At a workshop about Sister Care at the 2015 Mennonite World Conference assembly in Harrisburg, Pennsylvania, many Latin American women testified to the ways they have shared the program.[34] Martha Basualdo, a Paraguayan pastor, reported that they had done five more Sister Care trainings in her country. As a member of the board of the Evangelical Mennonite denomination in Paraguay, she hopes to make Sister Care a regular part of the denomination's ministry. "I don't want this to be a side group or something that we will do once in a year," she said. "You have brought something that has brought healing personally but also is bringing healing among churches and congregations." Ester Bornes shared about Argentinian women leading Sister Care trainings in Presbyterian and Baptist churches and at a daycare center for a group that included Catholics and a local officer in Argentina's Women's Department. "We have replicated it, but with something different," she said. "It's going beyond the Mennonite women." Brazilian pastor Deusilene Milhomen spoke about Sister Care seminars she had helped lead in four additional cities since

Heggen and Keener had been to the country just a few months earlier. By the summer of 2015, MW USA (with assistance from Linda Shelly, Mennonite Mission Network director for Latin America) had led eight Sister Care seminars in Latin America for a total of 467 women.[35] Shelly estimated that these women had taught nearly one hundred additional seminars, reaching more than 2,800 participants.[36]

Follow-Up and New Initiatives

The proliferation of Sister Care around the world (especially in Latin America) has brought new energy to MW USA and its supporters, who can follow events in almost real time through social media. Sister Care has not necessarily had the same level of follow-up energy in many U.S. settings, perhaps because of the abundance of materials, workshops, and retreats available in North America. As Heggen has noted, in contexts where people do not have public libraries or money to buy books, having written resources to use oneself and share with others can be a very empowering thing.[37] But North American women have genuinely responded to Sister Care's healing message, and many have found new ways to deepen relationships with one another as they use the materials in Sunday school classes, small groups, and other settings. (See Suzette Shreffler's story in the introduction.)

Mennonite Women USA has initiated conversations about Sister Care presentations for and by African American and Hispanic women in the United States, though there are significant challenges to these efforts. The variety of Hispanic cultures among U.S. Mennonites, the tensions around incorporating women of different cultures into the organization in the past, and the demands on women of color who serve as leaders in multiple contexts have made it difficult for the program to gain traction.[38] Another complicating factor is that Lancaster Conference, which contains a significant portion of the denomination's Hispanic and African American congregations, decided in 2015 to leave the denomination. Even so, in early 2017, several Hispanic Mennonite leaders began plans for presenting a Sister Care seminar in Spanish in the United States. Hyacinth Stevens and Ann Jacobs have planned a Sister Care event specifically for African American women in Elkhart in April 2017, which Stevens will lead. In a 2015 interview, Stevens noted her appreciation for Keener's willingness to let the program be used how other cultures see fit instead of just feeding it to them. "Then we begin to create a healed culture and a culture of healing," Stevens said.[39]

While North American Sister Care seminars may not have quite the same energy as the international events, the materials have been embraced by women from a variety of races, educational backgrounds, and ages. Ivorie Lowe attended two early Sister Care seminars and has been encouraged as she reads about the program's development. "I think what Sister Care is doing is hearing women," she said in a 2015 interview. "That's an important thing."[40] Beth Martin Birky, a Goshen College professor, admitted she was suspicious of Sister Care before she attended but said that "it turned out to be a really powerful interaction with other women."[41] Birky was impressed with how Keener and Heggen subtly integrated potentially controversial issues and approached tough topics through accessible stories.[42]

Birky helped organize a pilot Sister Care seminar for college-aged women at Goshen College in March 2015. Maggie Weaver, a Goshen sophomore who attended, appreciated the space to talk about challenging things, especially when Keener and Heggen allowed the group to veer off schedule for a longer discussion about rape and the college's specific policies around sexual assault.[43] For Weaver, the main benefit of the seminar—besides the homemade food provided by local congregations —was simply having time to connect with others on campus. "The community that blossomed from the weekend was fantastic," she wrote in a reflection on the event. "I was able to connect and have conversations with women that I knew, but may not have had the opportunity to spend as much time with without Sister Care."[44] MW USA executive director Marlene Bogard plans to stress connections with women in the local campus communities as she gives leadership to Sister Care for college students in the future.[45] By bringing in community members to help with the presentation, as Bogard did at the Bethel and Hesston College seminars in early 2016, college women can connect with local congregations and other resources for continued support.

One aspect of Sister Care that both Beth Martin Birky and Ivorie Lowe mentioned was an uncertainty about follow-up from the powerful seminar. In a reflection on her 2009 Sister Care experience, Lowe wrote, "I am left wondering what happened to the wounds that were opened that day. Are they healed? Are they being supported?"[46] Some area conferences have organized follow-up activities. Doris Diener, who served as Southeast Conference's minister of Mennonite women, led four Sister Care extension gatherings after the seminar there in 2011.[47] After a March 2012 Sister Care seminar for women from Eastern District and Franconia Conferences, local women formed a Sistering Committee. They have held an annual day of sharing stories and support; the March 2016 gathering was bilingual and included participants from a Philadelphia church with mostly immigrant members.[48]

After women from Akron (Pa.) Mennonite Church attended Sister Care together in 2014, they organized regular brown bag lunches at different people's homes and a Sunday school class where women shared stories of challenges in their lives.[49] The class grew to more than fifty people. Several other congregations have also started women's Sunday school classes in which participants explore their life timelines or continue sharing deeply together.[50] A twelve-session DVD of the Sister Care seminar was created by Eastern Mennonite University students in 2012 with an accompanying facilitator guide written by Keener and Heggen.

Rose Kennel, Sandie Glunt, and Karel Glunt (left to right) at a Sister Care Level 2 retreat in Pennsylvania in 2015.

Some groups have used the DVD to spend more time on the material in a congregational setting. MW USA has also developed a Sister Care Level 2 retreat for women who want to explore the topics further. The first such gathering was held in Pennsylvania in October 2015; two more are planned for 2017 in Kansas and Illinois.

For many women, attending a Sister Care seminar has simply re-invigorated already existing congregational women's activities. As Flo Harnish put it, "It's the stuff you know you're supposed to do anyway, but you're there with other women talking about it."[51] Nalungo Aduma attended an Ohio Sister Care seminar with several women from her Youngstown church. Aduma said that someone usually visits congregational members in the hospital, but more women think to do this since attending the seminar. Some women have also started meeting once a month with a congregation member who cannot easily leave home because of her husband's illness.[52] "Sister Care" has even entered the informal lexicon in some circles. In June 2015, Shirley Bustos (president of Indiana-Michigan Conference Mennonite Women) said she had recently received an email with the subject line "Sister Care meeting" that called women together to pray for a woman with a tumor.[53]

Sister Care seminars continue in North America and abroad. Additional international seminars took place in Cuba in November 2015, hosted by the Cuban Council of Churches, and in Kenya and Tanzania in April 2016, with women also attending from Uganda, Burkina Faso, and the Democratic Republic of Congo. Future international seminars are being planned for Indonesia, India, Thailand, and Vietnam, as well as an advanced training for Latin American leaders. The Sister Care manual has an international version and has been translated into five languages (French and Swahili in addition to Spanish, Kekchi, and Portuguese). At the time of this writing it is also being translated into Hindi, Indonesian, and Hmong.

Many church agencies and individuals have collaborated with MW USA to support the Sister Care ministry. A substantial grant from the United Service Foundation helped to launch Sister Care, and the foundation also helped to fund the DVD, college initiative, and many of the international seminars. The Schowalter Foundation funded translations of the manual and several cross-cultural and international seminars. Zion Mennonite Church (Souderton, Pa.) provided funds for a Sister Care presence at the 2015 Mennonite World Conference assembly. The Care and Prevention Fund of Mennonite Church USA has contributed to Sister Care, and Mennonite Central Committee has helped with costs to local hosts. In addition to funding, Mennonite Mission Network, Eastern Mennonite Missions, Virginia Mennonite Missions, the Latin American Women Theologians, and the Council of International Anabaptist Ministries' Latin America Committee have all provided invaluable help with understanding the different seminar contexts.[54]

Mennonite Women USA leadership continues to dream about the possibilities for Sister Care. Heggen imagines Sister Care seminars led for widows and for women who find themselves divorced or abandoned, along with initiatives that continue to forge connections with women around the world. One of the most meaningful moments in Heggen's work with Sister Care was an encounter she had with an indigenous woman at the 2013 Bolivia seminar. Though Martha Morales could not read and Spanish was not her first language, Heggen could tell she was very much following the presentation. During a break in the teaching, she pulled Heggen aside and told her about the incredible violence she had experienced, and Heggen shared some of her own story. The two women—one illiterate and one with a PhD—shared a long, intimate hug as their tears mingled. "It's hard to explain why experiences like that touch me, or touch her, so deeply, but somehow those images to me are the core of Sister Care," Heggen said.[55]

Martha Morales (left) and Carolyn Holderread Heggen after the Bolivia Sister Care seminar.

Heggen reflected that women in international contexts want the same things as women in North America. "We want relationship, and we want connections where we can feel safe and we can feel accepted, so that we can be transparent and then be healed," she said. "And we want to learn how to take what we've learned from our own healing journeys and walk with others on their path to healing." Because MW USA has moved in the direction of facilitating healing relationships and connections, especially through Sister Care, Heggen and others see great promise for the vitality of the organization as it continues into the future.

"A Wind Underneath My Wings"

After a term of service in Colombia with her family, Elizabeth Soto Albrecht had returned to United States and was a full-time mom. She was feeling edgy and was wondering what was next for her. She remembers setting her young daughter in front of her on the washing machine as she worked on household chores. Out of nowhere, her daughter asked, "What you do want to be when you grow up?"

"Mommy is already grown up," she replied, "but I wanted to be a doctor."

"You still could," her daughter said. Soto Albrecht was taken aback, and she felt God speaking to her in that moment. She soon decided to enter a doctoral program—in theology.[1]

MW USA was one of several groups that assisted Soto Albrecht in completing a degree in international feminism through San Francisco Theological Seminary. While MW USA's scholarship covered only a small part of her expenses, she felt supported by the denominational women's organization. "Mennonite Women was a type of wind underneath my wings, helping me accomplish what I needed to," she said in a 2015 interview.[2] In 2011, Soto Albrecht was affirmed as moderator-elect of Mennonite Church USA, the first Latina (or any person of Hispanic heritage) to hold the top volunteer position in the denomination. "Because Mennonite Women USA believed in me enough to support my theological education, their investment has helped me turn around and give

Elizabeth Soto Albrecht was affirmed as moderator-elect of Mennonite Church USA in 2011.

it back to the church in the form of ministry and service," she reflected soon after assuming the moderator-elect role.[3]

* * * * *

MW USA has been a wind—or least a gentle breeze—under the wings of many international women leaders. The 2015 Mennonite World Conference (MWC) assembly in Harrisburg, Pennsylvania, revealed how much these women's leadership gifts are being used not only in their congregations and communities but also in the worldwide Anabaptist fellowship. At the time of the 2015 assembly, four women in MWC leadership had received support from MW USA's International Women's Fund at some point: Ofelia García (Mission Commission), Alix Lozano and Rebecca Osiro (Faith and Life Commission), and Sandra Campos (Executive Committee). García and Lozano had also served as presidents of the Mennonite body in their countries (Mexico and Colombia, respectively). At the 2015 assembly, Osiro was commissioned as vice president of Mennonite World Conference.

By the 2010s, the International Women's Fund (IWF) had helped further the education of many female church leaders from Mennonite-related congregations. Speaking from her observations of the Latin American context, Linda Shelly said, "The more that IWF encourages women, the more they are coming forth. And the more they are coming forth, the more opportunities we have to provide not only dollars but the solidarity of spirit that strengthens relationships and connections across the globe as both men and women pursue God's mission together."[4] In a 2015 letter, Willi Hugo Perez, the president of the Anabaptist seminary in Guatemala, said that MW USA's support of women studying theology in Central America has led to more equitable relationships among Mennonites there, where increasing numbers of women were participating in denominational gatherings. "You have helped the women to affirm themselves as daughters of God with dignity, people with rights and opportunities to fulfill themselves," he wrote.[5]

The International Women's Fund has not only been significant for Latina women. In 2013, Nancy Myers and Charlie Malembe talked with several women in the Democratic Republic of the

Congo who had benefited from the fund. "Rev. Mimi Kanku attributes her ordination in 2012 directly to her MW USA scholarship," Myers and Malembe reported in an article posted on the blog of Mennonite Women USA. Though the scholarship did not cover her entire costs, it enabled Kanku to finish her second year of studies, after which she became the first woman ordained in the Evangelical Mennonite Church of Congo. Myers and Malembe also talked with former scholarship recipients Leya Mulobo, who was directing a volunteer exchange program for Congolese Mennonite young people, and Tatiana Mdjoko, who had founded a youth peace education program and was serving as a missionary in Angola.[6]

The fund has aided Asian women as well, such as 2015 recipients Priyanka Bagh (from India) and Jeongih Han (from South Korea), who both studied at Eastern Mennonite Seminary. Han's goal was to become a missionary in North Korea, while Bagh wanted to use her learning in psychology and theology to help women recover from trauma.[7] Priyanka is a second-generation Indian woman theologian; her mother, Rachel Bagh, received IWF assistance for her study at Eastern Mennonite University's Summer Peacebuilding Institute, which enriched her teaching at Union Biblical Seminary in Pune, India.

Many International Women's Fund recipients have been part of networks for Anabaptist women theologians in their regions. African women were the first to organize such a network, which MW USA accompanied through its Sister-Link program (see chapter 9). Inspired by the African women's activities at the 2003 MWC assembly in Zimbabwe, Latina theologians developed their own network, called the Movimiento Teólogas Anabautistas Latinoamericanas (MTAL). The Latin American women defined *theologian* broadly as anyone who reflects theologically and gives leadership in the congregations, not only those who have done formal biblical or theological study. Most of the leaders in this network have received International Women's Fund scholarships or been involved with MW USA's Sister Care seminars, or both. (The MTAL has also been supported by MWC's Global Gifts Sharing Project and other initiatives.)

The Latina network had a significant presence at the 2009 Mennonite World Conference assembly in Paraguay, where it hosted "the first-ever transcontinental gathering of Anabaptist women theologians" before the start of the full convention.[8] Patricia Burdette, MW USA's editor at the time, attended the gathering with about 130 others from Latin America, Africa, and North America. She described it as a "life-changing event" for her personally.[9] Burdette, who had been involved with MW USA for several years and taught at a Mennonite college, wrote, "This was the first time I had heard such strong and accurate words concerning the marginalization of women in the church—wherever it is located."[10] At this gathering, the women developed a declaration that three Latina leaders read from the stage to the full MWC assembly. The statement proclaimed that Anabaptist women and men constitute an interdependent community, and called on women to take church leadership roles.[11] It proposed dialogue that fostered equality, following in the liberating way of Jesus, and rereading the Bible through the eyes of women.[12] Press covering the assembly called it "a bold statement of solidarity with women leaders in the global Mennonite church."[13]

Anabaptist women from Asia noted the activities of the Latina and African women. At the All-India Mennonite Women's Conference in October 2012 (the same gathering where Sister Care was presented), Asian women theologians formed two networks. A network of theologically trained Indian women was initiated by Rachel Bagh, who had shared her dreams for such a group with Rhoda Keener when she was studying in the United States. A broader Asian network (which the Indian women would also participate in) was led by Cynthia Peacock, who had been encouraged in this task by MWC's Deacons Commission. Women from Indonesia, Japan, and Nepal joined the Indian women for the initial gathering. "The birth of these networks is a dream come true for me in working toward empowerment of women," said Elisabeth Kunjam, another former IWF recipient, who would later become coordinator of the Asian network.[14]

The 2015 Mennonite World Conference assembly marked a sort of culmination of the work of these networks as well as

Rachel Bagh (left) and Cynthia Peacock discussing plans at the All-India Mennonite Women Conference in Cuttack, India, 2012.

a potential new beginning. During each day of the weeklong assembly, space was set aside for a different regional grouping of women theologians to gather. At the end of the week, ninety-eight women—mostly North Americans and Latinas, with a handful of Asians, Africans, and Europeans—gathered to explore forming a global network of Anabaptist women theologians. The gathering, initiated by the Latin American theologians with facilitation help from Elizabeth Soto Albrecht, was a rich four hours of singing, conversation, brainstorming, and space to work on a collaborative art project. In an introductory presentation, Alix Lozano brought attention to the need not just for mutual encouragement but also for promoting women's voices within MWC. She had attended the delegate meeting before the assembly, where out of more than one hundred participants, only twelve were women.[15]

Latina leaders brainstorm at the gathering to form a global network of women theologians.

At the gathering, women split into continent groups to discuss whether there was need for a global network of women. As they reported back, each group's yes was met with cheers and murmurs of affirmation from the Latina theologians. North American and European women were not sure about the need for a network of women theologians in their own regions, but they expressed a desire to both share and receive gifts from the global members. Asian and African women came away with a renewed commitment to strengthen their own networks, which had not been meeting regularly, and then work on connecting more with the global body. "We are just beginning, but what we are beginning is something encouraging and real," said Angela Opimí, MTAL co-coordinator, to sum up the gathering. Opimí also recognized Rhoda Keener, noting that "she has accompanied us in many ways." The meeting closed with a ritual in which women passed a candle, representing God's Spirit, to each other and braided together cloths representing the different continents. Olga Piedrasanta, MTAL's other co-coordinator, expressed her satisfaction with the gathering. "We have been dreaming of this day for several years now, and today it has been fulfilled," she said.[16] She reflected further in an email, noting that the network was "a dream that must have a constant and adequate follow-up. If we achieve it, we will have the opportunity to learn from the experiences of each other, to share materials, to fraternize, to share with sisters who want to hear our stories, to pray for each other, to holistically support our problems as women."[17]

* * * * *

The future of a truly functioning global network of Anabaptist women is uncertain. But what was certain at the 2015 gathering was the giftedness of a multitude of women leaders, thinkers, and practitioners. In a program like MW USA's International Women's Fund, the money flows mostly in one direction: from the North American organization and its donors to the recipients in the majority world. But the greatest spiritual blessing perhaps flows the other way: from emerging women theologians, often living and working in extremely challenging contexts, to the rest of the world. Connections between women can be powerful, perhaps especially when women see themselves as both sisters and servants to each other. MW USA, often working with many other organizations, has been a facilitator of such connections for decades. And the organization continues to lift the wings of women as they care for each other in their communities, in their denominations, and in the worldwide church.

11
Local and Regional Activities

> Mennonite women are all ages and belong to many races and ethnic groups. We meet in Bible study groups, during seminars, mission and service groups, one-on-one in friendships, and at retreats. We are women who juggle work, family, and spiritual growth yet seek to be part of faith circles that fit our needs.
> —MW USA website[1]

Homestead Mennonite Church, near the southern tip of Florida, is far from Mennonite Church USA denominational centers. The congregation is small, but its women are vibrant and committed. Their endeavors in recent years give an example of the many activities of contemporary Mennonite women's groups.

Some years ago, the Homestead women hosted a monthly "craft and chat" Saturday event, where people would sew, quilt, paint, or work on other projects. The casual gathering included lunch and a devotional and drew community members. At another point in the church's history, the women held a "mothering" group, meeting weekly with young mothers from nearby migrant camps. A woman with connections in the community brought the mothers, most of them under age eighteen, to the church with their children. Together, the women ate meals, took field trips, celebrated milestones, and discussed childcare skills. The Homestead women helped the young mothers develop better relationships with their children, who were sometimes conceived and raised in very difficult circumstances. "It was a real privilege to work with them, to build relationships, to watch the children grow . . . [and] have them experience church life," said Donna Geib, a Homestead congregant.[2]

Retreats have also been important for the Homestead women. Most recently the group has enjoyed retreats with just the congregation, staying together at a member's lake house with a congregation member as the speaker. Sometimes the group attended Southeast Conference Mennonite Women's retreats as well. Alice Taylor, a leader among the Homestead women, remembers that they would gather a "ragtag" group of thirty or forty women connected with the small congregation and would travel several hours to most retreat locations. They had invigorating conversations on the way and "especially on the way home, because we'd just been inspired," Taylor said.

Debbie Lee, the pastor's wife, has led a weekly Bible study for seven years, which most of the women in the congregation have attended. "I've kind of selfishly kept it all women," she said. "When you have your spouse around or just men, there are certain things you don't say." Some women who do not attend church on Sunday have said that the

Women of Homestead Mennonite Church. Front row (left to right): Vivian O'Haber, Donna Geib, Alice Taylor, and Lorri Cutrer. Back row (left to right): Mary Hess, Debbie Lee, Amy Grimes, and Emma Lee.

Bible study is "church" for them. At age twenty, Debbie's daughter, Emma Lee, finds herself in a "generational gap" in the church. She participates in a young adult group at another church but has also found a place with the Homestead women. "I've been going to retreats, helping my mom, since I was fifteen or sixteen," she said. The women's invitations to participate have helped her become more involved not only with them, but also in the wider congregation and community.

Sometimes the women have staged elaborate events with extravagant decorations and well-orchestrated activities. At an Esther-themed evening, the women watched *One Night with the King* while lounging on Persian rugs, clanking their glasses when the actors did in the movie. In another event, attendees were detectives and went from room to room solving clues. The activities of the group have ebbed and flowed over the years, changing with the energy and interests of those involved. Taylor summed up the group's philosophy: "It has to be fun *and* important. If it's just important, it can be boring. If it's just fun, it's not meaningful."

Southeast Conference Inspiration Day

Homestead Mennonite hosted the 2015 annual Southeast Conference Mennonite Women Fall Inspiration Day. The creative talents of the Homestead women were on display in the colorful decorations, hand-embroidered crosses for each participant, and abundant food at the gathering. Southeast Conference is one of the denomination's most culturally diverse, and women from Hispanic, Anglo, and Garifuna backgrounds attended the event. (The conference also includes several Haitian churches.) The speaker for the day was Alma Perez Ovalle, a high school teacher and Southeast Mennonite Women leader, as well as Iglesia Menonita Hispana's representative on the MW USA board. Ovalle spoke with grounded wisdom from the prophet Micah, and women gathered in smaller groups to share examples of living with humility, love, and justice in their daily lives. The highlight of the day for many was the "prayer for the world" station, an idea borrowed from the recent Mennonite World Conference assembly. A huge world map drawn on two sheets was spread across the floor. Participants were invited to light candles and place them on countries they wanted to pray for. Prayers rang out in Spanish, English, and Garifuna as women

Alma Perez Ovalle leading women in worship at the 2015 Southeast Conference Mennonite Women Fall Inspiration Day.

lifted up their home countries, recent events from the news, or places far away in need of God's healing and peace.[3]

One woman who felt especially blessed by the Inspiration Day was Ovalle's mother, Elizabeth Perez. "I am just thankful that the Lord has opened doors for [my daughter] too as a woman," said Perez, who has served as a leader in the Hispanic women's conference, with her husband in Mathis, Texas, and in her current Sarasota church. Perez said she enjoys the feeling of togetherness among Mennonite women of many cultures in the Florida area.[4]

Elizabeth Perez's thoughts were shared by a group of Garifuna attendees, whose culture incorporates West African, Arawak (indigenous South American), and Hispanic elements. Loretta Dominguez first encountered Mennonites in New York and now copastors a Garifuna Mennonite church in Miami with her husband. For Dominguez, being Mennonite means learning to work with people who look and believe differently. At women's gatherings, everyone's gifts are appreciated, she said. A white woman might organize a sewing project, while Dominguez is asked to bake her signature coconut bread. "That's what I say when people ask me why I'm a Mennonite—I get to love everybody," she said. Blanca Gonzalez, whose aunt pastors a Garifuna

Mennonite church in Honduras, and Paula Suazo, Dominguez's daughter, said they appreciate the real-life, everyday emphasis of Mennonites, something Ovalle also stressed in her input. "We've talked today about being humble," said Suazo. "Sometimes things can be made super-spiritual, up there, extreme." Gonzalez added, "But we're down here, with the actions."[5]

Kathy Smith and Rebecca Zehr, who are part of a church-planting team in Key West, drove several hours to attend the Fall Inspiration Day; Smith also brought her teenage daughter. For Smith and Zehr, who live and minster in a largely post-Christian context, getting together with other Mennonites was a much-needed refreshment. "It's just a treat to be with people who *get* you," they said.[6]

While the Southeast Conference Fall Inspiration Day is unique in the cultural diversity of its participants, these days are a regular event for many regional Mennonite women's groups. Not all the denomination's area conferences have organized women's activities on a regional level. But those that do tend to plan three main events each year: a "day of inspiration"; a gathering, often over a meal, at their area conference's annual assembly; and a weekend retreat, usually at a campground associated with their conference.

Area Conference Retreats

As women's groups have continued to age, many retreat planners have tried to attract younger attendees. Western District and South Central Conferences collaborate for their annual "women and girls retreat," with some separate and some joint activities for the different generations. Indiana-Michigan Conference's 2015 retreat was called "Growing (Up) Together in Christ," and women were encouraged to invite their daughters and granddaughters. Several groups offer free retreat registration to women aged twenty-five and younger.

Area conference women's organizations also face a challenge in the recent splintering of the larger denomination (Mennonite Church USA). In some areas, women are hesitant to participate in anything they see as associated with the denomination. In others, significant numbers of congregations have already left the denomination and conference. This is the case in Gulf States Conference, though some there hope that women's events, which have always been open to people outside the denomination, can continue to involve as many women as possible. In 2015, Edith Michalovic noted that the previous year's retreat and conference quiltmaking event were both well-attended "in spite of all our differences." Michalovic herself has missed only one or two conference women's retreats in forty years, even though she no longer attends a Mennonite congregation.[7]

Black Mennonite Women ROCK

One of the most innovative and well-attended women's retreat in recent years was Central District Conference's 2014 retreat at Camp Friedenswald, planned by Chicago-area churches and called "Black Mennonite Women ROCK." Cynthea Millsaps, who led the planning, was inspired by the Black Entertainment Television (BET) show *Black Girls Rock*, with its message of empowering young black women.[8] The retreat program was intended to attract women of color—who tend to be hesitant about coming to an event at a rural campground—and still be welcoming for the usual white attendees.[9] Millsaps described the event this way: "Black Mennonite Women ROCK seeks to create safe places for uncomfortable conversations to take place between the women of Mennonite Church USA—through the lens of Black Mennonite Women. We are celebrating in a particular style, and all women are welcome!"[10] The event drew many from outside the conference. Of the 150 registrants, a third were women of color, and participants represented a range of ages.[11]

Hyacinth Stevens provided keynote sessions for the Black Mennonite Women ROCK retreat in 2014 in Michigan.

The retreat had typical elements such as worship, workshops, a campfire, and recreation options, but also some new components, such as line dancing, a screening of the documentary *Dark Girls*, and an "Ebony Café" talent show.[12] The featured speaker was Hyacinth Stevens, a pastor in the Bronx, New York, and a member of the MW USA board. She spoke on the complicated connection between Hagar and Sarah in Genesis. "We were challenged to recognize that as women we are all grafted together, we cannot be separated, and need to learn to overcome our discomfort with differences, celebrating our need for each other," wrote Ruth Lapp Guengerich, who attended the event in her role as MW USA coexecutive director.[13]

One significant element of the retreat was a quilt. A colorful quilted spread with images depicting African American history was displayed in the retreat space. The quilt had been made collaboratively by women from Hively Avenue Mennonite, a mostly white congregation in Elkhart, Indiana, and Community Mennonite, a racially diverse congregation in Markham, Illinois. The quilt project, led by Millsaps and Terri Geiser, came from an earlier initiative between the two congregations to promote racial and cultural understanding.[14] At the Black Mennonite Women ROCK retreat, participants created their own quilt squares representing their identity. Having a quilt feature prominently at the retreat was a powerful way to signal the event's connection to and expansion of traditional Mennonite gatherings. While quilting may be viewed as a white Mennonite practice, there is also a long and important history of African American quiltmaking, as Carolyn Mazloomi, founder of the Women of Color Quilters Network, has brought to light.[15] The potential for mutually inspiring interactions through cross-cultural quilt projects or retreats like Black Mennonite Women ROCK makes these efforts models for Mennonite women's groups to consider for the future.

Congregational Mennonite Women's Activities

Mennonite women continue to find freedom and meaningful connection not just in regional events but also in their local church groups. Congregational women's groups face similar challenges to those faced by regional and denomination organizations: the busyness of today's society, the broad interests among women of different ages and backgrounds, and dwindling participation in church in general. But stable women's groups still exist in many congregations. A glimpse into a few of these groups and their activities offers a window into the variety of contemporary Mennonite women's groups at the local level.

Bethel College Mennonite Church

The women's organization at Bethel College Mennonite Church (North Newton, Kans.) has a unique way of organizing its participants. Starting in 1964, the names of all the women in the congregation were written down and divided into eight separate smaller groups, which the women remained in for two years before assignments were rearranged. The process continues today, though most of the women involved are near or at retirement age and are now organized into five groups. These smaller groups have five meetings during the year using MW USA's Bible Study Guide; at other monthly meetings the groups unite for a speaker or special program. These groups of women are also the congregation's means of providing food at funerals and contacting people who are ill. Carol Peters, a Bethel College Mennonite Church member, thinks that women's activities at the congregation have stayed strong because the women get to know and appreciate so many congregation members as the groups reshuffle.[16]

Weavers Mennonite Church

Some congregational groups have continued sewing as their main activity, creating quilts for MCC relief sales and material aid for the local community. Women at Weavers Mennonite Church (Harrisonburg, Va.) regularly meet to quilt and make comforters as well as to share devotions using MW USA materials and engage in supportive conversations. In a 2015 interview, Edith Shenk Kuhns recalled that the congregation had recently received a call from the local immigration support network; the network was anticipating a group of forty individuals and needed a single-bed blanket for each person. The sewing group had that many comforters prepared, so they donated them. Kuhns said she can imagine why some might dismiss sewing circles as gossipy groups or a kind of undermining activity. "But I've not experienced that," she said. "It's always upbuilding and encouraging and just really helpful to be able to share together."[17]

Springdale Mennonite Church

Springdale Mennonite Church (Waynesboro, Va.) has also kept alive a sewing tradition that goes back to 1935. Meeting monthly, the group mostly works on quilts for the Virginia Relief Sale. A 2015 video on a local news website shows the women stitching with intense concentration but also telling jokes as they work. "We come because we like to sew and we like to be together," Sharon Shenk said in an accompanying article. "But we also do it because we love Jesus. It's a way for us to raise money to feed people around the world."[18] Shenk's comments articulate the dual purpose that Mennonite women's groups continue to have—giving women an outlet to serve others and to participate in an enjoyable activity for themselves. In a 2015 interview, Shenk mentioned another role of their group: it is a place where some newcomers can fit into congregational life. One newly retired woman who had just started attending the church joined the group and was already volunteering to bring things. "She doesn't have to know deep theology or singing in four parts," Shenk said. "It's a great way for her to connect."[19]

Calvary Community Church

Some Mennonite Church USA congregations with thriving women's ministries have little connection to traditional Mennonite activities or to the denominational women's organization. One outstanding example is Calvary Community Church, a large African American congregation in Hampton, Virginia. The church's size (more than twelve hundred members) enables it to run a variety of initiatives. Women of Worth and Worship is a program for mentoring and spiritual growth led by pastor Natalie Francisco. A cohort of women, including international participants who partake via online streaming, work closely with Francisco for several months. Women of Worth and Worship also runs a conference that sometimes takes place on a cruise ship, with workshops on women's everyday concerns and timely biblical topics and vendors offering Christian-themed products. Calvary also offers Women's Fellowship, a monthly gathering of women and girls of all ages for worship and sharing. This group hosts an annual mother-daughter banquet, a formal affair in which male congregation members serve as waiters and parking attendants. Ticket sales fund a scholarship for a congregation member preparing to attend college.[20]

Several years ago, Alicia Manning, a leader in Calvary's singles ministry, started a program called My Sister's Keeper. In a 2015 interview, Manning said the program seeks to address things women experience and need to talk about but may not know how to.[21] Manning planned target conversations around those subjects with teaching from one of the congregation's female ministers. The events were initially evening discussions, but Manning couldn't get people to leave. "People are hungry to have the conversation," she said. "Once they open up, they don't want to be abrupt about shutting down."[22] So the conversations became Friday to Saturday gatherings at someone's home. During the Friday evening session, Manning shares case studies with the group, and a minister presents a biblical perspective. Women talk with partners about how the issue relates to their lives. The women have dinner together and fellowship into the night, and on Saturday morning they do a community service project or recreation activity together. My Sister's Keeper has some interesting parallels to Mennonite Women USA's Sister Care ministry.

Bethesda Mennonite Church

A more traditional Mennonite women's group story comes from Bethesda Mennonite Church in Henderson, Nebraska. The long history of the women's organization in this congregation includes many of the activities and trends mentioned throughout this book. A women's group at Bethesda was first organized in 1898 with nineteen members. Early minutes record that one meeting started late because the group was waiting for the pastor to arrive to open the meeting with prayer, a story later women's group members found incredible. This original group purchased fabric and sewing supplies to make and mend clothing items and took additional offerings. Contributions were first sent to Africa, then (in the 1920s) to "Kinder in Russland" (children in Russia), then to Native Americans in Oklahoma and Arizona. By the 1930s, the group, then comprising about forty members, had started subscribing to *Missionary News and Notes* and connecting with Northern District Conference.[23]

In 1949 a second group started, called Young Women's Fellowship, with seventy-seven members. A local church "relief sale" began, and the women created many sewn items for the sale, some of which drew fierce bidding competition. In 1952 the younger group divided into two groups, known as Mission Circle II and Mission Circle III. Circle III had the youngest women, who "reminisce about taking their babies in infant seats, toddlers entertaining babies, and preschoolers running

Women working on projects at Bethesda Mennonite Church in Nebraska.

'to and fro' at Mission Circle meetings." Circle III developed more of a focus on personal relationships than on work projects.

For the next fifty or so years, work continued in three mission circles roughly grouped by age. In 2005, Circle I had sixty-four members, with nineteen "honorary members" who could no longer attend meetings. In 2004, this group of elderly women contributed $8,000 to mission work. The attendance of all three groups dwindled, as it did in the congregation overall, in the early 2000s. In 2011, the women started meeting in one group as they first had done more than one hundred years earlier. They took the name Bethesda Women's Ministries and adopted the mission and vision statement of MW USA and collected regular donations for the denominational organization and their subscriptions to *Timbrel* magazine.

The Bethesda's women's group continues to meet on the first Tuesday of each month with about fifty women attending. They use MW USA's annual Bible Study Guide, with a different woman presenting each month and incorporating her personal experience into the material. Guest speakers, often from the congregation, also share about their work with a community-based organization loosely related to the month's topic. The group also has two special programs, one in the spring and one in December, as well as six all-day sewing meetings during the winter months. In 2016, these work days produced ninety-four comforters for local needs and Mennonite Central Committee.

The reflections of group member Kathy Friesen on the history of Bethesda Mennonite women can speak for many existing congregational Mennonite women's groups: "Much has changed in the way women support the work of the church, yet much is the same, as we gather for a time of learning, sharing, fellowship around the table, and serving the needs here in our local community and that of the global Mennonite Church."

12
Future Directions for Mennonite Women's Groups

> I wanted greater connection with women—Mennonite women, spiritual women, professional women, smart women, and social justice-minded women. MW USA gave me that connected feeling. I have a home here.
> —Karen Wiens[1]

Several themes have emerged on this journey through one hundred years of Mennonite women's organizations. One theme, of course, is the dual purpose of Mennonite women's groups. As we have seen throughout these pages, women's groups have enabled their members to reach outward as they contribute to worldwide missions, offer tangible service to others, engage in evangelism, and strengthen local churches. Women's groups have also helped members develop bonds of sisterhood by providing places for women to connect with others socially, receive encouragement, worship in unique ways, and exercise gifts as spiritual leaders.

Not everyone, including some women previously involved in leadership of the denominational organizations, believes that church women's groups will or should exist in the future. Gloria Neufeld Redekop's 1989 study of Canadian Mennonite women's groups concluded that the groups were so important because they functioned as "parallel churches" for those involved.[2] With many more women participating in the "regular" church over the past few decades, women's groups no longer have quite the same function, even if they are mostly doing the same things. In many congregations, projects traditionally viewed as "women's projects," such as certain missions offerings or assembling school kits for Mennonite Central Committee, now involve the full church—which, as former Women in Mission coordinator Joan Wiebe said, is probably healthier for everyone.[3]

Service and Sisterhood

But for many women, having a denominational organization is still crucial. For some, the long-standing service orientation of church women's groups is the key to why they continue. "Are women's groups still useful?" reflected Pauline Toews in a 2014 interview. "Certainly! They do the drudge work no one else will do."[4] Christine Scheffel said that the hardworking sewing circle at her Oklahoma congregation may "fade into oblivion" in the next few years, but the women will continue to be involved in doing things for others.[5] "There will always be a need and always some women who will fill that need," she said. Scheffel noted that serving others is the purpose of not only the women's organization but also "the commission of the Christian."[6]

For some, a women's organization is valuable because of the continued need for women to support each other. Bek Linsenmeyer said that she has seen signs in many churches that people "still have a hard time embracing the legitimacy of women having a voice."[7] Women's gatherings can build bridges between church members and empower individuals. "It takes a lot of affirmation for people to be willing to start their journey, to be all they could be," Linsenmeyer said.[8] Although things are different from when Mim Book started in church leadership in the 1980s, as a female pastor she still encounters unique challenges that are helpful to talk about with other women. "Mennonite Women helps us to encourage each other, remember our foremothers, and stand on their shoulders," she said.[9] "I think it's awesome that we have a women's association," said Maggie Weaver, who first interacted with MW USA when she attended the 2015 Goshen College Sister Care seminar.[10] Weaver sees value in the organization's ability to bring awareness to women's issues and provide safe space to talk about them.

Some women also name the significance of the spiritual aspect of the women's organization. Dorothy Shank, who oversaw the spiritual dimension of the organization in her role as WMSC vice president, is "so happy" with what she sees MW USA, especially Sister Care, doing. "I think that's getting back to . . . the spiritual care and the spiritual formation of women, and the importance that carries in the Mennonite Church," she said.[11] Marlene Bogard, who was hired as MW USA executive director in 2015, has an interest in faith formation and wants to make resources about creative spiritual practices available to congregations. Her vision is that existing women's groups continue their service orientation but have it "coupled very strongly with a Christian formation aspect."[12]

The dual purpose of Mennonite women's groups—service to others and development of an empowering sisterhood—will be important if such groups are to thrive in the future. In today's atmosphere, different aspects of a faithful life can easily become dichotomized, whether within congregations or individuals. People of all ages are seeking ways to authentically hold together service and spirituality, action and prayer, an orientation toward others and an appreciation of self-care. Women's groups may be one place where these seemingly separate streams of faithfulness can converge.

Marlene Bogard, hired as MW USA executive director in 2015, speaking at the Mennonite Women of Virginia retreat in October 2016.

Cultural Groups

A second theme that emerged during this study, particularly in the history of the last fifty years, is the presence of various cultural groups within, on the fringes of, and outside the denominational women's organizations. Attention to Mennonites from a variety of backgrounds will continue to be important in the future. Conrad Kanagy's 2006 study of Mennonite Church USA revealed that membership in the denomination overall was aging and declining, but that "racial/ethnic" members were younger and increasing in numbers.[13] Kanagy concluded that finding ways to cross racial and ethnic boundaries was "perhaps the most important challenge and opportunity facing the denomination."[14] As the denomination and the country in general become more diverse, MW USA's sentiment that all women in Mennonite churches are Mennonite Women will need to include an increasingly diverse constituency.

The authentic engagement of various cultural groups has sometimes been a challenge for the Mennonite women's organization, as it has for the denomination overall. Hyacinth Stevens remembers walking past the Mennonite Women dinner at previous denominational assemblies and seeing no women of color, many women with head coverings, and quilts hanging on the walls. "Even though it said 'Mennonite Women,' my assumption was that I must not be one," Stevens said.[15] Stevens now serves as the African American Mennonite Association representative to MW USA's board and has sensed among board members "the desire for the lines to come down and be part of a sisterhood."[16] In 2015, Stevens wrote an article directed toward black Mennonite women titled "We Help Make the Circle Complete." Stevens wrote about using MW USA's 2013 Bible Study Guide (*Courageous Women of the Bible* by Linda Gehman Peachey) as the basis for a conference call-in meeting tailored to the busy lives of women in (and beyond) New York City. She also described the "healing, resourceful, empowering, and applicable" Sister Care materials, which she experienced at a 2013 seminar.[17] Stevens invited black women "not just to utilize resources but to contribute our voice, our hands, and culture to the circle of global impact Mennonite Women USA desires to have."[18]

Maria Tijerina, a former Iglesia Menonita Hispana representative to the MW USA board, also recalled some struggles in her role. In the past, she felt like "a minority, not fully part" of the organization and sensed that people had outdated views of Hispanic women.[19] "But the women on the board now are beautiful women," Tijerina said in a 2015 interview. "They're leaving that concept."[20] When Carol Roth, a Native Mennonite Ministries staff member of Choctaw heritage, was asked about appointing a Native representative to the MW USA board, she was unsure about the organization and wondered why previous Native representatives had only stayed for one or two meetings. "So I got in there and realized now that it is important," she said.[21] In a 2015 interview with *The Mennonite*, Roth listed former MW USA codirectors Ruth Lapp Guengerich and Rhoda Keener as some of her faith mentors.[22] Roth enjoys helping the women's organization change and grow through her presence on the board. If she had not been there, "I think the Native women would be left out," she said.[23]

At the prompting of Roth, Stevens, and Alma Ovalle (current Iglesia Menonita Hispana representative), MW USA is reevaluating its system of having one designated person on the board for each of the denomination's organized cultural groups. The board is considering how to use women's gifts in a variety of positions while still ensuring that different backgrounds are represented. MW USA leadership has also thought about groups that have not had a voice in the organization. Sue Park-Hur, a Korean American Mennonite from California, was asked to join the board but declined because she was unfamiliar with the organization and felt her gifts would be best used in other ways. In a 2016 interview, Park-Hur expressed a hope that MW USA would go and engage immigrant churches rather than simply send resources or ask people to come to the organization.[24] This, of course, is a challenge for an organization with a small staff and budget that seeks to minister to women across the entire country.

Park-Hur is one of several women who have noted the seeming discrepancy between MW USA's vibrant international connections and its work with women of different cultures in the United States.[25] "I know they do a lot of international ministry, but how about the immigrant churches here?" she asked.[26] Aveani Moeljono noted that the language barrier is the biggest challenge to the engagement of Indonesian American Mennonites, the denomination's largest Asian group.[27] Some of these congregations maintain strong connections with Mennonite denominations in Indonesia, so they may not necessarily experience a great need for the support of Mennonite Church USA or its women's organization. Still, Indonesian Mennonites are engaging in activities that could easily connect with MW USA's interests, such as women's Bible studies, women's worship services, and a "Mother, Daughter, and Friends" banquet with proceeds going to combat human trafficking.

For many Mennonite women of color, finding the support they need happens mostly in informal ways. For example, Erica Littlewolf, who works for Mennonite Central Committee's Indigenous Visioning Circle, said she often gathers for dinner or side conversations with other women of color at larger denominational conferences.[28] Littlewolf said that the women who influenced her as she grew up in a Northern Cheyenne (Tsitsistas) Mennonite context impressed her not so much with the organized things they did but through their humble, faithful way of being. "I think it's because it's the way they *are* that they don't get recognized," she said.[29] Littlewolf's reflections suggest that there may be ways MW USA could recognize and support the informal mentoring that happens among Mennonite women of color.

Relevance through Changing Times

A third theme that weaves its way throughout this history is the desire for the women's organization to be relevant for women of all ages in a changing world. Bogard is currently leading a discernment process with the MW USA board related to intentional mentoring relationships, an attempt to respond to the needs of women from older and younger generations. "For younger women, it might be the need to be listened to, prayed for, to connect to the wisdom of older women," Bogard said. "For the elders, it might be finding a way to pass on meaningful traditions, skills, and discovering a new purpose as formal women's groups disband." Bogard hopes a mentoring initiative could connect with and expand specific areas of Sister Care and provide even more practical resources for women.[30]

In Bogard's explanation of her mentoring idea in the Autumn 2015 issue of *Timbrel*, she described two realities: the rise in "spiritual but not religious" or "unaffiliated and uninterested" young adults, on the one hand, and declining participation in or floundering purpose of congregational women's groups, on the other.[31] It is not clear yet if or how the mentoring concept will take root among Mennonite women. But it is clear that new ideas are needed in today's context of "nones and dones"—people who mark "none" on surveys about religious affiliation or who say they are "done" with religion.[32] These new ideas may be able to draw on the long-standing structure that church women's groups provide.

Terri Plank Brenneman, who has continued working with women since her time leading the Women's Missionary and Service Commission board, said she continually hears people wanting contemplative space, especially in a Mennonite denomination that has often focused more on work and information. Younger people seem especially drawn to rituals and visuals. Mennonite Women always had a bit of that, Brenneman said, and the women's organization has been more open and engaging of art than the denomination as a whole, even if it was primarily the "accepted" art of quilting.[33] If tangible and artistic expressions of faith have flourished among Mennonite women's groups, as Brenneman suggests, it's possible that women's groups can help church members embrace a more experiential worship style that is more inviting to younger participants and to those on the fringes of church life.

Sue Park-Hur said that she often cautions Mennonites not to lose their distinctiveness in their effort to be relevant and inclusive. "We've grafted ourselves to the Mennonite community because you have something to offer," she said.[34] In her opinion, the cooking, the creating, the peacemaking, the "radical hospitality" should all continue but it doesn't always have to be German food or a certain kind of quilting. "How do we bring different pieces of life together and sit together and create something beautiful together?" she asked. "That's a value Mennonites have. It's deeper than making a quilt."[35] Rhoda Keener has articulated a similar idea as she leads Sister Care seminars. At the 2015 seminar in Lombard, Illinois, she noted that in previous generations the sewing circle or quilting frame may have been the perfect medium. "They're doing something worthwhile, something beautiful, something creative," she said. "And they have time to talk and share with each other." Then she asked, "What's the medium for 2015?"[36] For some Mennonite women, the medium for 2015 and beyond is sharing stories of loss and healing around the table at a Sister Care seminar or in a follow-up Sunday school class. For some, it may be in mentoring relationships, where women of different generations engage in service activities and faith formation together. For some, it may still be around the quilt frame—though they may find themselves piecing quilts with Choctaw colors or depicting scenes from African American history or inviting a new immigrant family in their neighborhood to join their work.

This third theme of Mennonite women's organizations includes not only staying relevant in a changing world but also dealing with realities in the wider denomination. As with broader church-related happenings, such as the beginnings of the mission movement, the fundamentalist-modernist debates, the Civilian Public Service program, and the growing acceptance of women pastors, the activities and issues in today's Mennonite Church USA closely affect the women's organization. In the fall of 2015, Lancaster Mennonite Conference voted to leave Mennonite Church USA over concerns about LGBT inclusion, scriptural interpretation, church authority, and other related topics. While Lancaster was the largest conference to announce a departure, it was not the only one. As of early 2016, North Central and Franklin Conferences had also decided to leave, and additional conferences have lost many of their congregations.

Some who are affiliated with Mennonite Women USA would like to do more to reach out to LGBT Mennonites, while others want the organization to uphold traditional understandings of Scripture and sexuality. There is great variety politically, socially, and theologically across and within area conferences and local congregations, and women with diverse perspectives and experiences are involved in congregational women's groups. Lesbian Mennonite women, though, tend to connect with more recently formed advocacy groups, such as Pink Menno and the Brethren Mennonite Council for LGBT Interests, rather than with congregational women's groups or the denominational women's organization. For some, MW USA's connection with Mennonite Church USA is problematic because they see the denomination as slow-moving and unaccepting. However, other women are hesitant about the organization's affiliation because they are troubled by what they see as the denomination's movement in a more open direction.

In October 2015, amid the uncertainty in the denomination, Bogard and Kathy Bilderback (MW USA board chair) released a statement that made it clear that MW USA is a constituency group of Mennonite Church USA, which means the organization is strongly affiliated with the denomination and collaborates with it, but does not receive funding from it. Bogard and Bilderback acknowledged the great diversity of views and the strong emotions around this topic. They concluded:

> We will continue to offer seminars, events, conferences, and retreats that offer encouragement, faith formation, and training in care and compassion. Our publications will continue to be centered in Christian Anabaptist faith, with a clear leaning toward the empowerment of women. We will make all our ministries, publications, and staff available to all who are interested, regardless of their membership in Mennonite Church USA member churches. We remain strongly committed to affiliating with Mennonite Church USA, and we strive to support and empower all women who identify themselves as Mennonites worldwide. . . . Mennonite Women all across the United States, please know: *you always have a home with our organization. We remain committed to you!*[37]

The statement was read in its entirety at several gatherings of Mennonite women in the subsequent months. For some women, it offered a sense of hope that relationships forged across congregations, conferences, and global contexts could continue.[38]

Elaine Maust is a pastor in Gulf States Conference, which has lost most of its congregations in recent years. For Maust, it is hard to tell what the future holds for the denomination and for society in general as religious institutions crumble. With this context in mind, Maust said she has no idea what will happen to women's groups. Or, she wondered, "Are small nuclear community-type organizations like the women's group going to be the way we head?"[39] Maust noted that throughout history, women have always found ways to be together, whether through washing clothes, grinding corn into flour, or helping to raise each other's children. Claire DeBerg also commented on women's need for each other, which has continued to express itself throughout many eras. "I honestly think if MW USA went away something else would grow and bloom," she said.[40] Women are looking for ways to care for each other, which programs like Sister Care address. "There's a hole there and they're filling that hole," DeBerg said.[41]

Throughout their history, Mennonite women have sought to make connections—between sewing circles and missionaries, through inter-Mennonite and ecumenical efforts, between North Americans and women theologians on other continents, among different women in the same congregation, and between individual women and God. The denominational women's organization has been an important facilitator of these connections. Even (and perhaps especially) today, many Mennonite women articulate the need to cultivate relationships with women of different ages, races, educational backgrounds, sexual orientations, and theological affinities. The sense of connectedness among women of faith inspires Bogard's work with MW USA. "I love being with women who are connected to Christ's church, because we are serving the same God, we are listening to the same Spirit, and we are empowered by Christ's life together," she said in a 2016 interview. "I like being with Mennonite women because I think we 'get' each other," she continued. "It's my sisterhood."[42] Rhoda Keener, now the director of Sister Care, often thinks about the three parts of MW USA's vision statement—connecting globally, providing resources, and speaking prophetically. Those simply stated but profound tasks are "the reason we need to exist for another one hundred years," she said.[43]

Time will tell if a denominational Mennonite women's organization will last another hundred years. Clearly, much will change in church, society, and the world during those years, just as much has changed since the formation of the first Mennonite women's organizations around 1917. But it seems likely that the desire for women to serve others and form bonds of sisterhood among themselves will remain. As long as women continue to seek connections with God and with each other, they will form circles of sisterhood, strengthening their own faith while reaching out to the world.

Epilogue

I came to this project at what felt like a time of crisis in the denomination and, to some extent, in Christianity. Mennonite Church USA was coming apart, it seemed, over irreconcilable differences in its members' views of sexuality, church polity, and other issues. News reports and surveys showed fewer and fewer people were attending church or claiming a religious faith. Like many people of my generation, I have often found myself disillusioned with the Mennonite church in particular and the Christian church in general. But then I spent the better part of two years researching and crafting this history. Hearing the stories of women who have participated in church-related efforts for sixty, seventy, or eighty years gave me hope. Their faithfulness, honesty, courage, and humor have helped me want to stay in and contribute to this broken, beloved denomination and the larger Christian body.

A special highlight during my research for this project was attending the 2015 Mennonite World Conference assembly in Harrisburg, Pennsylvania. I was inspired by the gathering on the last day of the assembly that explored forming a global network of women theologians. As someone with a theology degree myself, I was amazed to consider what it must be like to be a female seminary professor in Guatemala, a woman studying theology in Zambia, or the only female pastor in an entire Paraguayan denomination. An email I received later from Olga Piedrasanta, one of the conveners of the gathering, ended with this line: "Eres bienvenida al Movimiento" (You are welcome to the Movement). Something felt so right about being welcomed to an ongoing movement of faithfulness, struggle, and joy by an Anabaptist woman from a different culture, context, and generation. I am not sure how this global network will unfold, but I know I want to be part of it.

After all this work, I am left with an impression of the need for women to tell their stories. While several collections of Mennonite women's stories are available, and recently written histories give more attention to women, it is astonishing how few women appear in Mennonite history books, articles, and archival material—especially women of color. We need to hear stories from old women and young women; red, brown, yellow, black, and white women; conservative, liberal, and centrist women; lesbian, bisexual, and transgender women; women with PhDs and women with the wisdom that comes from living on the streets. We need stories of women who are mothers, grandmothers, stepmothers, and foster mothers; women who are widowed and divorced and child-free.

God works through women. This has always been recognized. Even in the earliest debates about women's roles in the church, it was clear that salvation came to women and men, that God's Spirit was "no respecter of persons" (Acts 10:34 KJV), including their gender. God will keep working even as organizations and denominational structures change and perhaps fade away. So, Mennonite women, tell your stories—because they are part of God's story. And that's a story we need to hear over and over again.

Relevant Organizations and Their Abbreviations

AAMA African American Mennonite Association, organization of African American and integrated MC USA congregations

AAWT African Anabaptist Women Theologians

AMBS Anabaptist (formerly "Associated") Mennonite Biblical Seminary, formed from merger of Mennonite Biblical Seminary (GCMC) and Goshen Biblical Seminary (MC) in 1958

BPW Business and Professional Women, a wing of the MC women's organization

CHM Commission on Home Ministries (GCMC)

CMC Conference of Mennonites in Canada, formed in 1952 with GCMC and MC churches

COE Commission on Education (GCMC)

COM Commission on Overseas Ministries (GCMC)

CPS Civilian Public Service, program of historic peace churches for alternative to military service during World War II

GCMC General Conference Mennonite Church, organized in 1860, many members of Russian Mennonite background, met in triennial assemblies

IMH Iglesia Menonita Hispana, organization of Hispanic MC USA congregations

IWF International Women's Fund, a ministry of Mennonite Women USA

MBMC Mennonite Board of Mission and Charities, later MBM Mennonite Board of Missions (MC)

MC "Old" Mennonite Church, first area conferences formed in 1700s, congregations mostly of Swiss-German Mennonite background, met in biennial assemblies starting in 1898

MC USA Mennonite Church USA, formed in 2002 merger of joint MC and GCMC denominations, minus Canadian congregations

MCC Mennonite Central Committee, inter-Anabaptist relief and service organization

MTAL Movimiento de Teólogas Anabautistas Latinoamericanas (Movement of Latin American Anabaptist Women Theologians)

MW Mennonite Women, joint MC/GCMC and U.S./Canada women's organization starting in 1997

MW USA Mennonite Women USA, women's organization of MC USA, 2003–present

MWC Mennonite World Conference, fellowship of worldwide Anabaptist groups, assembles every six years

MWMS Mennonite Women's Missionary Society, MC women's organization starting ca. 1916

WLP Women in Leadership Project, housed under MC USA Executive Board

WM Women in Mission, GCMC women's organization starting 1974

WMA Women's Missionary Association, GCMC women's organization starting ca. 1917

WMSA Women's Missionary and Service Auxiliary, MC women's organization starting 1954

WMSC Women's Missionary and Service Commission, MC women's organization starting 1971

WMSO Women's Missionary and Sewing Circle Organization, MC women's organization starting 1947

Timeline

Key:

* MC women's organizations
† GCMC women's organizations
‡ Mennonite Women
§ Mennonite Women USA, Sister Care

1860s–onward: Great Awakening spurs "quickening" among Mennonites

1860: General Conference Mennonite Church (GCMC) organized out of Mennonite Church (MC)

1868: Wadsworth Institute opens (GCMC), local women's societies furnish bedding and linens †

1870s–onward: Denominational women's mission organizations form in many denominations

1872: Foreign Mission Board (GCMC) is created

1880s–onward: Many local women's mission groups form in Mennonite contexts

1880: GCMC begins mission work among Native Americans

1885: GCMC starts publishing *The Mennonite* periodical

1890s–1920s: Progressive Era; "first-wave" feminism

1890s–onward: Women in charge of evening mission programs at regional and denominational assemblies †

1893: MC's first home mission opens in Chicago

1894: Elkhart Institute opens (MC)

1894: First printed record of contributions to MC missions from "sisters" (from Amish Mennonite church in Holden, Mo.) *

1895–96(?): Earliest Mennonite *Nähverein* (sewing circle) organized in Canada (Gretna, Man.) †

1898: MC starts gathering for biennial "General Conference" assembly

1899: MC begins overseas mission work in India; GCMC begins work there in 1900

1900–onward: Congregations across United States and Canada continue to form sewing circles and "sisters" groups; Middle District reports a women's mission society in every church in 1900 †

1903: Conference of Mennonites in Central Canada forms (becomes Conference of Mennonites in Canada in 1952)

1906: Mennonite Board of Mission and Charities organizes (MC)

1908: MC starts publishing *Gospel Herald* as merger of *Gospel Witness* and *Herald of Truth*

1909: GCMC city missions begin

1911: Associated Sewing Circles of Lancaster Conference forms *

1911: Clara Eby Steiner begins visiting and corresponding with local women's groups *

August 1915: First general meeting of sewing circle women held at MC assembly *

August 1916: Three officers elected at general sewing circle meeting *

April 1917: United States enters World War I

August 1917: District representatives elected at general meeting *

August 1917: At GCMC triennial assembly, women elect executive committee to organize sewing and mission societies, becomes known as the Women's Missionary Association (WMA) †

March 1919: Steiner starts regular newsletter, encourages groups to send in reports *

1920s and earlier: District associations are organized in United States †

1920s: Fundamentalist-modernist controversy in many denominations; conservative/liberal tension especially in MC, dress codes strictly enforced

1920: Nineteenth Amendment grants U.S. women the right to vote; granted in Canada in 1918

1920: Women push mission board for formal recognition, finally see reference to a "new GC women's organization" †

1920: Famine in Ukraine, migration of Mennonites to Canada (through 1940s); Mennonite Central Committee (MCC) begins

March 1921: Mennonite Women's Missionary Society (MWMS) has twelve regional branches, 131 societies, 3,721 members *

June 1921: Newsletter named *Monthly Letter* *

1924: MWMS issues *Booklet of Prayer for Missions of the Mennonite Church* *

1926: Resolutions passed to issue monthly letter and establish literature committee †

March 1926: *Gospel Herald* says that mission board has appointed committee in charge of sewing circle work; MWMS continues promoting missions amid confusion *

October 1926: *Missionary News & Notes* begins publication (in English and German) †

1929: MWMS issues final report transferring funds to mission board committee *

1929: WMA writes constitution and bylaws †

October 1929: Start of Great Depression

July 1930: *Missionary Sewing Circle Letter* begins circulation *

1930: First "Prayer Cycles" appears †

1933: Secretary of Junior and Intermediate Girls' societies appointed †

1933: "The General Sewing Circle Committee of the MBMC" name appears *

1935: WMA partially adopts Incapacitated Missionaries' Fund from mission board, members are asked to contribute "two cents a week and a prayer" for missionary pensions †

Late 1930s–1940s: Canadian provincial groups organize †

1940s–50s: "Golden age" for Mennonite women's societies

December 1941: United States enters World War II

1941–45: Many Mennonites do Civilian Public Service as alternative to military service; women's groups provide clothing, food, and other aid

1941: GCMC, Central Conference, Defenseless Mennonites form United Mennonite Women's Service Committee, place workers in migrant camps †

1941: Church Women United forms (group of denominational women's organizations connected with National Council of Churches)

1945: Mennonite Men (GCMC) organizes on denominational level

1947: WMA gets office and employee, has a budget for the first time, joins Congo Inland Mission Ladies' Auxiliary (becomes Africa Inter-Mennonite Mission in 1972) †

1947: Name change to Women's Missionary and Sewing Circle Organization (WMSO) *

1948: Mennonite Youth Fellowship organized (MC)

1950: Ruth Brunk Stoltzfus starts *Heart to Heart* radio broadcast for women

1950: MC committee says women can serve on church boards but not have chief executive or administrative responsibilities

1950: GCMC constitution revised, WMA identifies as an "auxiliary" to GCMC †

1952: Conference of Mennonites in Canada WMA organizes formally †

1954: Name change to Women's Missionary and Service Auxiliary (WMSA), publication changes name to *Women's Missionary and Service Monthly* *

1955–56: MC and GCMC declare racial discrimination contrary to work of church

1957: First MCC relief sale

1957: GCMC starts Women in Church Vocations program

1960s–70s: "Second-wave" feminism

1961: Magazine renamed *WMSA Voice* *

1962: First women's retreat in Lancaster Conference *

1965: Magazine renamed *Missions Today* †

1968: First WMA grants to Mennonite Biblical Seminary students †

1968: GCMC changes denominational structure from "boards" to "commissions"

1968: Urban Racial Council forms (MC), becomes Minority Ministries Council; eventual splits into African American Mennonite Association and Iglesia Menonita Hispana

1970: Lois Gunden Clemens (then WMSC editor) presents lectures on role of women in the church, published in 1971 as *Woman Liberated* *

1970: Betty Epp (WMA board president) first woman elected to MCC board †

1971: Fern Umble (WMSC) and Lora Oyer (WMA) join Peace Section of MCC board * †

1971: Name change to Women's Missionary and Service Commission (WMSC), relation with newly formed Board of Congregational Ministries *

1972: WMA asks for representatives on GCMC commissions, granted without voting privileges; Tina Block first woman on Africa Inter-Mennonite Mission board †

November 1972: Women's Caucus following MCC Peace Section assembly in Chicago

1973: Evangelical Women's Caucus forms; *Daughters of Sarah* feminist journal begins in 1974

Spring 1973: MCC Peace Section starts Task Force on Women in Church and Society, *Task Force Newsletter* begins, later *Women's Concerns Report* (discontinues 2004)

April 1973: First Hispanic Mennonite women's conference

July 1973: Emma Richards first ordained female pastor of an MC congregation

October 1973: Consultation on role of women in the church held at Mennonite Biblical Seminary

1974: Name change to Women in Mission (WM); *Window to Mission* starts publication as insert in *The Mennonite* †

1974: First MCC thrift shop opens

1974: GCMC resolves "Neither race, class, or sex should be considered barriers in calling a minister"; MC leaves the issue to area conferences

February 1974: WMA gets representation with voting power on GCMC commissions †

1976: First Women in Ministry conference (inter Anabaptist)

1976: Marilyn Miller first ordained female pastor of a GCMC congregation

1977: First black Mennonite women's retreat

1978: Women in Mission contributes scholarships for women to attend Mennonite World Conference in Kansas; Women's World Outreach fund begins in 1979 †

1980: *Women in Search of Mission: A History of the General Conference Mennonite Women's Organization* published (Gladys Goering) †

1982: MCC Peace Section appoints half-time staff person for Women's Concerns; Task Force changes to Committee on Women's Concerns

1983: *Mennonite Women: A Story of God's Faithfulness 1683–1983* published (Elaine Sommers Rich) *

1983: WMSC becomes associate group in MC; appoints Business and Professional Women secretary *

Summer 1983: First MC/GCMC joint denominational assembly

1987: South America learning tour †

1987: Florence Driedger becomes president of GCMC (first woman in top position of a Mennonite denomination)

1989: Women in Mission self-evaluation process is completed, new mission statement †

1990: WMSC completes self-study and celebrates its seventy-fifth anniversary *

1990s–onward: "Third-wave" feminism

1990–91: First joint devotional, becomes Bible Study Guide (continues to present in collaboration with Mennonite Women Canada) ‡

1991: "At Home with One Another" learning tour †

Spring 1992: Women Doing Theology seminar (at Conrad Grebel), several more follow

1995: "The Quiet in the Land? Women of Anabaptist Traditions in Historical Perspectives" conference

Summer 1995: MC and GCMC vote in favor of integration

1997: Women in Mission and WMSC merge into Mennonite Women; International Women's Fund supports women studying theology ‡

January 1998: *Timbrel* begins publication ‡

1999: First PREP (Preparing, Resourcing, Encouraging, Praising) retreat for regional leaders; first Women in Conversation retreat ‡

Summer 1999: MC, GCMC, and Conference of Mennonites in Canada vote to form two national bodies

February 2002: Official start of Mennonite Church USA (MC USA)

February 2003: Official split into Mennonite Women USA (MW USA) and Canadian Women in Mission (later Mennonite Women Canada) §

2004: Sister-Link with African Anabaptist Women Theologians begins (concludes 2009) §

June 2004: Latin American Anabaptist Women Theologians movement organizes

July 2006: Rhoda Keener (MW USA executive director) starts Sister Care exploratory group §

2007: *Timbrel* becomes U.S. magazine; end of annual group reporting §

2008: Sister Care pilot seminar in Virginia §

2009: Strategic planning retreat sets new mission and vision statement; Women in Leadership Project and Audit begins §

2010: Rewrite of Sister Care manual, Carolyn Holderread Heggen becomes cofacilitator §

Fall 2012: First international Sister Care seminars (India and Nepal); networks of theologically trained Anabaptist women in Asia and India form §

February 2013: Sister Care in Guatemala for Central American leaders §

July 2013: Elizabeth Soto Albrecht becomes first Latina moderator of MC USA

Fall 2013: Sister Care has been shared in all twenty-one area conferences of MC USA §

2014: Sister Care held in multiple Caribbean, South American, Canadian contexts §

February 2014: "All You Need Is Love" Women Doing Theology conference organized by Women in Leadership Project

March 2015: First college Sister Care (pilot seminar at Goshen College) §

July 2015: Gathering at Mennonite World Conference assembly to form global network of women theologians

Fall 2015: Lancaster Conference announces plans to leave MC USA, several other conferences and congregations have left

February 2016: College Sister Care seminars led by Marlene Bogard §

April 2016: Sister Care in Tanzania and Kenya §

October 2016: Sister Care leaders' training in Guatemala §

July 2017: MW USA centennial celebration §

Notes

Acknowledgments

1. Small grammatical errors in interview responses and typographical errors in written sources are silently corrected throughout this text, though no changes were made that influence the meaning of a statement.

Introduction: Service and Sisterhood

1. This and the subsequent three paragraphs are based on John Landis Ruth, *The Earth Is the Lord's: A Narrative History of the Lancaster Mennonite Conference* (Scottdale, PA: Herald Press, 2001), 740–41, 834, 867–68.
2. Joyce Shutt, "I Never Intended to Be a Pastor," in *She Has Done a Good Thing: Mennonite Women Leaders Tell Their Stories*, ed. Mary Swartley and Rhoda Keener (Scottdale, PA: Herald Press, 1999), 117.
3. Ibid.
4. Joyce Shutt, interview by author, October 16, 2014.
5. Ibid. See also Joyce Shutt, chap. 12 in *Our Struggle to Serve: The Stories of Fifteen Evangelical Women*, ed. Virginia Hearn (Waco, TX: Word Books, 1979), 142–52.
6. Suzette Shreffler, interview by author, December 7, 2015.
7. Ibid.
8. Suzette Shreffler, Facebook message to author, April 21, 2016.
9. Nadine Busenitz, interview by author, January 4, 2015.
10. "Sister Question Responses," *Timbrel*, March/April 2010, 22.

Chapter 1: Beginnings of Mennonite Women's Groups

1. Magdalene Redekop, "Through the Mennonite Looking Glass," in *Why I Am a Mennonite: Essays on Mennonite Identity*, ed. Harry Loewen (Scottdale, PA: Herald Press, 1988), 240, 242.
2. Thieleman J. van Braght, *Martyrs Mirror: The Story of Seventeen Centuries of Christian Martyrdom from the Time of Christ to A.D. 1660*, trans. Joseph F. Sohm (Scottdale, PA: Herald Press, 1950), 505.
3. Ibid., 516.
4. Ibid., 517. Jerome was referencing Luke 10:42, which refers to Mary, sister of Martha. Whether Mary Magdalene and Mary, sister of Martha, were one and the same person remains a matter of debate.

5. Lois Barrett Janzen, "Three Portraits of Mennonite Women," *The Mennonite*, March 20, 1973, 188.
6. C. Arnold Snyder and Linda A. Huebert Hecht, *Profiles of Anabaptist Women: Sixteenth-Century Reforming Pioneers* (Waterloo, ON: Wilfrid Laurier University Press, 1996), 1–12.
7. Barrett Janzen, "Three Portraits," 188.
8. Snyder and Hecht, *Profiles of Anabaptist Women*, 10.
9. Melvin Gingerich, "The Mennonite Woman's Missionary Society," *Mennonite Quarterly Review* 37, no. 2 (1963): 114.
10. Sycamore Grove Centennial 1866–1966, box 1, folder 1, Sycamore Grove Mennonite Church (Garden City, Mo.) Records, 1868–2012 (III-25-002), Mennonite Church USA Archives, Elkhart, Indiana (hereafter abbreviated MCUSAA–Elkhart).
11. Sewing Circle Record Book, 1914–1927, box 1, folder 2, Sycamore Grove Mennonite Church (Garden City, Mo.) Records, MCUSAA–Elkhart.
12. Ibid.
13. Sewing Circle Records 1908–1922, box 5, folder 1, Prairie Street Mennonite Church (Elkhart, Ind.) Records, 1872–2001 (III-14-002), MCUSAA–Elkhart.
14. Gingerich, "Mennonite Woman's Missionary Society," 113.
15. Marlene Epp, "Women in Canadian Mennonite History: Uncovering the 'Underside,'" *Journal of Mennonite Studies* 5 (1987): 94.
16. Ibid., 95.
17. Gladys V. Goering, *Women in Search of Mission* (Newton, KS: Faith & Life Press, 1980), 16.
18. James C. Juhnke, *A People of Mission: A History of General Conference Mennonite Overseas Missions* (Newton, KS: Faith & Life Press, 1978), 101.
19. Goering, *Women in Search*, 1. It seems that sometimes these programs were attended only by members of women's groups, while other times they were presented to the entire gathered session.
20. Gingerich, "Mennonite Woman's Missionary Society," 113.
21. Ibid.
22. See Sharon L. Klingelsmith, "Steiner, Clara Daisy Eby (1873–1929)," *Global Anabaptist Mennonite Encyclopedia Online*, 1989, http://gameo.org/index.php?title=Steiner,_Clara_Daisy_Eby_(1873-1929)&oldid=112838.
23. Gingerich, "Mennonite Woman's Missionary Society," 124.
24. Sharon Klingelsmith, "Women in the Mennonite Church, 1900–1930," *Mennonite Quarterly Review* 54, no. 3 (1980): 167.
25. Melvin Gingerich, "The Mennonite Woman's Missionary Society: II," *Mennonite Quarterly Review* 37, no. 3 (1963): 215. "Woman's" was the term used at the time.
26. Ibid., 216.
27. Ibid., 216–17.
28. Ibid., 217.
29. Ibid., 218.
30 Ibid., 219.
31. The current publication, *Rejoice!*, has less of a focus on prayers for missions and more reflections on Scripture passages. It is published quarterly by MennoMedia.

32. Goering, *Women in Search*, 5.
33. Ibid., 1.
34. Ibid., 17.
35. Ibid., 18.
36. Ibid., 19.
37. Ibid., 3.
38. Emma H. Shank to "My Dear Sisters of the Sewing Circles," June 15, 1924, in *Monthly Letter*, September 1, 1924, 1.
39. Lydia Lehman to "the Missionary Circles in America," November 12, 1924, in *Monthly Letter*, February 1, 1925, 1.
40. Goering, *Women in Search*, 15.
41. Ibid., 7–10.
42. Klingelsmith, "Women in the Mennonite Church," 196.
43. See Carolyn DeSwarte Gifford, "Nineteenth- and Twentieth-Century Protestant Social Reform Movements in the United States," in *Encyclopedia of Women and Religion in North America*, ed. Rosemary Skinner Keller and Rosemary Radford Ruether (Bloomington: Indiana University Press, 2006), 1027.
44. Cited in Gloria Neufeld Redekop, *The Work of Their Hands: Mennonite Women's Societies in Canada* (Waterloo, ON: Wilfrid Laurier University Press, 1996), 4.
45. Ibid.
46. Margaret Lamberts Bendroth and Virginia Lieson Brereton, eds., *Women and Twentieth-Century Protestantism* (Chicago: University of Illinois Press, 2001), 2.
47. Ibid.
48. Jennifer Graber, "Mennonites, Gender, and the Bible in the 1920s and '30s," *Conrad Grebel Review* 21, no. 2 (Spring 2003), https://uwaterloo.ca/grebel/publications/conrad-grebel-review/issues/spring-2003/mennonites-gender-and-bible-1920s-and-30s.
49. Paul Toews, "Fundamentalism," *Global Anabaptist Mennonite Encyclopedia Online*, 1990, http://gameo.org/index.php?title=Fundamentalism.
50. See Marlene Epp, *Mennonite Women in Canada: A History* (Winnipeg: University of Manitoba Press, 2008), 185–86.
51. Ibid.
52. Paul Toews, *Mennonites in American Society, 1930–1970: Modernity and the Persistence of Religious Community* (Scottdale, PA: Herald Press, 1996), 60. For example, in the early twentieth century, MC leaders also brought John F. Funk's publishing company and Goshen College (after a temporary closure in 1923) under closer denominational control.
53. Klingelsmith, "Women in the Mennonite Church," 194–99.
54. Ibid., 199.
55. Gingerich, "Mennonite Woman's Missionary Society: II," 225.
56. Ibid.
57. Klingelsmith, "Women in the Mennonite Church," 201.
58. Gingerich, "Mennonite Woman's Missionary Society: II," 229.
59. Klingelsmith, "Women in the Mennonite Church," 203.
60. Elaine Sommers Rich, *Mennonite Women: A Story of God's Faithfulness* (Scottdale, PA: Herald Press, 1983), 204.

61. Susan M. Yohn, "'Let Christian Women Set the Example in Their Own Gifts': The 'Business' of Protestant Women's Organizations," in Bendroth and Brereton, *Women and Twentieth-Century Protestantism*, 214.
62. Loretta M. Long, "Christian Church/Disciples of Christ Tradition and Women," in Keller and Ruether, *Encyclopedia of Women and Religion*, 303.
63. Lois A. Boyd, "Presbyterian Women in America," in Keller and Ruether, *Encyclopedia of Women and Religion*, 356.
64. Barbara Brown Zikmund, "Women in the United Church of Christ," in Keller and Ruether, *Encyclopedia of Women and Religion*, 374.
65. Yohn, "'Let Christian Women,'" 214.
66. Ibid.
67. Rich, *Mennonite Women*, 201.
68. Ibid., 205.
69. Gingerich, "Mennonite Woman's Missionary Society," 232.
70. James C. Juhnke, *Vision, Doctrine, War: Mennonite Identity and Organization in America, 1890–1930* (Scottdale, PA: Herald Press, 1989), 270–73.
71. Ibid.
72. In addition, Martha Goerz's father was "one of the early giants" in the GCMC, and Anna Isaac's brother and sister-in-law, Peter A. and Elizabeth Penner, went to India as the GCMC's first missionaries. Goering, *Women in Search*, 3–4.
73. Toews, *Mennonites in American Society*, 61.
74. See Klingelsmith, "Women in the Mennonite Church," 190–91.
75. Gingerich, "Mennonite Woman's Missionary Society: II," 219.
76. Quoted in ibid., 220.
77. Goering, *Women in Search*, 24.
78. Esther Patkau, *Canadian Women in Mission: 1895–1952–2002* (Saskatoon, SK: Canadian Women in Mission, 2002), 1.
79. Ibid., 9.
80. Redekop, *Work of Their Hands*, 45.
81. Valerie S. Rake, "A Thread of Continuity: Quiltmaking in Wayne County, Ohio, Mennonite Churches, 1890s–1990s," *Uncoverings* 20 (1999): 35.
82. Ibid.
83. Dema G. Horst, untitled report of sewing circle and missionary society meeting, June 16, 1921. Box 5, Folder 49. Women's Missionary and Service Commission District Conferences Records, 1921-1983. IV-20-14. MCUSAA–Elkhart.
84. Epp, *Mennonite Women in Canada*, 160.
85. Ibid.
86. Rosemary Skinner Keller, "Leadership and Community Building in Protestant Women's Organizations," in Keller and Ruether, *Encyclopedia of Women and Religion*, 857.
87. Ibid., 852.
88. Jeannie Zehr, "History of General Conference Mennonite Church Women's Organization," *Mennonite Women Voices* (blog), May 17, 2013 [prepared in 2008], http://mennonitewomenusa.org/2013/05/history-general-conference-mennonite-church-womens-organization/.
89. Edith C. Loewen, "Women in Mission (General Conference Mennonite Church)," *Global Anabaptist Mennonite Encyclopedia Online*, 1989, http://gameo.org/index.php?title=Women_in_Mission_General_Conference_Mennonite_Church)&oldid=78870.

Chapter 2: Years of Quiet Faithfulness

1. Gingerich, "Mennonite Woman's Missionary Society: II," 232.
2. Rich, *Mennonite Women*, 206.
3. Toews, *Mennonites in American Society*, 54, 187.
4. Hope Kauffman Lind, *Apart and Together: Mennonites in Oregon and Neighboring States, 1876–1976* (Scottdale, PA: Herald Press, 1990), 241.
5. Toews, *Mennonites in American Society*, 40.
6. Ibid., 50.
7. Ibid., 51.
8. Ibid.
9. Rich, *Mennonite Women*, 206.
10. Toews, *Mennonites in American Society*, 60.
11. Qtd. in Goering, *Women in Search*, 59.
12. Goering, *Women in Search*, 59–60.
13. Ibid., 107.
14. Ibid., 26.
15. Goering notes that the portion of women's contributions may be higher than two-thirds, since the numbers at that time did not include the contributions of Canadian women.
16. Ibid., 69.
17. Ibid., 59.
18. Fanny Stoll, "Memories of Sewing Circle Days," *Voice*, May 1988, 14.
19. Ibid.
20. Barbara Brown Zikmund, "Women's Organizations: Centers of Denominational Loyalty and Expressions of Christian Unity" in *Beyond Establishment: Protestant Identity in a Post-Protestant Age*, ed. Jackson Carroll and Wade Clark Roof (Louisville, KY: Westminster/John Knox Press, 1993), 123.
21. Goering, *Women in Search*, 28.
22. Ibid.
23. Toews, *Mennonites in American Society*, 160.
24. Goering, *Women in Search*, 29.
25. Calvin Redekop, "The Mennonite Central Committee: A Review Essay," *Mennonite Quarterly Review* 67 (1993), 84, n2.
26. Toews, *Mennonites in American Society*, 185.
27. Patkau, *Canadian Women in Mission*, 340. The presentation was given in German but appears in English in Patkau.
28. Qtd. in Epp, *Mennonite Women in Canada*, 52–53.
29. Epp, "Women in Canadian Mennonite History," 99.
30. Ibid.
31. Goering, *Women in Search*, 29.
32. Rachel Waltner Goossen, *Women against the Good War: Conscientious Objection and Gender on the American Home Front, 1941–1947* (Chapel Hill: University of North Carolina Press, 1997), 123.
33. Ibid., 130.
34. Ibid.
35. Albert N. Keim, *The CPS Story: An Illustrated History of Civilian Public Service* (Intercourse, PA: Good Books, 1990), 103–5.

36. Harold S. Bender and Harold A. Penner, "Voluntary Service," *Global Anabaptist Mennonite Encyclopedia Online*, 1989, http://gameo.org/index.php?title =Voluntary_Service&oldid=133942.
37. Sandy Dwayne Martin, "Women in African American Denominations," in Keller and Ruether, *Encyclopedia of Women and Religion*, 259.
38. "Our Story," Church Women United, accessed December 7, 2016, http://www .churchwomen.org/?page_id=45.
39. Ibid.
40. See "Celebrate," Church Women United, accessed December 7, 2016, http://www .churchwomen.org/index.php/celebrate/
41. Phyllis D. Airhart, "Women in the United Church of Canada," in Keller and Ruether, *Encyclopedia of Women and Religion*, 363–64; Martin, "Women in African American Denominations," 260.
42. Janet Blosser and Rachel Schrock, "Vignettes for Annual Day, 2003," electronic copy in author's possession.
43. Patkau, *Canadian Women*, 22.
44. Eleanor Yoder, *Iowa-Nebraska Sewing WMSC* (Kalona, IA: Kalona Printing, 1989), 15, 31.
45. Epp, "Women in Canadian Mennonite History," 99.
46. Rich, *Mennonite Women*, 215. Florence Shantz was executive secretary from 1956 to 1958.
47. Ibid., 207.
48. Eleanor Graber Kreider, "Meet Minnie Graber," *Voice*, May 1990, 7.
49. Goering, *Women in Search*, 64.
50. Ibid., 74.
51. Ibid., 70–71.
52. Ibid., 71.
53. Ibid.
54. Rich, *Mennonite Women*, 230.
55. Edith (Mrs. O'Ray) Graber, "Women in Church Vocations (General Conference Mennonite Church)," *Global Anabaptist Mennonite Encyclopedia Online*, 1959, http://gameo.org/index.php?title=Women_in_Church_Vocations_(General_ Conference_Mennonite_Church)&oldid=86225.
56. While Stoltzfus promoted the view that woman's primary place was in the home, she modeled other options by leaving her home duties to host a radio broadcast and speak across the country. In 1989, she became the first woman ordained by Virginia Mennonite Conference.
57. Frieda Amstutz's role in the women's organization was clearly a meaningful part of her life. When she died in 2015 at the age of almost 104, the family directed memorial contributions to the local church camp, her church's sewing group, and Mennonite Women USA.
58. Frieda (Mrs. George) Amstutz, "Girls' Missionary and Service Auxiliary," ca. 1955, p. 5, from the files of Nettie Hooley, copy in author's possession.
59. Yoder, *Iowa-Nebraska Sewing WMSC*, 60.
60. Rich, *Mennonite Women*, 207.
61. Nettie (Mrs. Clarence) Hooley, "With Our Girls," *WMSA Monthly*, 1956, 6.
62. Ibid.

63. Phyllis Baumgartner, interview by author, October 14, 2015.
64. Goering, *Women in Search*, 38.
65. Ibid.
66. According to *Global Anabaptist Mennonite Encyclopedia Online* articles, in 1956 there were 77,369 Mennonite Church members in the United States and Canada, and in 1958 there were 15,690 WMSC members. If women composed about half the Mennonite Church membership, then about half the women members were part of the women's organization. See Harold S. Bender and Beulah Stauffer Hostetler, "Mennonite Church (MC)," *Global Anabaptist Mennonite Encyclopedia Online*, 2013, http://gameo.org/index.php?title=Mennonite_Church_(MC) &oldid=146617; Melvin Gingerich and Barbara K. Reber, Women's Missionary and Service Commission (Mennonite Church)," *Global Anabaptist Mennonite Encyclopedia Online*, 1989, http://gameo.org/index.php?title=Women%27s_Missionary_and_Service_Commission_(Mennonite_Church)&oldid=143794).
67. J. C. Wenger, *The Mennonite Church in America* (Scottdale, PA: Herald Press, 1966), 227.
68. Quoted in Yoder, *Iowa-Nebraska Sewing WMSC*, 9.
69. Zikmund, "Women United Church of Christ," 375.
70. Ibid.
71. Airhart, "Women in the United Church of Canada," 366.
72. Joan C. LaFollette, "Money and Power: Presbyterian Women's Organizations in the Twentieth Century," in *The Organizational Revolution: Presbyterians and American Denominationalism*, ed. Milton J. Coater et al. (Louisville, KY: Westminster/John Knox Press, 1992), 202.
73. Redekop, *Work of Their Hands*, 65.
74. Ibid., 67.
75. Lois Gunden Clemens, "Editorially Speaking," *WMSA Voice*, July 1961, 2.
76. Goering, *Women in Search*, 50.
77. Ibid., 51.

"More Than Sewing"

1. Qtd. in Klingelsmith, "Women in the Mennonite Church," 188.
2. Ibid., 189.
3. Goering, *Women in Search*, 106. Italics are in the original (as quoted by Goering).
4. Lora Oyer, interview by author, October 6, 2014.
5. Lora Oyer to MW USA, May 23, 2014, copy in author's possession.
6. Vel Shearer, interview by author, May 5, 2015.
7. Letha Froese, "There Is a Time!" *Gospel Herald*, February 7, 1989, 90.
8. Kathy Bilderback, interview by author, July 3, 2015.
9. Marlene Bogard, interview by author, December 2, 2015.
10. Quoted in Patricia Burdette, "A Discerning Woman," *The Mennonite*, January 2012, 15.
11. Hyacinth Stevens, interview by author, July 3, 2015.
12. Joan Wiebe, interview by author, November 5, 2014.
13. Esther Yoder, interview by author, July 19, 2015.
14. Elaine Widrick, interview by author, May 7, 2015.

15. Carolyn Holderread Heggen, interview by author, February 11, 2015.
16. Carmen Miller, interview by author, October 31, 2015.
17. Jodi H. Beyeler, "Quilting Connects Generations of Women," *The Mennonite*, November 3, 2009, 21; Jennifer Speight, "Passing on a Living Tradition between Generations," *Record* (Goshen College), March 17, 2011, https://record.goshen.edu/2011/03/14651-passing-on-a-living-tradition-between-generations.
18. Rhoda Charles, interview by author, July 25, 2015. See also Jeff Hawkes, "Burmese Refugees and Mennonites Sew Hope and Warmth for the World," Lancaster (Pa.) Online, January 15, 2015, http://lancasteronline.com/features/burmese-refugees-and-mennonites-sew-hope-and-warmth-for-the/article_8cd65b56-9d03-11e4-b94b-abf87a2c49b6.html.
19. Although several congregations have left this conference because of concerns about the larger denomination, many women hope they will still meet to work on the quilt, which is sold to support the local Christian camp.
20. Edith Michalovic, interview by author, July 17, 2015.
21. Serena Tubby, interview by author, July 17, 2015.

Chapter 3: Woman Liberated

1. Dorothy Nickel Friesen, "Resources for Women and the Church," *The Mennonite*, March 20, 1973, 97.
2. The Conrad Grebel Lectures were established in 1950 to support a Mennonite Church scholar's work on a topic of relevance to Mennonites and other Christians. The first fourteen lecturers in the series were all men.
3. Lois Gunden Clemens, *Woman Liberated* (Scottdale, PA: Herald Press, 1971), 117.
4. See Mary Jean Gunden, "Lois Gunden: A Righteous Gentile," *The Mennonite*, September 2013, 12–16.
5. Jocele Meyer, interview by author, April 23, 2015.
6. Epp, *Mennonite Women in Canada*, 178.
7. Ibid.
8. Flora Davis, *Moving the Mountain: The Women's Movement in America since 1960* (New York: Simon & Schuster, 1991), 27–28.
9. Ibid., 15; Sara Evans, *Personal Politics: The Roots of Women's Liberation in the Civil Rights Movement and the New Left* (New York: Vintage Books, 1979).
10. Davis, *Moving the Mountain*, 15.
11. Ibid.; Evans, *Personal Politics*, 21–23.
12. Evans, *Personal Politics*, 16–17; Davis, *Moving the Mountain*, 34–38.
13. Evans, *Personal Politics*, 17.
14. Katie Funk Wiebe, "The Feminine Mystique (Part 2)," *Canadian Mennonite*, April 5, 1966, 10.
15. Ibid.
16. Susan Martin Weber, "God Made Me a Woman," *Gospel Herald*, April 25, 1967, 369.
17. Elsie Flaming, interview by author, May 20, 2015.
18. Shutt, "I Never Intended to Be a Pastor," in Swartley and Keener, *She Has Done*, 117.
19. Oyer to MW USA, May 23, 2014.
20. The article mentioned is from *Gospel Herald*, January 9, 1973, 30.

21. Reta Halteman Finger, "Who Does the Dirty Work of the Kingdom?" *Gospel Herald*, June 24, 1975, 461–62.
22. Reta Halteman Finger, interview by author, October 30, 2015; Reta Halteman Finger, "Standing in the Gap," in Swartley and Keener, *She Has Done*, 47–56.
23. See especially the letters in the April 24, 1973, issue of the *The Mennonite*.
24. This group continues today as the Evangelical and Ecumenical Women's Caucus (EEWC) and maintains a website at www.eewc.com, which Finger still contributes to.
25. Oyer to MW USA, May 23, 2014.
26. Rhoda Keener, email to author, April 26, 2016. Ruth Lapp Guengerich, another future Mennonite women's organization leader, faithfully read the magazine as well.
27. Finger, interview.
28. See Toews, *Mennonites in American Society*, 257.
29. See Felipe Hinojosa, *Latino Mennonites: Civil Rights, Faith, and Evangelical Culture* (Baltimore: Johns Hopkins University Press, 2014), 51.
30. Ibid., 49.
31. See Tobin Miller Shearer, "A Prophet Pushed Out: Vincent Harding and the Mennonites," *Mennonite Life* 69 (May 2015), https://ml.bethelks.edu/issue/vol-69/article/a-prophet-pushed-out-vincent-harding-and-the-menno/; see also other articles about Harding in this May 2015 issue.
32. Toews, *Mennonites in American Society*, 255.
33. Hinojosa, *Latino Mennonites*, 49.
34. Ibid., 49–50.
35. Ibid., 49.
36. See chapter 4 of Hinojosa, *Latino Mennonites* for a detailed account of this conference.
37. Eleanor High to Beulah (Mrs. Alvin) Kauffman, 1969, box 1, folder 58, Women's Missionary and Service Commission Executive Secretary (Beulah Kauffman) Files, 1953–87 (IV-20-023), MCUSAA–Elkhart.
38. Ibid.
39. Davis, *Moving the Mountain*, 356.
40. Ibid., 359.
41. Ibid., 364.
42. Ibid., chapter 9.
43. "Women," UFCW Canada, accessed January 24, 2017, http://ufcw.ca/index.php?option=com_content&view=category&id=36&Itemid=155&lang=en.
44. Davis, *Moving the Mountain*, 16.
45. Oyer (to MW USA, May 23, 2014) suggests this was the case.
46. This and other Women's Concerns background information in subsequent paragraphs is from Dorothy Yoder Nyce, "And So It Began: On Birthing an Organization," *Conrad Grebel Review* 23, no. 1 (Winter 2005): 55–78, https://uwaterloo.ca/grebel/publications/conrad-grebel-review/issues/winter-2005/30th-anniversary-mcc-womens-concerns-committee.
47. Luann Habegger Martin, "The Thirtieth Anniversary of the MCC Women's Concerns Committee," *Conrad Grebel Review* 23, no. 1 (Winter 2005): 53, https://uwaterloo.ca/grebel/publications/conrad-grebel-review/issues/winter-2005/30th-anniversary-mcc-womens-concerns-committee.

48. Katie Funk Wiebe, "My Impressions of the Early Years of the Women's Task Force," *Conrad Grebel Review* 23, no. 1 (Winter 2005): 84, https://uwaterloo.ca/grebel/publications/conrad-grebel-review/issues/winter-2005/my-impressions-early-years-womens-task-force.
49. Nyce, "And So It Began," 65. The comment was made by Lee Roy Berry, who was supportive of the formation of the task force.
50. Emily Will, "Women's Advocacy Era Ends," *Mennonite World Review*, February 13, 2012, http://www.mennoworld.org/archived/2012/2/13/womens-advocacy-era-ends/?print=1.
51. Ann J. Allebach was ordained for congregational ministry by Mennonite leaders in 1911, but she never held an official post at a Mennonite congregation.
52. John A. Esau, "Ordination," *Global Anabaptist Mennonite Encyclopedia Online*, 1989, http://gameo.org/ index.php?title=Ordination&oldid=101100.

Chapter 4: Women's Missionary and Service Commission

1. Quoted in Helen Good Brenneman, *Ring a Dozen Doorbells: Twelve Women Tell It Like It Is* (Scottdale, PA: Herald Press, 1973), 126.
2. Ibid.
3. Rich, *Mennonite Women*, 208.
4. Louise Stoltzfus, *Quiet Shouts: Stories of Lancaster Mennonite Women Leaders* (Scottdale, PA: Herald Press, 1999), 123.
5. Ibid. The quote is from a 1981 *Missionary Messenger* article by Lauver and Diffenbach.
6. Dorothy Shank, interview by author, October 30, 2015.
7. Meyer, interview.
8. Angie Williams, interview by author, October 30, 2015.
9. Ibid.
10. Royden Loewen and Steven M. Nolt, *Seeking Places of Peace: A Global Mennonite History* (Intercourse, PA: Good Books, 2012), 265.
11. Ibid.
12. Grace Brunner, "By the Grace of God" in Swartley and Keener, *She Has Done*, 68.
13. Ibid.
14. Loewen and Nolt, *Seeking Places of Peace*, 266.
15. Ibid.
16. Ibid.
17. Elizabeth McLaughlin, "Engendering the *Imago Dei*: A Rhetorical Study of Quilts and Quiltmaking as Metaphor and Visual Parable in the Anabaptist Peace Tradition" (PhD diss., Regent University, 2008), 225 (Mennonite Historical Library, Goshen, Ind.).
18. Ibid., iv.
19. Ibid., 225.
20. Rake, "Thread of Continuity," 51. In *MennoFolk: Mennonite and Amish Folk Traditions* (Scottdale, PA: Herald Press, 2004), Ervin Beck notes that the quilt auction was 41 percent of the Michiana Relief Sale's total proceeds in 2001 and that the Elkhart County Convention and Visitors Bureau calls the whole event "The Quilt Auction" (198). At the 2016 Kansas Mennonite Relief Sale, the highest-priced auction item was a 1948 Oldsmobile, but the runner-up was a

quilt—which sold for $11,900 ("48th Kansas Mennonite Relief Sale—April 8 and 9, 2016," accessed July 15, 2016, http://kansas.mccsale.org/).

21. Ruth, *The Earth Is the Lord's*, 834.
22. McLaughlin, "Engendering the *Imago Dei*," 296.
23. Daniel Born, "From Cross to Cross-Stich: The Ascendancy of the Quilt," *Mennonite Quarterly Review* 79, no. 2 (April 2005), https://www.goshen.edu/mqr/2005/06/april-2005-born/.
24. Ibid.
25. Ibid.
26. McLaughlin, "Engendering the *Imago Dei*," 317.
27. Ibid., 259.
28. Christine Scheffel, email to author (information from Zion Mennonite Church's 2011 centennial book), December 5, 2015.
29. Yoder, *Iowa-Nebraska Sewing WMSC*, 52.
30. Alma Yoder mentioned these examples in an interview by author, October 31, 2015.
31. E. Jane Burkholder, interview by author, October 31, 2015.
32. Yoder, interview.
33. Letters," *Voice*, May 1974, 12.
34. Ibid.
35. Quoted in Saralyn Yoder, "Barbara Reber: Happy with Women's Changing Roles," *Voice*, October 1990, 13.
36. Angie Williams, interview by author, May 5, 2015.
37. See Hinojosa, *Latino Mennonites*, 80–82.
38. Williams, interview, May 5, 2015.
39. Vel Shearer, "On the Possibility That There Are Megs in the Mennonite Family," *Voice*, January 1986, 15.
40. Shearer, interview.
41. Ibid.
42. See Rachel Waltner Goossen, "'Defanging the Beast': Mennonite Responses to John Howard Yoder's Sexual Abuse" *Mennonite Quarterly Review* 89, no. 1 (January 2015): 44–48.
43. Ibid., 39–44.
44. See Linda Gehman Peachey, "Naming the Pain, Seeking the Light: The Mennonite Church's Response to Sexual Abuse," *Mennonite Quarterly Review* 89, no. 1 (January 2015): 111–28.
45. Mim Book, interview by author, April 30, 2015.
46. Melanie Zuercher, "Expanding the (Sewing) Circle," *Gospel Herald*, August 6, 1985, 545.
47. Quoted in Yoder, "Barbara Reber," 12.
48. Zuercher, "Expanding the (Sewing) Circle," 545.
49. Mrs. Lester Koch and Mrs. Ronald Zehr, "Ontario WMSA Observes Golden Anniversary," *WMSA Voice*, May 1967, 7.
50. "Facts Over Time: Women in the Labor Force," United States Department of Labor, https://www.dol.gov/wb/stats/facts_over_time.htm.
51. Grace Brunner, interview by author, December 11, 2015.
52. Quoted in Zuercher, "Expanding the (Sewing) Circle," 545.

53. Book, interview.
54. Susan Gingerich, interview by author, November 10, 2014.
55. Meyer, interview.
56. McLaughlin, "Engendering the *Imago Dei*," 224.
57. Yoder, *Iowa-Nebraska Sewing WMSC*, 8.
58. "WMSC Report to the Delegate Session," *Voice*, October 1987, 4.
59. Joan Kern, "New Holland Spanish Mennonite Church to Hold International Food Festival," Lancaster Online, November 4, 2011, lancasteronline.com/features/faith_values/new-holland-spanish-mennonite-church-to-hold-international-food-festival/article_e33f45d4-a754-53e6-b78e-bbc415000efa.html.
60. Wanda Gonzalez Coleman, interview by author, January 5, 2016.
61. Ibid.
62. Kathy Zendt, interview by author, October 31, 2015.
63. Charles, interview.
64. Brunner, interview.
65. Donella Clemens, interview by author, August 15, 2015.
66. Book, interview.
67. Ibid.
68. Levina Huber, interview by author, May 4, 2015.
69. Shearer, interview.
70. Angie Williams, interview by author, October 29, 2015.
71. Quoted in Yoder, "Barbara Reber," 12.
72. See Eve MacMaster, "Ruth and Me," *Mennonite Life* 58, no. 2 (June 2003), https://ml.bethelks.edu/issue/vol-58-no-2/article/ruth-and-me/.
73. Widrick, interview.
74. Yoder, "Barbara Reber," 13.
75. Rich, *Mennonite Women*, 201–6; Klingelsmith, "Women in the Mennonite Church," 163–207.
76. "WMSC Report to General Assembly," *Voice*, November 1985, 9.
77. Alice W. Lapp, "WMSC: Whence and Whither?" *Gospel Herald*, August 6, 1985, 544.

"Are Mennonite Women's Groups Feminist?"

1. bell hooks, *Feminism Is for Everybody: Passionate Politics* (London: Pluto Press, 2000), 1.
2. Leonard Swidler, *Jesus Was a Feminist: What the Gospels Reveal about His Revolutionary Perspective* (Lanham, MD: Sheed and Ward, 2007), 17.
3. *Merriam-Webster Online*, s.v. "Feminism," accessed January 24, 2017, http://www.merriam-webster.com/dictionary/feminist.
4. The conference was "Mennonite/s Writing VII: Movement, Transformation, Place" (Fresno, CA, March 12–15, 2015).
5. Katie Funk Wiebe, "The Place of Women in the Work of the Church," *Canadian Mennonite*, March 1, 1963, 5.
6. Elaine Penner, "Few Church Women Aspire to 'Male' Jobs—At Least Not Yet," *Canadian Mennonite*, May 9, 1969, 5.
7. Zikmund, "Women's Organizations," 133.
8. Ibid.

9. LaFollette, "Money and Power," 200.
10. Ibid.
11. Nyce, "And So It Began," 73.
12. Ella May Miller to Beulah Kauffman, 1968, box 1, folder 26, Women's Missionary and Service Commission Executive Secretary (Beulah Kauffman) Files, 1953–87 (IV-20-23), MCUSAA–Elkhart.
13. Nyce, "And So It Began," 56. In 1976, the *Heart to Heart* broadcast shifted to a different program (a show for "personal growth for women") with a new host.
14. Beulah Kauffman, "The Role of Women: Time for a Fresh Look" *Gospel Herald*, January 8, 1974, 26.
15. Ibid.
16. Saralyn Yoder, "Cautious Progress in a Time of Change: WMSC in the '60s and '70s" *Voice*, July–August 1990, 9.
17. Joyce Shutt, "Linked in Love," *Window to Mission*, October–November 1980, 11.
18. For example, the excerpted quote references John Milton's poem "When I Consider How My Light Is Spent," which contains the line "They also serve who only stand and wait."
19. Gladys Goering, "Still Going after All These Years" *Window to Mission*, December 22, 1992, 3.
20. Ibid.
21. Marian Hostetler, interview by author, October 3, 2014.
22. Susan Rempel Letkemann, "University Group Questions Changing Role of Women in the Church," *Mennonite Reporter*, February 22, 1982, section B, 3.
23. Ibid.
24. Keller, "Leadership and Community Building," in Keller and Ruether, *Encyclopedia of Women and Religion*, 851.
25. Ibid., 851–52.
26. Susan Jantzen, interview by author, December 8, 2014. Since her time leading the women's organization, Jantzen has served as a pastor in several congregations.
27. Ivorie Lowe, interview by author, June 4, 2015.
28. Irene Bechler, interview by author, November 4, 2014.
29. Sylvia Shirk, interview by author, July 2, 2015.
30. Ibid.
31. "Introducing: Womensage," *Womensage Resource Center for Mennonite Women* 1 (1982). (This resource can be found in the Mennonite Historical Library–Goshen, IN).
32. See "Women in Leadership Project," Mennonite Church USA @ Work, http://mennoniteusa.org/what-we-do/peacebuilding/women-in-leadership-project/.
33. Marlene Bogard, email to author, May 4, 2016.
34. Jennifer Castro, interview by author, October 12, 2015.
35. "About Us," Mennonite Women USA, accessed December 16, 2016, https://mennonitewomenusa.org/about-us/.
36. Claire DeBerg, interview by author, March 3, 2015.

Chapter 5: Hispanic Mennonite Women's Conferences and Black Mennonite Women's Retreats

1. Quoted in Vel Shearer, "An Open Letter to All Black Mennonite Women," *Voice*, September 1979, 15.
2. Ella May Miller, "We Met to Pray," *Voice*, October 1973, 5.
3. A note on language: I use the terms *Hispanic Mennonite women* and *Latina Mennonites* somewhat interchangeably. *Latina / Latino* are used more often in academic circles and indicate people from Latin American heritage regardless of the language they speak; *Hispanic* or *Hispana* denotes Spanish-speaking people in the United States and is currently used in Mennonite organizational names. I will also use both *black* and *African American*. The Mennonite women who gathered during the 1970s and 1980s generally used the term *Black* (or *black*), which could (and often did) include people of African descent around the world. Some black people in the United States prefer *African American* because it connects them with the history of a distinct people; this is the term used by today's African American Mennonite Association.
4. Chapter 6 of Hinojosa's *Latino Mennonites* is a good start in terms of the history of Hispanic Mennonite women's organizing efforts.
5. Hinojosa, *Latino Mennonites*, 152. Maria Bustos is often referred to as "Mary Bustos" in publications, since there were many other Marias involved with the organization. I follow Hinojosa in using "Maria."
6. Ibid., 152–53.
7. Lupe Bustos, "Historic Women's Assembly," *Voice*, April 1973, 5.
8. Ibid.
9. This event is also written about in several other places, including Hinojosa, *Latino Mennonites*, 153.
10. Bustos, "Historic Women's Assembly," 5–6.
11. Mary Bustos, "Report to the Executive Committee," November 10, 1978, box 1, folder 3, Women's Missionary and Service Commission Partnerships Records, 1973–92 (IV-20-008), MCUSAA–Elkhart.
12. Beulah Kauffman to district WMSC presidents, April 3, 1974, box 4, folder 19, Women's Missionary and Service Commission Executive Committee Records, 1917–97 (IV-20-001), MCUSAA–Elkhart.
13. Lois Gunden Clemens, "Editorially Speaking," *Voice*, July 1974, 2.
14. Enriqueta Díaz, "Hispanic Women's Conference," *Voice*, August 1974, 11.
15. Mary Bustos to Beulah Kauffman, June 12, 1974, box 1, folder 2, Women's Missionary and Service Commission Partnerships Records, MCUSAA–Elkhart.
16. Beulah Kauffman to "Committee Ladies," July 10, 1974, box 1, folder 2, Women's Missionary and Service Commission Partnerships Records, MCUSAA–Elkhart.
17. Seferina De León, interview by author, May 7, 2015.
18. Enriqueta Díaz, "Reflections from Corpus Christi," *Voice*, August 1976, 12.
19. Ibid.
20. WMSC Executive Committee Minutes, September 1976, box 2, folder 1, Women's Missionary and Service Commission Executive Committee Records, MCUSAA–Elkhart.
21. Mary Bustos, "Hispanic Women's Conference," *Voice*, April 1978, 7.

22. See Felipe Hinojosa, "Truth Teller," *The Mennonite*, February 2016, 27–28.
23. Juanita Nuñez, "Reporte de la Coordinatora," 1999, from the files of Maria Tijerina, copy in author's possession.
24. Ibid.
25. Untitled document (in Spanish), 1999, from the files of Maria Tijerina, copy in author's possession.
26. Maria Tijerina, interview by author, February 18, 2015.
27. Elizabeth Perez, interview by author, November 7, 2015.
28. Hinojosa, *Latino Mennonites*, 211.
29. Ibid.
30 Steve Bustos, interview by author, February 10, 2015.
31. Ibid.
32. I also was unable to get in touch with many women who were involved in leading the retreats. Many of them are no longer connected to the Mennonite church, probably for a variety of reasons, including the racism or marginalization they experienced. Le Roy Bechler's 180-page book *The Black Mennonite Church in North America 1886–1986*, which focuses on specific congregations, does not mention the retreats.
33. Information in this paragraph is drawn from materials in Black Women's Fellowship Conferences, 1977–79, box 4, folder 3, African American Association Records, MCUSAA–Elkhart.
34. Information in this paragraph is drawn from *Voice*, September 1979, 11.
35. Rose Harding, "Love and Accepting Myself," *Voice*, September 1979, 4–5, 10, 14. For more on Rosemarie and Vincent Harding, see chapters 1 and 2 in *Widening the Circle: Experiments in Christian Discipleship*, ed. Joanna Shenk (Harrisonburg, VA: Herald Press, 2011).
36. Quoted in Shearer, "Open Letter", 15.
37. Ibid.
38. Unless otherwise noted, information in this paragraph is drawn from materials in Black Women's Fellowship Conference, 1981, box 4, folder 9, African American Association Records, MCUSAA–Elkhart.
39 Rose Covington, interview by author, January 11, 2016.
40. David R. Swartz, *Moral Minority: The Evangelical Left in an Age of Conservatism* (Philadelphia: University of Pennsylvania Press, 2012), 190.
41. The number of black and integrated congregations comes from Bechler, *The Black Mennonite Church*, 109; Joy Lovett mentioned the mostly-female makeup of African American congregations during her "Black Concerns Report" at a WMSC leadership meeting ("Minutes: WMSC Executive Committee, November 5–7, 1987, Elkhart, Indiana," box 2, folder 2, Women's Missionary and Service Commission Executive Committee Records, MCUSAA–Elkhart).
42. Swartz, *Moral Minority*, 210.
43. "Black Mennonite Women's Retreat," *Gospel Herald*, August 9, 1983, 555.
44. "Black Women's Retreat—Changing Women: An Unchanging God, by Goldie Ivory, Parts I–II, 1983," box 21, audiocassettes 21–22, African American Mennonite Association Records, 1969–2001 (I-06-007), MCUSAA–Elkhart.
45. This paragraph is drawn from materials in Black Women's Retreat, 1983, box 5, folder 3, African American Association Records, MCUSAA–Elkhart.

46. See Miriam Sweigart, "Three Generations Share," *Voice*, June 1967, 5.
47. Black Women's Retreat, 1985–87, box 5, folder 7, African American Association Records, MCUSAA–Elkhart.
48. WMSC Executive Committee Minutes, October 1993, box 2, folder 3, Women's Missionary and Service Commission Executive Committee Records, MCUSAA–Elkhart.
49. Rose Covington, interview by author, March 10, 2016.
50. Addie Banks, interview by author, March 29, 2016.
51. Covington, interview, January 11, 2016.
52. Mertis Odom, interview by author, May 28, 2015.
53. Banks, interview.
54. For more on the wearing of a prayer covering, particularly in Lancaster Conference, see Donald B. Kraybill, "Mennonite Woman's Veiling: The Rise and Fall of a Sacred Symbol," *Mennonite Quarterly Review* 61, no. 3 (July 1987): 298–320.
55. Tobin Miller Shearer, *Daily Demonstrators: The Civil Rights Movement in Mennonite Homes and Sanctuaries* (Baltimore: Johns Hopkins University Press, 2010), 33.
56. Banks, interview.
57. Ibid.
58. Ibid.
59. See Laurie Oswald Robinson, "First African-American Woman Ordained by Lancaster Mennonite Conference," *Mennonite Weekly Review*, September 26, 2011, http://www.mennoworld.org/archived/2011/9/26/first-african-american-woman-ordained-lancaster-co/?print=1.
60. Tijerina, interview.
61. Ibid.
62. Untitled document in Black Women's Retreat, 1985–87, box 5, folder 7, African American Association Records, MCUSAA–Elkhart.
63. Seferina De León, "HMC SDCA Report," February 25–27, 1999, 1, from the files of Maria Tijerina, copy in author's possession.

Chapter 6: Women in Mission

1. Naomi Lehman, "Which Way Are We Heading?" *Window to Mission*, April 1974, 4.
2. Goering, *Women in Search*, 90–92.
3. Flaming, interview.
4. At that time, the Commissions on Overseas Ministries and Education had women members not connected to the women's organization, though women made up a very small percentage of the commissions and there were no measures to ensure their representation.
5. Goering, *Women in Search*, 92–93.
6. Lehman, "Which Way?" 3.
7. Ibid.
8. Gladys Goering, memo to General Board, January 1977, box 19, folder 248, Women in Mission 1973–77 (VII.N.1), Mennonite Library and Archives, Bethel College, North Newton, Kansas (hereafter abbreviated MLA–Newton).

9. Ibid.
10. Jeannie Zehr, interview by author, December 9, 2014.
11. Ibid.
12. Zehr, "History of Women's Organization."
13. Gladys Goering, "From Gladys Goering in the WMA Office" *Window to Mission*, April 1974, 21.
14. Self Study Report, 1974, box 19, folder 246, Women in Mission 1973–77, MLA–Newton.
15. Goering, *Women in Search*, 108.
16. Ibid., 107–8.
17. See Susan Jantzen, *Gems from the Files: Past Women in Mission Programs from the 1940s to 1980s* (Newton, KS: General Conference Women in Mission, 1995).
18. Baumgartner, interview.
19. Lowe, interview.
20. Ibid.
21. Patkau, *Canadian Women in Mission*, 165.
22. Ibid., 166.
23. Ibid., 169.
24. Ibid.
25. Goering, *Women in Search*, 80.
26. Ibid., 81.
27. Ibid., 98.
28. Gladys Goering, "Saskatoon Report," 1986, MLA–Newton.
29. Quoted in Zehr, "History of Women's Organization."
30. Keller, "Leadership and Community Building," in Keller and Ruether, *Encyclopedia of Women and Religion*, 857.
31. Ibid.
32. Ibid.
33. Gladys Goering, untitled, *Window to Mission*, April–May 1984, 12–13.
34. Jeannie Zehr, interview by author, October 10, 2014.
35. Kay Ann Fransen, "No Simple Answers: Let's Look at Abortion," *Window to Mission*, October–November 1979, 7–10.
36. David E. Shelly, "Abortion Fallacies in Window to Mission Insert,"*The Mennonite*, October 23, 1979, 683. Shelly did note that he appreciated parts of the material but he felt that abortion categorically went against a Mennonite commitment to nonviolence, which was not discussed in the material.
37. "A Letter to You," *Window to Mission*, April–May 1980, 12.
38. Ibid., 13.
39. Pearl Bartel, "In Response . . .," *Window to Mission*, April–May 1980, 13.
40 Jeannie Zehr, "Happy Birthday, Window" *Window to Mission*, April–May 1989, 3.
41. Bek Linsenmeyer, interview by author, February 21, 2015.
42. Ibid.
43. Lois Deckert, interview by author, December 10, 2014.
44. Zehr, "Happy Birthday, Window," 3.
45. Jeannie Zehr, interview, December 9, 2014.
46. Goering, *Women in Search*, 118.

47. Quoted in Patkau, *Canadian Women in Mission*, 172.
48. Wiebe, interview.
49. Sara Regier, interview by author, December 10, 2014.
50. Bogard, interview.
51. Ibid.
52. "WM Learning Tour Participants Multiply Linkages in Churches," *The Mennonite*, August 23, 1988, 373.
53. Carla Reimer, "South Americans' Faith Impresses Women," *The Mennonite*, March 22, 1988, 139.
54. Beth Hege, "Women Tell Stories from Learning Tour," *The Mennonite*, March 26, 1991, 133–34.

"A Mission to Themselves"

1. Parts of this interlude (with additions from other parts of this book) were first published in Anita Hooley Yoder, "A Mission to Themselves: Changing Views of Mission in Mennonite Women's Organizations," *Anabaptist Witness* (December 2016): 17–27.
2. Goering, *Women in Search*, 99.
3. Ibid., 106.
4. Ibid.
5. Ibid.
6. "WMSC Report to Assembly," August 16, 1979, box 3, folder 17, Women's Missionary and Service Commission Executive Committee Records, MCUSAA–Elkhart.
7. According to Redekop's 1988 survey, this was the most frequently cited verse by women's groups connected to the Conference of Mennonites in Canada. Redekop, *Work of Their Hands*, 112.
8. LaFollette, "Money and Power," 215.
9. Ibid.
10. Wilbert R. Shenk, *By Faith They Went Out: Mennonite Missions 1850–1999* (Elkhart, IN: Institute of Mennonite Studies, 2000), 61.
11. Ibid., 62.
12. Ibid.
13. Ibid., 83.
14. Patkau, *Canadian Women in Mission*, 176.
15. Thanks to Gerald Mast for pointing to this insight in comments on an early draft of this project.
16. Marlene Epp, "Women of Anabaptist Traditions," in Keller and Ruether, *Encyclopedia of Women and Religion*, 267.
17. For example, see Goossen, "'Defanging the Beast,'" 42–44.
18. Regier, interview.
19. Ibid.
20. Deckert, interview.
21. Ibid.
22. Patkau, *Canadian Women in Mission*, 208.
23. Ibid.
24. Hostetler, interview.

25. Rhoda Keener, interview by author, October 16, 2014.
26. Rhoda Keener, "To Know We Have Worth," *Timbrel*, May–June 2007, 15.
27. "About Us," Mennonite Women USA, accessed December 16, 2016, https://mennonitewomenusa.org/about-us/.

Chapter 7: Decline and New Vision

1. Terri Plank Brenneman, "Creating a Vision," *Voice*, October 1992, 5.
2. Robert D. Putnam, *Bowling Alone: The Collapse and Revival of American Community* (New York: Simon and Schuster, 2000). Thanks to Amy Gingerich for alerting me to this resource and providing me with her own interviews with Mennonite women's organization members conducted in 2003.
3. Ibid., 61.
4. Ibid., 72.
5. Ibid.
6. Ibid.
7. Zikmund, "Women's Organizations," 133.
8. Redekop, *Work of Their Hands*, 101.
9. Ibid., 130.
10. This and the next two sentences are from Regier, interview.
11. Quoted in Patkau, *Canadian Women in Mission*, 212.
12. Ibid.
13. Hostetler, interview.
14. Redekop, *Work of Their Hands*, 107.
15. Helen Friesen, "Twenty-Fifth Triennial Session of Women in Mission," August 5, 1989, box 1, folder 28, Women in Mission Minutes, reports, etc. 1960s–1990s (VII.N.15), MLA–Newton.
16. Women in Mission brochure, ca. 1980, box 1, folder 3, Women in Mission Promotional items/printed matter 1980s–early 1990s, MLA–Newton.
17. Susan Jantzen, "1991 Coordinator's Report to Women in Mission," box 1, folder 29, Women in Mission Minutes, reports, etc. 1960s–1990s, MLA–Newton.
18. GCMC Women in Mission and MC Women's Missionary and Service Commission, "Program and Reports," 1995, p. 18, MLA–Newton.
19. Susan Jantzen, "1995 Women in Mission Coordinator's Report," p. 14, box 1, folder 33, Women in Mission Minutes, reports, etc. 1960s–1990s, MLA–Newton.
20. GCMC Women in Mission and MC Women's Missionary and Service Commission, "Program and Reports," p. 19, Women in Mission 1990s files from Susan Jantzen, MLA–Newton.
21. Ruth Lapp Guengerich, WMSC Executive Committee Minutes, July 1993, box 1, folder 3, Women's Missionary and Service Commission Executive Committee Records, MCUSAA–Elkhart.
22. Ibid.
23. Mary Ellen Kauffman, "Treasurer's Report," *Voice*, April 1997, 5.
24. Ibid.
25. Marian Hostetler, "The Most-Often-Asked-Question," *Voice*, July–August 1993, 4.
26. Susan Gingerich, interview; Ruth Lapp Guengerich, interview by author, October 2, 2014.

27. GCMC Women in Mission and MC Women's Missionary and Service Commission, "Program and Reports," p. 16, Women in Mission 1990s files from Susan Jantzen, MLA–Newton.
28. See WMSC Executive Committee Minutes, October 1994 and March 1995, box 1, folder 3, Women's Missionary and Service Commission Executive Committee Records, MCUSAA–Elkhart.
29. Jantzen, interview.
30. Phyllis Schultz, "Church Visitation Report to Women in Mission," MLA–Newton.
31. Ibid.
32. Quoted in Redekop, *Work of Their Hands*, 100.
33. Ibid.
34. Lapp, "Whence and Whither?" 544.
35. Marian Hostetler, "WMSC Self-Study: A Valuable Process," *Voice*, July–August 1990, 4.
36. Quoted in Ruth Lapp Guengerich, "A History of the Mennonite Women's Organization," Mennonite Women USA, posted June 25, 2013, http://mennonitewomenusa.org/2013/06/history-womens-missionary-and-service-commission/.
37. Redekop, *Work of Their Hands*, 101.
38. Leslie L. Heywood, "Introduction: A Fifteen-Year History of Third-Wave Feminism" in *The Women's Movement Today: An Encyclopedia of Third-Wave Feminism* (Westport, CT: Greenwood Press, 2006), xvi. Heywood specifically mentions *The Beauty Myth* by Naomi Wolf and *Backlash* by Susan Faludi, both published in 1991.
39. Ibid., xx.
40. Jantzen, interview.
41. Ibid.
42. Brenneman, "Creating a Vision," 4. See also Terri J. Brenneman, "Sisterhood Is a Painful, Joyful, Powerful, and Enduring Affiliation," *Gospel Herald*, May 9, 1995, 1–2, 8.
43. Siegrid K. Richer, "Do Mennonite Women Really Feel Connected through WMSC?" *Ohio Evangel*, March–April 1996, 2.
44. Zelma Kauffman, "Reflections on WMSC at Lockport Mennonite Church," *Ohio Evangel*, June 1996, 3.
45. Ibid.
46. Ibid.
47. "49th Annual Conference of Alberta Women in Mission," May 3–4, 1996, from the files of Rhoda Keener, copy in author's possession. The women who gave reports on their groups were Tena Quiring (Taber), Erna Goerzen and Frieda Derksen (Bergthal), and Agnes Schroeder (Tofield).
48. "Minutes: WMSC Executive Committee, November 5–7, 1987, Elkhart, Indiana," box 2, folder 2, Women's Missionary and Service Commission Executive Committee Records, MCUSAA–Elkhart.
49. Ibid.
50. WMSC Executive Committee Minutes, October 1991, box 2, folder 3, Women's Missionary and Service Commission Executive Committee Records, MCUSAA–Elkhart; WMSC Executive Committee Minutes, March 1994, box 2, folder 3,

Women's Missionary and Service Commission Executive Committee Records, MCUSAA–Elkhart.

51. Doris Schmidt, "Joint WMSC/WM Meeting Verbatim Notes," October 18, 1996, box 1, folder 31, Women in Mission Files from Carol Peterson (VII.N.14), MLA–Newton.
52. Covington, interview, January 11, 2016.
53. De León, interview.
54. Quoted in Schmidt, "Verbatim Notes."
55. Valerie Weaver, "Women's Groups Continue Work of Integration," *The Mennonite*, November 12, 1996, 15.
56. Bek Linsenmeyer, "Journey Thoughts," *Window to Mission*, December 24, 1996, 9.
57. WMSC Executive Committee Minutes, May 1996, box 1, folder 3, Women's Missionary and Service Commission Executive Committee Records, MCUSAA–Elkhart.
58. Covington, interview, January 11, 2016.
59. Minutes of Joint WMSC and WM Committees, October 17, 1996, p. 3, box 2, folder 3, Women's Missionary and Service Commission Executive Committee Records, MCUSAA–Elkhart.

"We Moved Our Two Tables to Make It One"

1. Hostetler, interview.
2. Melanie A. Zuercher, "Integration Groundbreakers: Mennonite Women Celebrate Ongoing Work with *Timbrel*," *Gospel Herald*, November 18, 1997, 9.
3. Susan Gingerich, interview.
4. Ibid.
5. Pauline Toews, interview by author, December 11, 2014.
6. David L. Swartz, "Would Women Split?" *Mennonite World Review*, February 1, 2016, http://mennoworld.org/2016/02/01/letters/would-women-split/.
7. Ibid., comments by Sally Miller and Elaine Fehr.
8. Zikmund, "Women's Organizations," 116.
9. Ibid.
10. Bendroth and Brereton, *Women and Twentieth-Century Protestantism*, xiv.
11. Toews, *Mennonites in American Society*, 152.
12. Ibid.
13. Ibid., 267.
14. Rich, *Mennonite Women*, 186–87.
15. Patkau, *Canadian Women in Mission*, 21, 53.
16. Brian Froese, *California Mennonites* (Baltimore: Johns Hopkins University Press, 2015), 111.
17. Ibid, 129.
18. Ibid, 131–32.
19. Goering, *Women in Search*, 35. Goering provides an interesting summary of this partnership (see pp. 30–36), including some tensions when Mennonite Central Committee began its own migrant work. The woman quoted is Emma Ruth.

20. "Notes from the History and Proceedings of the Union Missionary Society of the Mennonites of Indiana," box 2, folder 10, Indiana Mennonite Women's Missionary Rally Committee Records (X-060), MCUSAA–Elkhart.
21. Ibid.
22. "Welcome to Indiana Mennonite Women's Missionary Rally 50th Celebration," box 2, folder 10, Indiana Mennonite Women's Missionary Rally Committee Records, 1937–2003 (X-060), MCUSAA–Elkhart.
23. Ibid.
24. Sarah J. Yoder, Minutes of the 66th Annual Indiana All-Mennonite Women's Missionary Rally, box 2, folder 10, Indiana Mennonite Women's Missionary Rally Committee Records (X-060), MCUSAA–Elkhart.
25. Carol Peters, interview by author, October 13, 2015.
26. Lindsey Bauman, "Photos: Day 1 of the MCC Comforter Blitz 2016," *Hutchinson (KS) News*, March 7, 2016, http://www.hutchnews.com/multimedia/photos-day-of-the-mcc-comforter-blitz/collection_494bd36a-6bc5-5a14-8207-923d12631700.html?utm_medium=social&utm_source=facebook&utm_campaign=user-share#20.
27. Peters, interview.
28. Ibid.
29. See Diana Williams, "Groceries: From Donation to Distribution," Mennonite Central Committee U.S., October 14, 2016, https://mcc.org/stories/groceries-donation-distribution.
30. Paul Schrag, "Kansas Thrift Shop Celebrates Forty Years, Honors a Founder," *Mennonite World Review*, May 9, 2016, 14.
31. Patkau, *Canadian Women in Mission*, 285.
32. Schrag, "Kansas Thrift Shop," 14.
33. Charles, interview. While I was interviewing Charles at the Mennonite World Conference assembly, Roth happened to walk by and joined in the conversation!

Chapter 8: Mennonite Women

1. Susan Jantzen, "1998 Co-Executive Coordinator Report," box 1, folder unknown, Women in Mission Minutes, reports, etc. 1960s–1990s, MLA–Newton.
2. Cathleen Hockman-Wert, "Mennonite Women Becomes a Reality," *Timbrel*, January/February 1998, 3.
3. On the other hand, Jantzen notes that a couple of local groups actually formed because they noticed the term *missionary* was no longer in the organization's name, though she does not indicate anything more about the motivations of these new groups. Susan Jantzen to Lara Hall Blosser, email, January 7, 1998, box 2, folder "January–February Emails," Women in Mission 1990s files from Susan Jantzen, MLA–Newton.
4. Guengerich, interview.
5. Jantzen, interview.
6. Susan Jantzen, "We Continue a Venture of Faith and Hope," *Timbrel*, January/February 1998, 5.
7. Lara Hall Blosser and Susan Jantzen, "Is Mennonite Women for Support or Outreach?" *Timbrel*, May/June 1998, 15.
8. Ibid.

9. See "Why a Lower Contribution?" Mennonite Women newsletter, November 15, 1997, 3.
10. "What Do Your Contributions Provide?" Mennonite Women newsletter, November 15, 1997, 2.
11. From a Mennonite Women survey at the 1999 Saint Louis assembly, published in *Timbrel*, November/December 1999, 4.
12. Cathleen Hockman-Wert, application for Mennonite Women Editor, July 18, 1997, copy in author's possession.
13. Ibid.
14. Cathleen Hockman-Wert, interview by author, May 3, 2015.
15. Cathleen Hockman-Wert, "And Our Survey Said," *Timbrel*, May/June 1998, 14.
16. Hockman-Wert, interview.
17. Susan Gingerich, interview.
18. Ibid.
19. Ibid.
20. Susan Gingerich, "Board Composition Marks Milestone for Women," *Timbrel*, July/August 1999, 19.
21. Ibid.
22. "Bylaws for Mennonite Church USA," Mennonite Church USA, rev. July 2013, http://mennoniteusa.org/wp-content/uploads/2015/03/MCUSA_Bylaws_APPROVED_2013_July.pdf.
23. Ibid., 11.
24. See "Executive Board Members," Mennonite Church USA, http://mennoniteusa.org/who-we-are/structure/executive-board-members/.
25. Paula Brunk Kuhns, interview by author, May 5, 2015.
26. Keener, interview, October 16, 2014.
27. Ibid.
28. Rhoda Keener, interview by author, September 22, 2014.
29. Keener, interview, October 16, 2014. Some of the information in this paragraph was first published in Anita Hooley Yoder, "A Turnaround for Mennonite Women," *The Mennonite*, June 2015, 27–30.
30. "SisterLink Brings Special Delivery to New Mothers," Mennonite Mission Network 2003–2004 Annual Report, 17.
31. Rhoda Keener, "Relationships at the Heart of Sister-Link," *Timbrel*, March/April 2003, 15.
32. Cathleen Hockman-Wert, "Sister-Link Helping to Forge New Relationships," *Mennonite Weekly Review*, April 28, 2003, 7.
33. Elizabeth Klassen, interview by author, June 2, 2015.
34. Keener, interview, October 16, 2014.
35. Amy Gingerich, interview by author, September 26, 2014; Guengerich, interview.
36. Doris Schmidt, interview by author, December 10, 2014.
37. Ibid.
38. Keener, interview, October 16, 2014.
39. Ibid.
40. Paula Brunk Kuhns, interview.
41. Ibid.
42. Klassen, interview.

Chapter 9: Mennonite Women USA

1. Quoted in Laurie L. Oswald, "Growing Circle of Funding Expands Ministry of Mennonite Women USA," *Mennonite Weekly Review*, May 9, 2005, http://www.mennoworld.org/archived/2005/5/9/growing-circle-funding-expands-ministry-mennonite-/?page=1.
2. Goering, *Women in Search*, 71.
3. Rhoda Keener, "The Story behind Our Missionary Pension Fund" (paper presented at Mennonite Health Assembly seminar, 2007).
4. Rhoda Keener, email to author, April 26, 2016.
5. "Missionary Pension Fund," Mennonite Women USA, accessed December 15, 2016, https://mennonitewomenusa.org/ministries/missionary-pension-fund/.
6. Ibid.
7. Shirk, interview.
8. Ibid.
9. Cathleen Hockman-Wert, "Moved by the Spirit," *The Mennonite*, November 3, 2009, 9.
10. Ibid., 8–10.
11. Les Amies newsletter, November 2009, 4.
12. Ibid.
13. Shirk, interview.
14. Bethany Keener, "Pen Pals Connect the Continents," *Timbrel*, May/June 2006, 15.
15. "Rebecca Osiro Becomes First Ordained Pastor in Kenyan Mennonite Church," Les Amies newsletter, November 2008, 1.
16. See Nancy Myers, "Congo Mennonites Celebrate Women's Ordination," Mennonite World Conference News, November 12, 2013, https://www.mwc-cmm.org/content/congo-mennonites-celebrate-women%E2%80%99s-ordinations?language=en.
17. Hockman-Wert, "Moved by the Spirit," 10.
18. I was unable to locate the original source of this quote, which was cut out of a magazine and included in a binder of MW USA publicity in the files of Rhoda Keener, copy in author's possession.
19. Gloria Diener, "African Kaleidoscope: Quilted Batiks Blend Two Cultures," source unknown, n.d., copy included in binder of MW USA publicity in the files of Rhoda Keener, copy in author's possession.
20. See Laurie L. Oswald, "Sister-Link Bonds Students with Africa AIDS Patients," *Mennonite Weekly Review*, April 5, 2004, 9.
21. Rhoda Keener, "Threads of Hope Sister-Link Markets $4,815 for Guatemalan Weavers," *Burning Bush* (Franklin Mennonite Mission Board), February 12, 2006, 1–2.
22. "Gift Exchange Forges Transatlantic Friendship," *Mennonite Weekly Review*, June 4, 2007, 6.
23. Elaine Maust, interview by author, July 17, 2015.
24. Laurie Oswald Robinson and Elaine Good, "Gifts of Prayer in Katrina's Wake," *Mennonite World Review*, April 3, 2006, http://www.mennoworld.org/archived/2006/4/3/gifts-prayer-katrinas-wake/?print=1.
25. Ibid.
26. Maust, interview.

27. Rebecca Sommers, interview by author, October 4, 2014.
28. "MW USA Announces New Ministry Name and Coordinator: The Housewarmer Project," *Mennonite Women Voices* (blog), September 28, 2015, https://mennonitewomenusa.org/2015/09/mw-usa-announces-new-ministry-name-and-coordinator-the-housewarmer-project/.
29. Laurie Oswald Robinson, "Needles Stitch Healing into Storm-Ripped Lives," *Mennonite World Review*, May 26, 2008, http://www.mennoworld.org/archived/2008/5/26/needles-stitch-healing-storm-ripped-lives/?print=1.
30. "Your Gifts Matter!" *Timbrel*, May–June 2004, 19.
31. Keener, interview, October 16, 2014.
32. Ibid.
33. By 2015 the endowment stood at $161,742, thanks largely to two generous gifts in that year.
34. "Financial Report," Mennonite Women USA Annual Report, August 2013–July 2014.
35. Ibid.
36. Guengerich, interview.
37. Rebekah Basinger, interview by author, January 22, 2015.
38. Diana Butler Bass, *Christianity after Religion: The End of the Church and the Birth of a New Spiritual Awakening* (New York: HaperCollins, 2012), 15.
39. Phyllis Tickle, *The Great Emergence: How Christianity Is Changing and Why* (Grand Rapids, MI: Baker Books, 2012), 16. Tickle credits the "rummage sale" concept to Anglican bishop Mark Dyer.
40. Ibid.
41. See ibid., 159; Bass, *Christianity after Religion*, 201–4.
42. Bass, *Christianity after Religion*, 203.
43. Tickle, *Great Emergence*, 159.
44. Rhoda Keener, email to author, June 2, 2016.
45. Quoted in ibid.
46. Rhoda Keener, "Giving Circles in Changing Times," *Timbrel*, September/October 2008, 23.
47. Twila King Yoder, "Twila Yoder on the Work of MW USA and the Woman Who Ushered Her In," *Mennonite Women Voices* (blog), April 28, 2015, https://mennonitewomenusa.org/2015/04/twila-yoder-on-the-work-of-mw-usa-and-the-woman-who-ushered-her-in/.
48. Ibid.
49. Patricia Burdette, "*Timbrel* as a Talking Circle," *Timbrel*, November/December 2008, 24.
50. DeBerg, interview.
51. Dawn Araujo-Hawkins, email to author, December 2, 2016.
52. See Brenda Martin Hurst (with seminar participants), "Naming Porn: Mennonite Women Speak Out about Pornography," *The Mennonite*, September 20, 2005, 14–15.
53. See Paul Schrag, "Human Trafficking Opposed; Health Care Access Supported," *Mennonite Weekly Review*, June 13, 2009, http://www.mennoworld.org/archived/2009/7/13/human-trafficking-opposed-health-care-access-suppo/?print=1.
54. Susan Gingerich, interview

55. Ibid.
56. Email messages and other documents in Women in Conversation binder, in the files of Rhoda Keener, copy in author's possession.
57. Mennonite Women USA board and staff members, "God Calls Women to Share Their Gifts," *The Mennonite*, April 3, 2007, 2.
58. Jerry Roth, email to Rhoda Keener, April 10, 2007, from the files of Rhoda Keener, copy in author's possession.
59. Carol O., email to Rhoda Keener, March 19, 2007, from the files of Rhoda Keener, copy in author's possession.
60. Joanna Shenk, "Survey: More Women in Leadership but Still Not Enough," *The Mennonite*, March 2010, 45–47.
61. Quoted in Laurie Oswald Robinson, "Mennonite Women Find Their Voices," *The Mennonite*, November 2011, 48.
62. Quoted in Laurie Oswald Robinson, "A Drink of Living Water," *Mennonite Weekly Review*, March 26, 2007, 2.
63. Quoted in Rhoda Keener, "Mennonite Women USA's Legacy Circle Grows," *Mennonite Women Voices* (blog), September 24, 2014, https://mennonitewomenusa.org/2014/09/legacy/.
64. Elizabeth Goering, interview by author, December 10, 2014.
65. Alix Lozano, presentation at Mennonite Women USA dinner, trans. Linda Shelly (Mennonite Church USA Assembly, Kansas City, MO, July 2, 2015).
66. Olga Piedrasanta, presentation at Mennonite Women USA dinner, trans. Linda Shelly (Mennonite Church USA Assembly, Kansas City, MO, July 2, 2015).

Chapter 10: Sister Care

1. Ibid.
2. Twila Miller, "I Am Meena," *Timbrel*, January–March 2013, 18.
3. Ibid.
4. Rhoda Keener, "Meena's Story" (sermon, Marion Mennonite Church, January 13, 2013).
5. Ibid.
6. Ibid.
7. Carolyn Holderread Heggen, journal entry, private collection.
8. Cynthia Peacock, interview by author, June 25, 2015.
9. Ibid.
10. Mennonite Women USA, "Sister Care Shared Globally," Mennonite World Conference News, September 30, 2013, https://www.mwc-cmm.org/content/sister-care-shared-globally? language=en.
11. Unless otherwise noted, this and the next four paragraphs are drawn from Keener, interview, October 16, 2014.
12. See Al Dueck, "Congregational Care Needs and Resources Survey: A Summary," *Direction* 21, no. 1 (Spring 1992): 26–40.
13. Anna Groff, "Women Learn to Set Boundaries in Caring," *The Mennonite*, February 19, 2008, 24.
14. Heggen, interview.
15. Keener, interview, September 22, 2014.
16. Heggen, interview.

17. Carolyn Heggen, Ofelia García, and Olga Piedrasanta, facilitators, "Sister Care: Global Contextualization and Testimonials," trans. Lizette Flores (workshop, Mennonite World Conference Assembly, Harrisburg, PA, July 22, 2015).
18. Quoted in Claire DeBerg, "Sister Care Spreads to Guatemala," *The Mennonite*, April 2013, 41.
19. Mennonite Women USA, "Sister Care Manual Translated into K'ekchi'," *The Mennonite*, May 2014, 41.
20. Ofelia García, "Latin American Anabaptist Women Theologians Movement Celebrates Ten Years," trans. Anna Mary Yoder, Mennonite World Conference News, March 30, 2013, https://www.mwc-cmm.org/content/latin-american-anabaptist-women-theologians-movement-celebrates-ten-years?language=en.
21. Linda Shelly, "Sister Care Eases Pain of Loss," *Mennonite World Review*, July 8, 2013, http://www.mennoworld.org/archived/2013/7/8/sister-care-eases-pain-loss/.
22. A description of Giesbrecht's work—and several other items in this chapter—first appeared in Anita Hooley Yoder, "Global Connections of Mennonite Women," *The Mennonite*, November 2015, 21–23. Giesbrecht's comments, from an interview by the author, June 22, 2015, were translated by the author with help from Sheri Banks.
23. Giesbrecht, interview.
24. Ofelia García, email to Rhoda Keener and Carolyn Heggen, November 25, 2015, author's trans. Giesbrecht has plans to reach more German Colony women with the materials, working through existing women's groups run by people like Helena Thiessen. Thiessen grew up in a Low German–speaking community in Chihuahua and leads two groups of Old Colony women who meet weekly for mutual support and spiritual growth. In July 2015, Thiessen said her groups affirmed a need for a program like Sister Care when Giesbrecht came and spoke about it to them (Helena Theissen, interview by author, July 22, 2015).
25. Rhoda Keener, email message to author, May 2, 2016.
26. Elizabeth Soto Albrecht, interview by author, July 25, 2015.
27. Ibid.
28. Alix Lozano, presentation at Lydia Tea, trans. Linda Shelly (Mennonite Church USA Assembly, Kansas City, MO, July 4, 2015).
29. Angela Opimí, presentation at Lydia Tea, trans. Linda Shelly (Mennonite Church USA Assembly, Kansas City, MO, July 4, 2015).
30. "Taking Sister Care 'Home' to Puerto Rico," *Mennonite Women Voices* (blog), June 3, 2014, https://mennonitewomenusa.org/2014/06/pr/.
31. Mennonite Women USA, "Sister Care Seminar Presented in All 21 Mennonite Church USA Conferences," *Mennonite Women Voices* (blog), November 12, 2013, https://mennonitewomenusa.org/2013/11/sister-care-seminar-presented-in-all-21-mennonite-church-usa-conferences/.
32. Heggen, interview.
33. Carol Roth, interview by author, April 17, 2015.
34. The following quotations were shared during Heggen, García, and Piedrasanta, "Sister Care: Global Contextualization and Testimonials."
35. See statistics at "Sister Care Seminars," Mennonite Women USA, accessed January 25, 2017, https://mennonitewomenusa.org/sistercare/.

36. Laurie Oswald Robinson, "Timing Is Everything," *Beyond Ourselves*, November 2015, 7.
37. Heggen, interview.
38. Wanda Gonzalez Coleman (interview) mentioned the challenge of having a presentation that is relevant to the variety of Spanish speakers in the United States. Kelly Bates Oglesby noted the busyness of "the same black people" who seem to be called on to do everything in the denomination. Kelley Bates Oglesby, interview by author, December 10, 2015.
39. Stevens, interview.
40. Lowe, interview.
41. Beth Martin Birky, interview by author, October 3, 2014.
42. Ibid.
43. Maggie Weaver, interview by author, August 4, 2015.
44. Maggie Weaver, "Sister Care Goes to College: Creating Affirmation through Community," *Mennonite Women Voices* (blog), April 8, 2015, https://mennonitewomenusa.org/2015/04/maggie/.
45. Bogard, interview.
46. Ivorie Lowe, "The Circle of Sisters," *Timbrel*, November–December 2009, 6.
47. "Sister Care Extension Offered in Southeast Mennonite Conference," A Postcard and a Prayer email, June 2012, http://archive.constantcontact.com/fs070/1101337334910/archive/1110191858442.html.
48. Anne M. Yoder, "Women Meet to Tell Their Sacred Stories," *Mennonite Women Voices* (blog), April 26, 2016, https://mennonitewomenusa.org/2016/04/women-meet-to-tell-their-sacred-stories/.
49. Flo Harnish, interview by author, April 23, 2015; Twila Miller, "Next Steps at AMC with Sister Care," *Timbrel*, Summer 2014, 18.
50. Ridgeway (Va.) Mennonite Church and Lombard (Ill.) Mennonite Church are just two of many places that have had Sister Care follow-up Sunday school classes or groups (Shank, interview; Deborah Wetherill, "Sister Care Sparks . . . Sister Stories Sunday School," *Sowing Sisterhood,* July 2015, 1).
51. Harnish, interview.
52. Nalungo ("Jackie") Aduma, interview by author, October 15, 2015.
53. Shirley Bustos, interview by author, June 1, 2015.
54. The Council of International Anabaptist Ministries (CIM) is a group of agencies that has included Eastern Mennonite Missions, Evangelical Mennonite Conference (Steinbach), Mennonite Brethren Missions, MCC Canada, MCC U.S., Mennonite Church Canada Witness, Mennonite Mission Network, and Rosedale Mennonite Missions.
55. This and the next paragraph are from Heggen, interview.

"A Wind Underneath My Wings"

1. Soto Albrecht, interview.
2. Ibid.
3. Robinson, "Mennonite Women Find Their Voices," 48.
4. Ibid.

5. Olga Piedrasanta, presentation at Lydia Tea, trans. Linda Shelly (Mennonite Church USA Assembly, Kansas City, MO, July 4, 2015). Piedrasanta read Perez's letter to the group.
6. Nancy Myers and Charlie Malembe, "A Small Fund Makes a Big Difference for Women Theologians," *Mennonite Women Voices* (blog), November 20, 2013, https://mennonitewomenusa.org/2013/11/a-small-fund-makes-a-big-difference-for-women-theologians/.
7. Jeongih Han and Priyanka Bagh, interview by Rhoda Keener and Ruth Lapp Guengerich, October 10, 2013, notes, copy in author's possession.
8. Ferne Burkhardt, "Women Theologians: A Great Spiritual Festival Glorifying God," *Mennonite World Conference Courier* 25, no. 1 (2010), 7.
9. Patricia Burdette, "A Life-Changing Event," *The Mennonite*, November 3, 2009, 12.
10. Ibid., 13.
11. Burkhardt, "Women Thelogians," 7.
12. Ibid.
13. Dick Benner, "Thursday, July 16: Women Call for Solidarity," in "Paraguay 2009 Daily Worship," US Mennonite Brethren News, September 1, 2009, http://www.usmb.org/news/article/Paraguay-2009-daily-worship.html# sthash.QN1eqm1D.dpuf.
14. Mennonite Women USA, "Indian and Asian Women Theologians Form Two Networks," Mennonite World Conference News, November 12, 2012, https://www.mwc-cmm.org/content/indian-and-asian-women-theologians-form-two-networks?language=en.
15. Unless otherwise noted, information in this and the next paragraph is from my observations of Ofelia García, Angela Opimí, Olga Piedrasanta, Linda Shelly, Elizabeth Soto, facilitators,"Connecting Globally, Forming a Global Women's Network" (workshop, Mennonite World Conference Assembly, Harrisburg, PA, July 24, 2015).
16. Robinson, "Timing Is Everything," 6.
17. Olga Piedrasanta, email to author, October 7, 2015, author trans.

Chapter 11: Local and Regional Activities

1. "About Us," Mennonite Women USA, accessed December 16, 2016, https://mennonitewomenusa.org/about-us/.
2. This and the next three paragraphs draw upon a conversation I had with women at Homestead (Fla.) Mennonite Church, November 8, 2015. Participants were Lorri Cutrer, Donna Geib, Amy Grimes, Mary Hess, Debbie Lee, Emma Lee, Vivian O'Haber, and Alice Taylor.
3. This paragraph is drawn from my observations at the Southeast Conference Fall Inspiration Day, Homestead, Florida, November 7, 2015.
4. Perez, interview.
5. Loretta Dominguez, Blanca Gonzalez, and Paula Suazo, interview by author, November 7, 2015.
6. Kathy Smith and Rebecca Zehr, interview by author, November 7, 2015.
7. Michalovic, interview.

8. Ruth Lapp Guengerich, "150 Join for Black Mennonite Women ROCK," *The Mennonite*, October 9, 2014, https://themennonite.org/daily-news/150-join-black-mennonite-women-rock/.
9. Ibid.
10. "Black Mennonite Women ROCK: Event + Information," *Mennonite Women Voices* (blog), June 23, 2014, https://mennonitewomenusa.org/2014/06/bmwr/#more-2127.
11. Guengerich, "150 Join."
12. Rosalie Grove, "Selected Reflections from Black Mennonite Women ROCK," *Mennonite Women Voices* (blog), October 23, 2014, https://mennonitewomenusa.org/2014/10/selected-reflections-from-black-mennonite-women-rock-by-rosalie-grove/.
13. Guengerich, "150 Join."
14. Rich Preheim, "Quilting Cultures," *Mennonite World Review*, June 16, 2014, http://mennoworld.org/2014/06/16/ feature/quilt-tells-the-story-of-african-americans/.
15. See Carolyn Mazloomi, *Spirits of the Cloth: Contemporary African American Quilts* (New York: Clarkson Potter, 1998).
16. Peters, interview.
17. Edith Shenk Kuhns, interview by author, October 31, 2015.
18. Patricia Borns, "Will the (Sewing) Circle Be Unbroken?" *News Leader* (Staunton, VA), March 19, 2015, http://www.newsleader.com/story/news/2015/03/17/mennonite-sewing-circle-quilting-80-years-and-counting/24892949/.
19. Sharon Shenk, interview by author, October 31, 2015.
20 Alicia Manning, interview by author, December 7, 2015.
21. Ibid.
22. Ibid.
23. The information in this and the next four paragraphs are drawn from a document compiled by Bethesda member Kathy (Koop) Friesen: "Bethesda Women's Ministries," April 7, 2016, document sent via email to author, April 17, 2016.

Chapter 12: Future Directions for Mennonite Women's Groups

1. Karen Wiens, "Finding a Home with MW USA," *Timbrel*, Autumn 2015, 17.
2. Redekop, *Work of Their Hands*, 12.
3. Wiebe, interview.
4. Toews, interview.
5. Christine Scheffel, email to author, December 8, 2015.
6. Ibid.
7. Linsenmeyer, interview.
8. Ibid.
9. Book, interview.
10. Weaver, interview.
11. Shank, interview.
12. Bogard, interview.

13. Conrad L. Kanagy, *Road Signs for the Journey: A Profile of Mennonite Church USA* (Scottdale, PA: Herald Press, 2007), 57, 64.
14. Ibid., 65.
15. Stevens, interview.
16. Ibid.
17. Hyacinth Stevens, "We Help Make the Circle Complete," *Mennonite Women Voices* (blog), March 30, 2015, https://mennonitewomenusa.org/2015/03/we-help-make-the-circle-complete-hyacinth-stevens-on-mw-usa/.
18. Ibid.
19. Tijerina, interview.
20. Ibid.
21. Roth, interview.
22. "Seven Questions with Carol . . . Roth," *The Mennonite* blog, December 31, 2015, https://themennonite.org/seven-questions-with-carol-roth/.
23. Roth, interview.
24. Sue Park-Hur, interview by author, April 6, 2016. Park-Hur noted how valuable it was for her to have a later in-person conversation with Ruth Lapp Guengerich when she was in Indiana.
25. In 2015, Kelly Bates Oglesby (interview) applauded MW USA's work for education overseas, but said, "I don't think they see that it's needed here. Put it into black women here in America." In a 2006 devotional shared with MW USA leadership, Irene Bechler wrote, "I continue to look for articles and involvement from our women of color . . . We seem to do better with stories from women abroad and I do not minimize that but I wonder why this is true?" Irene Bechler, untitled devotional for Mennonite Women board, April 22, 2006, copy in author's possession.
26. Park-Hur, interview.
27. Aveani Moeljono, email to author, April 7, 2016.
28. Erica Littlewolf, interview by author, April 26, 2016.
29. Ibid.
30. Marlene Bogard, email to author, May 4, 2016.
31. Marlene Bogard, "On the Horizon: Become a Sage," *Timbrel*, Autumn 2015, 30.
32. See, for example, Michael Lipka, "A Closer Look at America's Rapidly Growing Religious 'Nones,'" Pew Research Center, May 13, 2015, http://www.pewresearch.org/fact-tank/2015/05/13/a-closer-look-at-americas-rapidly-growing-religious-nones/; John Longhurst, "The Rise of the Dones—Done with Church, That Is," *Mennonite World Review* blog, April 28, 2015, http://mennoworld.org/2015/04/28/the-world-together/the-rise-of-the-dones-done-with-church-that-is/.
33. Brenneman, interview.
34. Park-Hur, interview.
35. Ibid.
36. Rhoda Keener, presentation at Sister Care seminar (Lombard, IL, May 15, 2015).
37. Marlene Bogard and Kathy Bilderback, "We Remain Committed to You, Mennonite Women," *Mennonite Women Voices* (blog), October 28, 2015, https://mennonite womenusa.org/2015/10/we-remain-committed-to-you-mennonite-women-mw-usa-responds-to-clc-question/.

38. In some contexts, women have expressed frustration with decisions of mostly male church leaders to withdraw from the denomination or their area conference, even if they might align with them theologically. For example, Carol Roth ("Seven Questions with Carol Roth") said, "I still personally struggle with the way the Native American Mennonites often did not feel that they had a voice in this decision. I personally feel that the pastors and leaders made that choice for them and didn't give the congregation a chance to vote for what they wanted." Speaking about the Lancaster Conference decision, which Spanish-speaking churches in the conference followed, Wanda Gonzalez Coleman (interview) said, "I'm saddened by the division. I don't think that the women want to split . . . I don't think they [the male leaders] realize how much this change is going to affect us."
39. Maust, interview.
40. DeBerg, interview.
41. Ibid.
42. Bogard, interview.
43. Keener, interview, September 22, 2014.

Selected Bibliography

Archive Collections

Mennonite Church USA Archives, Elkhart, Indiana (abbreviated MCUSAA–Elkhart)

African American Association Records, 1969–2001 (I-06-007)

Indiana Mennonite Women's Missionary Rally Committee Records, 1937–2003 (X-060)

Prairie Street Mennonite Church (Elkhart, Ind.) Records, 1872–2001 (III-14-002)

Sycamore Grove Mennonite Church (Garden City, Mo.) Records, 1868–2012 (III-25-002)

Women's Missionary and Service Commission Executive Committee Records, 1917–97 (IV-20-001)

Women's Missionary and Service Commission Executive Secretary (Beulah Kauffman) Files, 1953–87 (IV-20-023)

Women's Missionary and Service Commission Partnerships Records, 1973–92 (IV-20-008)

Mennonite Library and Archives, North Newton, Kansas (abbreviated MLA–Newton)

Women in Mission 1973–77 (VII.N.1)

Women in Mission Annual Reports to the Council of Commissions (VII.N.11)

Women in Mission Files from Carol Peterson (VII.N.14)

Women in Mission Minutes, reports, etc. 1960s–1990s (VII.N.15)

Women in Mission Promotional items/printed matter 1980s–early 1990s (VII.N.3)

Books and Articles

Bass, Diana Butler. *Christianity after Religion: The End of the Church and the Birth of a New Spiritual Awakening*. New York: HarperCollins, 2012.

Bechler, Le Roy. *The Black Mennonite Church in North America 1886–1986*. Scottdale, PA: Herald Press, 1986.

Bender, Harold S. and Harold A. Penner. "Voluntary Service." *Global Anabaptist Mennonite Encyclopedia Online*. 1989. http://gameo.org/index.php?title=Voluntary_Service&oldid=133942.

Bendroth, Margaret Lamberts and Virginia Lieson Brereton, eds. *Women and Twentieth-Century Protestantism*. Chicago: University of Illinois Press, 2001.

Born, Daniel. "From Cross to Cross-Stitch: The Ascendancy of the Quilt." *Mennonite Quarterly Review* 79, no. 2 (April 2005). https://www.goshen.edu/mqr/2005/06/april-2005-born/.

Brenneman, Helen Good. *Ring a Dozen Doorbells: Twelve Women Tell It Like It Is*. Scottdale, PA: Herald Press, 1973.

Brunner, Grace. "By the Grace of God." In *She Has Done a Good Thing: Mennonite Women Leaders Tell Their Stories*, edited by Mary Swartley and Rhoda Keener, 65–73. Scottdale, PA: Herald Press, 1999.

Clemens, Lois Gunden. *Woman Liberated*. Scottdale, PA: Herald Press, 1971.

Davis, Flora. *Moving the Mountain: The Women's Movement in America since 1960*. New York: Simon & Schuster, 1991.

Dueck, Al. "Congregational Care Needs and Resources Survey: A Summary." *Direction* 21, no. 1 (Spring 1992): 26–40.

Epp, Marlene. *Mennonite Women in Canada: A History*. Winnipeg: University of Manitoba Press, 2008.

———. "Women in Canadian Mennonite History: Uncovering the 'Underside.' " *Journal of Mennonite Studies* 5 (1987): 90–107.

———. "Women of Anabaptist Traditions." In *Encyclopedia of Women and Religion in North America*, edited by Rosemary Skinner Keller and Rosemary Radford Ruether, 262–69. Bloomington: Indiana University Press, 2006.

Esau, John A. "Ordination." *Global Anabaptist Mennonite Encyclopedia Online*. 1989. http://gameo.org/index.php?title=Ordination&oldid=101100.

Evans, Sara. *Personal Politics: The Roots of Women's Liberation in the Civil Rights Movement and the New Left*. New York: Vintage Books, 1979.

Finger, Reta Halteman. "Standing in the Gap." In *She Has Done a Good Thing: Mennonite Women Leaders Tell Their Stories*, edited by Mary Swartley and Rhoda Keener, 47–56. Scottdale, PA: Herald Press, 1999.

Froese, Brian. *California Mennonites*. Baltimore: Johns Hopkins University Press, 2015.

Gifford, Carolyn DeSwarte. "Nineteenth- and Twentieth-Century Protestant Social Reform Movements in the United States." In *Encyclopedia of Women and Religion in North America*, edited by Rosemary Skinner Keller and Rosemary Radford Ruether, 1021–38. Bloomington: Indiana University Press, 2006.

Gingerich, Melvin. "The Mennonite Woman's Missionary Society." *Mennonite Quarterly Review* 37, no. 2 (1963): 113–25.

———. "The Mennonite Woman's Missionary Society: II." *Mennonite Quarterly Review* 37, no. 3 (1963): 214–33.

Goering, Gladys V. *Women in Search of Mission*. Newton, KS: Faith & Life Press, 1980.

Goossen, Rachel Waltner. "'Defanging the Beast': Mennonite Responses to John Howard Yoder's Sexual Abuse." *Mennonite Quarterly Review* 89, no. 1 (January 2015): 7–80.

———. *Women against the Good War: Conscientious Objection and Gender on the American Home Front, 1941–1947*. Chapel Hill: University of North Carolina Press, 1997.

Graber, Jennifer. "Mennonites, Gender, and the Bible in the 1920s and '30s." *Conrad Grebel Review* 21, no. 2 (Spring 2003). https://uwaterloo.ca/grebel/publications/conrad-grebel-review/issues/spring-2003/mennonites-gender-and-bible-1920s-and-30s.

Graber, Edith (Mrs. O'Ray). "Women in Church Vocations (General Conference Mennonite Church)." *Global Anabaptist Mennonite Encyclopedia Online*. 1959. http://gameo.org/index.php?title=Women_in_Church_Vocations_(General_Conference_Mennonite_Church)&oldid=86225.

Guengerich, Ruth Lapp. "A History of the Mennonite Women's Organization." Mennonite Women USA. Posted June 25, 2013. http://mennonitewomenusa.org/2013/06/history-womens-missionary-and-service-commission/.

Heywood, Leslie L. "Introduction: A Fifteen-Year History of Third-Wave Feminism." In *The Women's Movement Today: An Encyclopedia of Third-Wave Feminism*, edited by Leslie L. Heywood, xv–xxii. Westport, CT: Greenwood Press, 2006.

Hinojosa, Felipe. *Latino Mennonites: Civil Rights, Faith, and Evangelical Culture*. Baltimore: Johns Hopkins University Press, 2014.

hooks, bell. *Feminism Is for Everybody: Passionate Politics*. London: Pluto Press, 2000.

Jantzen, Susan. *Gems from the Files: Past Women in Mission Programs from the 1940s to 1980s*. Newton, KS: General Conference Women in Mission, 1995.

Juhnke, James C. *A People of Mission: A History of General Conference Mennonite Overseas Missions*. Newton, KS: Faith & Life Press, 1978.

———. *Vision, Doctrine, War: Mennonite Identity and Organization in America, 1890–1930*. Scottdale, PA: Herald Press, 1989.

Kanagy, Conrad L. *Road Signs for the Journey: A Profile of Mennonite Church USA*. Scottdale, PA: Herald Press, 2007.

Keim, Albert N. *The CPS Story: An Illustrated History of Civilian Public Service*. Intercourse, PA: Good Books, 1990.

Keller, Rosemary Skinner. "Leadership and Community Building in Protestant Women's Organizations." In *Encyclopedia of Women and Religion in North America*, edited by Rosemary Skinner Keller and Rosemary Radford Ruether, 851–64. Bloomington: Indiana University Press, 2006.

Keller, Rosemary Skinner and Rosemary Radford Ruether, eds. *Encyclopedia of Women and Religion in North America*. Bloomington: Indiana University Press, 2006.

Klingelsmith, Sharon L. "Steiner, Clara Daisy Eby (1873–1929)." *Global Anabaptist Mennonite Encyclopedia Online*. 1989. http://gameo.org/index.php?title=Steiner,_Clara_Daisy_Eby(1873-1929)&oldid=112838.

———. "Women in the Mennonite Church, 1900–1930." *Mennonite Quarterly Review* 54, no. 3 (1980): 163–207.

LaFollette, Joan C. "Money and Power: Presbyterian Women's Organizations in the Twentieth Century." In *The Organizational Revolution: Presbyterians and American Denominationalism*, edited by Milton J. Coater et al., 199–232. Louisville, KY: Westminster John Knox Press, 1992.

Lind, Hope Kauffman. *Apart and Together: Mennonites in Oregon and Neighboring States, 1876–1976*. Scottdale, PA: Herald Press, 1990.

Loewen, Edith C. "Women in Mission (General Conference Mennonite Church)." *Global Anabaptist Mennonite Encyclopedia Online*. 1989. http://gameo.org/index.php?title=Women_in_Mission_General_Conference_Mennonite_Church)&oldid=78870.

Loewen, Royden and Steven M. Nolt. *Seeking Places of Peace: A Global Mennonite History*. Intercourse, PA: Good Books, 2012.

MacMaster, Eve. "Ruth and Me." *Mennonite Life* 58, no. 2 (June 2003). https://ml.bethelks.edu/issue/vol-58-no-2/article/ruth-and-me/.

Martin, Luann Habegger. "The Thirtieth Anniversary of the MCC Women's Concerns Committee." *Conrad Grebel Review* 23, no. 1 (Winter 2005). https://uwaterloo.ca/grebel/publications/conrad-grebel-review/issues/winter-2005/30th-anniversary-mcc-womens-concerns-committee.

Mazloomi, Carolyn. *Spirits of the Cloth: Contemporary African American Quilts*. New York: Clarkson Potter, 1998.

McLaughlin, Elizabeth. "Engendering the *Imago Dei*: A Rhetorical Study of Quilts and Quiltmaking as Metaphor and Visual Parable in the Anabaptist Peace Tradition." PhD diss., Regent University, 2008. Mennonite Historical Library, Goshen, IN.

Nyce, Dorothy Yoder. "And So It Began: On Birthing an Organization," *Conrad Grebel Review* 23, no. 1 (Winter 2005): 55–78.

Patkau, Esther. *Canadian Women in Mission: 1895–1952–2002*. Saskatoon, SK: Canadian Women in Mission, 2002.

Peachey, Linda Gehman. "Naming the Pain, Seeking the Light: The Mennonite Church's Response to Sexual Abuse." *Mennonite Quarterly Review* 89, no. 1 (January 2015): 111–28.

Putnam, Robert D. *Bowling Alone: The Collapse and Revival of American Community*. New York: Simon and Schuster, 2000.

Rake, Valerie S. "A Thread of Continuity: Quiltmaking in Wayne County, Ohio, Mennonite Churches, 1890s–1990s." *Uncoverings* 20 (1999): 31–62.

Redekop, Calvin. "The Mennonite Central Committee: A Review Essay." *Mennonite Quarterly Review* 67 (1993): 84–103.

Redekop, Gloria Neufeld. *The Work of Their Hands: Mennonite Women's Societies in Canada*. Waterloo, ON: Wilfrid Laurier University Press, 1996.

Redekop, Magdalene. "Through the Mennonite Looking Glass." In *Why I Am a Mennonite: Essays on Mennonite Identity*, edited by Harry Loewen, 226–53. Scottdale, PA: Herald Press, 1988.

Rich, Elaine Sommers. *Mennonite Women: A Story of God's Faithfulness*. Scottdale, PA: Herald Press, 1983.

Ruth, John Landis. *The Earth Is the Lord's: A Narrative History of the Lancaster Mennonite Conference*. Scottdale, PA: Herald Press, 2001.

Shearer, Tobin Miller. "A Prophet Pushed Out: Vincent Harding and the Mennonites." *Mennonite Life* 69 (May 2015). https://ml.bethelks.edu/issue/vol-69/article/a-prophet-pushed-out-vincent-harding-and-the-menno/.

———. *Daily Demonstrators: The Civil Rights Movement in Mennonite Homes and Sanctuaries*. Baltimore: Johns Hopkins University Press, 2010.

Shenk, Wilbert R. *By Faith They Went Out: Mennonite Missions 1850–1999*. Elkhart, IN: Institute of Mennonite Studies, 2000.

Shutt, Joyce. Chapter 12. In *Our Struggle to Serve: The Stories of Fifteen Evangelical Women*, edited by Virginia Hearn, 142–52. Waco, TX: Word Books, 1979.

———. "I Never Intended to Be a Pastor." In *She Has Done a Good Thing: Mennonite Women Leaders Tell Their Stories*, edited by Mary Swartley and Rhoda Keener, 114–23. Scottdale, PA: Herald Press, 1999.

Snyder, C. Arnold and Linda A. Huebert Hecht. *Profiles of Anabaptist Women: Sixteenth-Century Reforming Pioneers*. Waterloo, ON: Wilfrid Laurier University Press, 1996.

Stoltzfus, Louise. *Quiet Shouts: Stories of Lancaster Mennonite Women Leaders*. Scottdale, PA: Herald Press, 1999.

Swartley, Mary and Rhoda Keener, eds. *She Has Done a Good Thing: Mennonite Women Leaders Tell Their Stories*. Scottdale, PA: Herald Press, 1999.

Swartz, David R. *Moral Minority: The Evangelical Left in an Age of Conservatism*. Philadelphia: University of Pennsylvania Press, 2012.

Swidler, Leonard. *Jesus Was a Feminist: What the Gospels Reveal about His Revolutionary Perspective*. Lanham, MD: Sheed and Ward, 2007.

Tickle, Phyllis. *The Great Emergence: How Christianity Is Changing and Why*. Grand Rapids, MI: Baker Books, 2012.

Toews, Paul. "Fundamentalism." *Global Anabaptist Mennonite Encyclopedia Online*. 1990. http://gameo.org/index.php?title=Fundamentalism.

———. *Mennonites in American Society, 1930–1970: Modernity and the Persistence of Religious Community*. Scottdale, PA: Herald Press, 1996.

van Braght, Thieleman J. *Martyrs Mirror: The Story of Seventeen Centuries of Christian Martyrdom from the Time of Christ to A.D. 1660*. Translated by Joseph F. Sohm. Scottdale, PA: Herald Press, 1950.

Wenger, J. C. *The Mennonite Church in America*. Scottdale, PA: Herald Press, 1966.

Wiebe, Katie Funk. "My Impressions of the Early Years of the Women's Task Force." *Conrad Grebel Review* 23, no. 1 (Winter 2005). https://uwaterloo.ca/grebel/publications/conrad-grebel-review/issues/winter-2005/my-impressions-early-years-womens-task-force.

Yoder, Anita Hooley. "A Mission to Themselves: Changing Views of Mission in Mennonite Women's Organization." *Anabaptist Witness* 3, no. 2 (December 2016): 17–27.

Yoder, Eleanor. *Iowa-Nebraska Sewing WMSC*. Kalona, IA: Kalona Printing, 1989.

Yohn, Susan M. "'Let Christian Women Set the Example in Their Own Gifts': The 'Business' of Protestant Women's Organizations." In *Women and Twentieth-Century Protestantism*, edited by Margaret Lamberts Bendroth and Virginia Lieson Brereton, 214–33. Chicago: University of Illinois Press, 2001.

Zehr, Jeannie. "History of General Conference Mennonite Church Women's Organization." *Mennonite Women Voices* (blog). May 17, 2013 [prepared in 2008]. http://mennonitewomenusa.org/2013/05/history-general-conference-mennonite-church-womens-organization/.

Zikmund, Barbara Brown. "Women's Organizations: Centers of Denominational Loyalty and Expressions of Christian Unity." In *Beyond Establishment: Protestant Identity in a Post-Protestant Age*, edited by Jackson Carroll and Wade Clark Roof, 116–38. Louisville, KY: Westminster John Knox Press, 1993.

Illustration Credits

Page 3: Courtesy of Joyce Shutt.
Page 4: Courtesy of Suzette Shreffler.
Page 10: Women of Science Ridge Mennonite Church courtesy of Women's Missionary and Service Commission Publications Committee Records, 1927-1997. IV-20-003, Box 3, Folder 1, Photo #917. Mennonite Church USA Archives, Elkhart, Indiana.
Page 13: 1992-14-2971: Mennonite Archives of Ontario.
Page 15 (two photographs): Mennonite Library and Archives, Bethel College, North Newton, Kansas.
Page 17: Mennonite Library and Archives, Bethel College, North Newton, Kansas.
Page 18: Lester and Charity Hostetler Photograph Collection. HM4-273, Box 1, Folder 1, Photo #193. Mennonite Church USA Archives, Elkhart, Indiana.
Page 35: C. J. Rempel/Mennonite Archives of Ontario.
Page 38: Mennonite Board of Missions Photographs. Eureka, Illinois, Home for the Aged, 1950-1956. IV-10-7.2, Box 3, Folder 72. Mennonite Church USA Archives, Elkhart, Indiana.
Page 40: Courtesy of Carol Peters.
Page 41: Mennonite Community Photographs. HM4-134, Box 1, Photo #091-10. Mennonite Church USA Archives, Elkhart, Indiana.
Page 43: Mennonite Board of Missions Photographs. Eureka, Illinois, Home for the Aged, 1950-1956. IV-10-7.2, Box 3, Folder 72, Photo #29. Mennonite Church USA Archives, Elkhart, Indiana.
Page 44: Mennonite Library and Archives, Bethel College, North Newton, Kansas.
Page 50: Courtesy of Jane Yoder.
Page 52: Courtesy of Jonathan Charles.
Page 54: Iowa cutting room courtesy of Mennonite Community Photographs. HM4-134, Box 1, Photo #091-03. Mennonite Church USA Archives, Elkhart, Indiana.

Page 56: Woman standing in WMSA session courtesy of Mennonite Board of Missions Photograph Collection. MBM Annual Meeting, June 1964, La Junta, Colorado. IV-10-7.2, Box 3, Folder 6, Photo 6. Mennonite Church USA Archives, Elkhart, Indiana.
Page 58: Women's Missionary and Service Commission Photographs, 1960-1967. IV-20-009, Box 1, Folder 2. Mennonite Church USA Archives, Elkhart, Indiana.
Page 64: Women's Missionary and Service Commission Photographs, 1960-1967. IV-20-009, Box 1, Folder 2. Mennonite Church USA Archives, Elkhart, Indiana.
Page 70: Gulf States conference quilt courtesy of Courtesy of Edith Michalovic.
Page 73: Women's Missionary and Service Commission Photographs, 1960-1967. IV-20-009, Box 1, Folder 2. Mennonite Church USA Archives, Elkhart, Indiana.
Page 76: Michiana Mennonite Relief Sale Records, 1968-2005. X-034, Box 1, Folder 5. Mennonite Church USA Archives, Elkhart, Indiana.
Page 78: Michiana Mennonite Relief Sale Records, 1968-2005. X-034, Box 1, Folder 14. Mennonite Church USA Archives, Elkhart, Indiana.
Page 89: Courtesy of *Mennonite World Review.*
Page 92: Mennonite Board of Missions Photographs. MBM Staff, 1950-1970. IV-10-7.2, Box 8, Folder 40. Mennonite Church USA Archives, Elkhart, Indiana.
Page 101: Mennonite Board of Missions Evangelism and Church Development Data Files, Part 4, 1970-1980. IV-16-21.4, Box 1, Folder 68. Mennonite Church USA Archives, Elkhart, Indiana.
Page 103: Mennonite Board of Missions Evangelism and Church Development Data Files, Part 4, 1970-1980. IV-16-21.4, Box 1, Folder 68. Mennonite Church USA Archives, Elkhart, Indiana.
Page 105: Courtesy of Maria Tijerina.
Page 106: Courtesy of Maria Tijerina.
Page 109: Mennonite Publishing House Photographs. VI-10-001, Drawer 3, Folder 46. Mennonite Church USA Archives, Elkhart, Indiana.
Page 116: Courtesy of Rhoda Keener.
Page 123: Mennonite Library and Archives, Bethel College, North Newton, Kansas.
Page 124: Mennonite Library and Archives, Bethel College, North Newton, Kansas.
Page 127: Courtesy of Rhoda Keener.
Page 131: Courtesy of Rhoda Keener.

Page 142: Hispanic MW banners courtesy of Maria Tijerina.
Page 146: Courtesy of Doris Schmidt.
Page 153: Women's Missionary and Service Commission Executive Committee Records, 1917-1997. IV-20-001, Box 2, Folder 8. Mennonite Church USA Archives, Elkhart, Indiana.
Page 162: Courtesy of Rhoda Keener.
Page 164: Atlanta quilt courtesy of Rhoda Keener.
Page 166: TabasaranSister-Link courtesy of AliceShenk.
Page 174: Courtesy of Alice Shenk.
Page 175: Courtesy of Rhoda Keener.
Page 181: Courtesy of Steve Keener.
Page 183: Courtesy of Rhoda Keener.
Page 184: Courtesy of Hellen Bradburn.
Page 187: Courtesy of Rhoda Keener.
Page 188: Graphic by Merrill Miller.
Page 190: Courtesy of Rhoda Keener.
Page 192: Courtesy of Paul Schrag and *Mennonite World Review.*
Page 193: Courtesy of Rhoda Keener.
Page 195: Courtesy of Rhoda Keener.
Page 197: Courtesy of Carolyn Holderread Heggen.
Page 198: Leya Muloba and Tatiana Mdjoko courtesy of Rhoda Keener.
Page 200: Courtesy of Rhoda Keener.
Page 204: Courtesy of Mennonite Women USA.
Page 206: Courtesy of Linda Shelly.
Page 208: Courtesy of Carolyn Holderread Heggen.
Page 210: Courtesy of Rhoda Keener.
Page 213: Courtesy of Mennonite Women USA.
Page 215: Courtesy of Rhoda Keener.
Page 217: Courtesy of Laurie Oswald Robinson.
Page 221: Courtesy of Rhoda Keener.
Page 222: Courtesy of Jonathan Charles.
Page 224: Women's Missionary and Service Commission Photographs, 1960-1967. IV/20/009, Box 1, Folder 2. Mennonite Church USA Archives, Elkhart, Indiana.
Page 226: Author photo.
Page 228: Author photo.
Page 230: Courtesy of Ruth Lapp Guengerich.
Page 235: Courtesy of Rhoda Keener.
Page 239: Courtesy of Deb Pardini.

Index

Studies in Anabaptist and Mennonite History Series

Series editor Gerald J. Mast; with editors Geoffrey L. Dipple, Marlene G. Epp, Rachel Waltner Goossen, Leonard Gross, Thomas J. Meyers, Steven M. Nolt, John D. Roth, Theron F. Schlabach, and Astrid von Schlachta.

The Studies in Anabaptist and Mennonite History Series is sponsored by the Mennonite Historical Society. Beginning with volume 8, titles were published by Herald Press unless otherwise noted.

1. Harold S. Bender. *Two Centuries of American Mennonite Literature, 1727–1928*. 1929.
2. John Horsch. *The Hutterian Brethren, 1528–1931: A Story of Martyrdom and Loyalty*. 1931. Reprint, Macmillan Hutterite Colony, Cayley, Alberta, 1985.
3. Harry F. Weber. *Centennial History of the Mennonites in Illinois, 1829–1929*. 1931.
4. Sanford Calvin Yoder. *For Conscience' Sake: A Study of Mennonite Migrations Resulting from the World War*. 1940.
5. John S. Umble. *Ohio Mennonite Sunday Schools*. 1941.
6. Harold S. Bender. *Conrad Grebel, c. 1498–1526, Founder of the Swiss Brethren*. 1950.
7. Robert Friedmann. *Mennonite Piety Through the Centuries: Its Genius and Its Literature*. 1949.
8. Delbert L. Gratz. *Bernese Anabaptists and Their American Descendants*. 1953.
9. A. L. E. Verheyden. *Anabaptism in Flanders, 1530–1650: A Century of Struggle*. 1961.

10. J. C. Wenger. *The Mennonites in Indiana and Michigan*. 1961.
11. Rollin Stely Armour. *Anabaptist Baptism: A Representative Study*. 1966.
12. John B. Toews. *Lost Fatherland: The Story of Mennonite Emigration from Soviet Russia, 1921–1927*. 1967.
13. Grant M. Stoltzfus. *Mennonites of the Ohio and Eastern Conference, from the Colonial Period in Pennsylvania to 1968*. 1969.
14. John A. Lapp. *The Mennonite Church in India, 1897–1962*. 1972.
15. Robert Friedmann. *The Theology of Anabaptism: An Interpretation*. 1973.
16. Kenneth R. Davis. *Anabaptism and Asceticism: A Study in Intellectual Origins*. 1974.
17. Paul Erb. *South Central Frontiers: A History of the South Central Mennonite Conference*. 1974.
18. Fred R. Belk. *The Great Trek of the Russian Mennonites to Central Asia, 1880–1884*. 1976.
19. Werner O. Packull. *Mysticism and the Early South German-Austrian Anabaptist Movement, 1525–1531*. 1976.
20. Richard K. MacMaster, with Samuel L. Horst and Robert F. Ulle. *Conscience in Crisis: Mennonites and Other Peace Churches in America, 1739–1789*. 1979.
21. Theron F. Schlabach. *Gospel Versus Gospel: Mission and the Mennonite Church, 1863–1944*. 1980.
22. Calvin Wall Redekop. *Strangers Become Neighbors: Mennonite and Indigenous Relations in the Paraguayan Chaco*. 1980.
23. Leonard Gross. *The Golden Years of the Hutterites: The Witness and Thought of the Communal Moravian Anabaptists during the Walpot Era, 1565–1578*. 1980. Rev. ed., Pandora Press Canada, 1998.
24. Willard H. Smith. *Mennonites in Illinois*. 1983.
25. Murray L. Wagner. *Petr Chelcický: A Radical Separatist in Hussite Bohemia*. 1983.

26. John L. Ruth. *Maintaining the Right Fellowship: A Narrative Account of Life in the Oldest Mennonite Community in North America*. 1984.
27. C. Arnold Snyder. *The Life and Thought of Michael Sattler*. 1984.
28. Beulah Stauffer Hostetler. *American Mennonites and Protestant Movements: A Community Paradigm*. 1987.
29. Daniel Liechty. *Andreas Fischer and the Sabbatarian Anabaptists: An Early Reformation Episode in East Central Europe*. 1988.
30. Hope Kauffman Lind. *Apart and Together: Mennonites in Oregon and Neighboring States, 1876–1976*. 1990.
31. Paton Yoder. *Tradition and Transition: Amish Mennonites and Old Order Amish, 1800–1900*. 1991.
32. James R. Coggins. *John Smyth's Congregation: English Separatism, Mennonite Influence, and the Elect Nation*. 1991.
33. John D. Rempel. *The Lord's Supper in Anabaptism: A Study in the Theology of Balthasar Hubmaier, Pilgram Marpeck, and Dirk Philips*. 1993.
34. Gerlof D. Homan. *American Mennonites and the Great War, 1914–1918*. 1994.
35. J. Denny Weaver. *Keeping Salvation Ethical: Mennonite and Amish Atonement Theology in the Late Nineteenth Century*. 1997.
36. Wes Harrison. *Andreas Ehrenpreis and Hutterite Faith and Practice*. 1997. Copublished with Pandora Press Canada.
37. John D. Thiesen. *Mennonite and Nazi? Attitudes among Mennonite Colonists in Latin America, 1933–1945*. 1999. Copublished with Pandora Press Canada.
38. Perry Bush. *Dancing with the Kobzar: Bluffton College and Mennonite Higher Education, 1899–1999*. 2000. Copublished with Pandora Press U.S. and Faith & Life Press.
39. John L. Ruth. *The Earth Is the Lord's: A Narrative History of the Lancaster Mennonite Conference*. 2001.
40. Melanie Springer Mock. *Writing Peace: The Unheard Voices of Great War Mennonite Objectors*. 2003. Copublished with Cascadia Publishing House.

41. Mary Jane Lederach Hershey. *This Teaching I Present: Fraktur from the Skippack and Salford Mennonite Meetinghouse Schools, 1747–1836*. 2003. Published by Good Books.
42. Edsel Burdge Jr. and Samuel L. Horst. *Building on the Gospel Foundation: The Mennonites of Franklin County, Pennsylvania, and Washington County, Maryland, 1730–1970*. 2004.
43. Ervin Beck. *MennoFolk: Mennonite and Amish Folk Traditions*. 2004.
44. Walter Klaassen and William Klassen. *Marpeck: A Life of Dissent and Conformity*. 2008.
45. Theron F. Schlabach. *War, Peace and Social Conscience: Guy F. Hershberger and Mennonite Ethics*. 2009.
46. Ervin R. Stutzman. *From Nonresistance to Justice: The Transformation of Mennonite Church Peace Rhetoric, 1908–2008*. 2011.
47. Nathan E. Yoder. *Together in the Work of the Lord: A History of the Conservative Mennonite Conference*. 2014.
48. Samuel J. Steiner. *In Search of Promised Lands: A Religious History of Mennonites in Ontario*. 2015.
49. Perry Bush. *Peace, Progress, and the Professor: The Mennonite History of C. Henry Smith*. 2015.
50. Rich Preheim. *In Pursuit of Faithfulness: Conviction, Conflict, and Compromise in Indiana-Michigan Mennonite Conference*. 2016.
51. Anita Hooley Yoder. *Circles of Sisterhood: A History of Mission, Service, and Fellowship in Mennonite Women's Organizations*. 2017.

The Author

Anita Hooley Yoder is a freelance writer, campus minister, and theopoet living in Cleveland Heights, Ohio. Her essays have appeared in *CrossCurrents*, *Anabaptist Witness*, *Center for Mennonite Writing Journal*, and other Anabaptist-related publications. She has also written devotionals and Sunday school curricula for Brethren Press and MennoMedia.

A native of Canton, Ohio, Yoder earned a degree in English and secondary education at Goshen (Ind.) College and a master of divinity degree at Bethany Theological Seminary (Richmond, Ind.). She and her husband, Benjamin Yoder, are members of Friendship Mennonite Church.

Yoder works as Campus Ministry Coordinator at Notre Dame College (South Euclid, Ohio). There she organizes service and immersion opportunities, promotes spiritual growth for students and staff, and enjoys making multicultural and ecumenical connections.

CPSIA information can be obtained
at www.ICGtesting.com
Printed in the USA
LVOW06*2301181217
560156LV00003B/7/P

9 781513 801438